HarperCollins*Publishers*

HarperCollins books may be purchased for educational, business, or sales promotional use. For information, please write: Special Markets Department, HarperCollins Publishers Inc., 10 East 53rd Street, New York, NY 10022.

FIRST EDITION

Designed by Elliott Beard

Printed on acid-free paper

Library of Congress Cataloging-in-Publication Data

Magnuson, Mike.
    Lummox : the evolution of a man / Mike Magnuson.— 1st ed.
      p. cm.
    ISBN 0-06-019372-7
      1. College students — Fiction. 2. Young men —Fiction. 3. Feminists—
Fiction. I. Title.
    PS3563.A35214 L86 2002
    813'.54—dc21   2001039436

02 03 04 05 06 ❖/RRD 10 9 8 7 6 5 4 3 2 1

For Robert Jones

I have an important message to deliver to all the cute people all over the world. If you're out there and you're cute, maybe you're beautiful, I just want to tell you something: There's a lot more of us ugly motherfuckers than you are. So watch out.

—FRANK ZAPPA

Part One
An Animal

Chapter 1

CALL HIM LUMMOX.

He's your *guy* guy, your *man's* man, your guy-with-a-spare-tire guy, your guy whose clothes don't fit quite the way they should. He drinks too much beer and likes the National Football League and SportsCenter and NASCAR and bowling and fishing and doing *anything* that keeps him from having to hang around with his girlfriend or his wife or his children or anybody who is not a lummox like himself. He's your guy who calls women *girls* and *chicks*, calls his wife or his girlfriend *his old lady*. He's been known to stare at fine pussy when he sees it in public places. He's been known to scratch himself at inappropriate times. And he leaves pizza boxes in the living room, drops his socks on the floor. He doesn't give a crap about ironing his shirts or making his bed or changing his sheets. He farts and he belches without excusing himself, and he doesn't put the toilet lid down or clean the crud from the toilet base once a week. He doesn't even wash his hands after he pisses, if he bothers to go indoors in the first place instead of watering the lilac hedge alongside his house, which is a perfectly natural spot for the lummox to do his duty (Outdoors! A night with an easy breeze and a kickass tapestry of stars overhead!) because a lummox, no matter what you might say about him, he knows his place in the universe: Indoors, outdoors, he's the same lummox he's always been. He's an animal, and he doesn't have problems with that.

You know him, right? He's *that* guy. Used to be every man in America was *that* guy—or a variation of that guy—and the people were totally cool about it. He would go ahead and do his lummoxy thing, whatever it was, and people were, like, "That's my *uncle*. That's my *grandpa*. That's my *brother*. That's my *dad*. He's just being the way he *is*." But not anymore. Women with a certain type of education, for instance, they don't want that guy around anymore. They don't see the *need* for him. They've heard *enough* about him. "Civilization has been built upon that guy," they say, "and civilization has failed us." And there's plenty of men, too—men who believe they're enlightened and hip, which means they're trying to think the way women think—who don't want that guy around anymore. The enlightened men say, "I'm no animal! I don't *need* to behave like he does! I've gone *beyond* being that guy."

Nevertheless, your lummox is still out there in the wide world, having himself a kickass time doing the kickass shit he loves, and even though he knows people believe his way of living has outgrown its usefulness, he sees no reason to change. Your lummox is by definition a person regarded by most people as clumsy and stupid or oafish, even if his inner lummox might not really be clumsy and stupid and oafish. And your lummox knows that being a lummox is equivalent to being a Neanderthal, a person also regarded as clumsy and stupid and oafish, even if, as happened to be the case with many *real* Neanderthals, the inner Neanderthal might be in point of fact as graceful at heart and as facile-minded as a Greek poet. So if somebody informs your lummox that he's not a genius and that he's not conducting himself like the refined citizenry is conducting itself, hell, he already knows *that*. Tell him something *new* for once.

Let's get one thing straight right here and now: A lummox is and has always been male. A *man*. Seems obvious, right?

Try this then: Go over to your local university and find the Hag Studies Department, and when you get there find the Hag in Charge and tell her that a lummox is a man. She might not answer you at first; she might snigger or roll her eyes and suggest that you move on to more important matters like sexual exploitation and unjust gender hegemony in the workplace or the aggregate horrors of living in a country not *educated* enough to elect a woman to its presidency. But if you tell her again that a lummox is a man, if you insist because you know it's true, she'll say, "No, you Neanderthal dolt. The word *lummox* is not gender specific."

She'll be extremely informed about the word *gender*, as long as it applies to hers, and if she's really the on-top-of-it type, she might point out that the definitive example of a lummox in American literature is actually a female. "See," she will say—and in a tone of voice she might use talking to a fourth-grader about the birds and the bees—"if you were educated properly, you'd know that the distinguished American woman novelist Fannie Hurst published a novel in 1923 called *Lummox*."

You will not have been educated properly, of course; the chances of your having heard of Fannie Hurst's *Lummox* are about the same as your getting abducted by aliens on your drive home from the tavern. It's possible. But not probable.

Here's what the Hag in Charge is saying, anyway: The lummox character in Fannie Hurst's *Lummox* is sure enough a female; she's this supersize chick with no tits named Bertha. This is the way Fannie Hurst describes her: "She was five feet nine and a half, of flat-breasted bigness and her cheekbones were pitched like a Norn's."

Big Bertha. You know her, or someone like her. You've seen her around town, at Hardee's or at Wal-Mart or at the Pizza Hut lunch buffet, or maybe she's one of your co-workers, or maybe you've taken some university courses from her. Whatever. She's the off-the-assembly-line Big Bertha type.

So Big Bertha in Fannie Hurst's *Lummox* is female, is five feet nine and a half, et cetera, and principal among her many miseries are her feet, which are so enormous that she can't find shoes big enough for them, and consequently she's always suffering in too-tight shoes. And she's an orphan, too, which figures, and she grows up in a whorehouse-type establishment that isn't really a whorehouse but seems like one because females are forever getting fucked over in the place, and when she's all grown and decides to strike out in life on her own, she gets a kitchen gig at some rich people's mansion. She washes beets and cleans chickens and shit like that and is in charge of making delicate dishes for this dainty twenty-five-year-old male *poet*, who is the rich people's son.

This *poet* is named Rollo, and apparently he can't eat fish or roast or any of the other stuff that rich people eat. His digestion is frail. His health is tenuous. He probably discovered the meaning of his poetic life when he was nine years old and consumptive and someone gave him a cup of tea and a *petite madeleine*. Bertha's job is to cook things Rollo can eat without embarrassing himself in front of the important guests who are constantly dining with him and his parents. So Bertha makes him aspic jellies and forms them into blobs that resemble the fish or the roast or whatever's on the menu on a given night.

You can see this coming: One lovely summer night Bertha's done working in the kitchen for the day, and she goes to the servants' porch to give her enormous feet some air. This is a starry night, a pleasantly cool one, and the air is fragrant with summertime foliage. She wiggles her huge toes in the night breeze, probably causing a nearby hydrangea to wilt. And here comes Rollo sniffing around for a taste of some Bertha. He can't eat fish, but hey: Bertha. *That's* tasty. He hangs with her a bit, talks to her about sonnets and how beautiful the night is, and she lets out a few grunts in response. Then he says to her, "Your problems are husky ones, Bertha." Then he checks out her feet and says, "Why, Bertha . . . your feet are like two big white magnolias off our tree."

He doesn't fuck her right then. He lets her mull things for a few hours and get all juicified thinking about him; then he shows up in her room in the servants' quarters. She's been sitting shirtless on the bed, in the dark, pondering the underdevelopment of her tits, and, sure enough, here's Rollo entering her room, saying, "I can see you, Bertha, because you are whiter than the darkness is black."

She puts up the obligatory protest, tells him to leave, but her underside's gushing with the thought of him.

Rollo holds her hand, rubs her. Says, "Strong Bertha." Then "You are a—a tower of silence that is buried under some sea. I want to write you into oxen words."

And there you go: She spreads and lets him stick his little poetic noodle into her, and of course he knocks her up, and it's a scandal, and she gets fired and has to go work for another rich family. Really breaks your heart in half, thinking about it.

So here's the deal: Any real lummox will tell you flat-out that Big Bertha is not a lummox. No way. Big Bertha is a stupid fat chick. That's what she is. Because only a stupid fat chick would go ahead and fuck some guy who just told her he wants to write her into oxen words.

The Hag in Charge of the Hag Studies Department, however, does not share the real lummox's view. Here is what one of her colleagues has to say about Fannie Hurst's *Lummox*:

> This book takes a harsh look at class value, self-worth, and the treatment and expectations of women in the early part of the century. It teaches one to look at the bright side of life no matter how tarnished it may be. It also made [sic] me feel lucky to be in this era where it is much harder to be pushed under by others' prejudices. It is a life lesson to remember so it can't happen in our society again!

Now, were there another book called *Lummox*, and were this book about a man who looks stupid and acts stupid but in fact really isn't stupid and in fact is only looking and acting stupid because people will think he's looking and acting stupid no matter what he does, were this book called *Lummox* to appear suddenly in the world, the Hag in Charge would say, "Not *another* book about a boy and his dick!"

So ALL RIGHT, GODDAMMIT. Go ahead and call Mike Magnuson Lummox.

He's your typical *guy* guy, your guy-with-spare-tire guy, et cetera. He's got *lummox* written all over him when he's born: nine pounds six ounces, full head of hair, cries to the delivery-room doctor for a cigarette and a beer, thinks about plooking the nurses in the nursery. Probably. He's nothing fancy, as lummoxes go, but he's raised into the full flower of his lummoxness in an era when the widespread cry in America is for lummoxness to come to an end.

The year he turns eighteen, 1981, is the year Ronald Reagan takes the oath of office for the Presidency of the United States.

Ronald Reagan's advice to young lummoxes, the way Mike figures it, is as follows:

1. Don't fuck anybody but your wife.

2. If you don't have a wife, don't fuck.

3. Don't get stoned and drunk and listen to heavy metal records.

4. Don't have any fun, for any reason, at any time, anywhere.

And also round about the year 1981 is when all those feminist activists from the sixties have grown old enough to do stuff like occupy official positions in universities and control the curricula with the ideas they came up with, over herbal tea and macrobiotic hors d'oeuvres, when they were twenty-two years old and meeting with their study groups and contemplating the overthrow of their oppressors.

These women's advice to young lummoxes is as follows:

1. Don't think with your dick.

Bᴜᴛ sɪɴᴄᴇ ᴇᴠᴇʀʏʙᴏᴅʏ knows that a lummox is guided in life by his dick, let's examine the circumstances of the inner Mike Magnuson from the front end.

This is one chick Mike knows in May of 1983: She's Karen Neilson. A girl with a wholesome-sounding name. A girl a lot of guys want to mount. That's a flat-out fact about Karen Neilson, and she'll totally tell you that. She's fourteen years old, olive-skinned, but looks way older and thicker than a fourteen-year-old. She's got hips the amplitude of a woman in her hard-luck twenties, and the muscular arms, the veins protruding from her forearms and from the tops of her hands. *Acts* older, too: She's been dicked already by every*thing* and every*body*. Her hair's the color of a cast-iron skillet, a rusty black, and she wears it long and in tangles and shakes it whenever a thought crosses her mind—a happy thought, a sad thought, it doesn't matter—as if to say she's been through this before. She's been there, seen it, experienced it already. Here's what she'll tell you: *Nothing's ever new.* And she's probably right.

Her father's a veterinarian in Milwaukee, Wisconsin. His practice specializes in household pets: dogs and cats and an occasional tropical bird—a steady-Eddie suburban-type business—and Karen specializes in making pot pipes out of apples. She's a priestess with an apple. She'll take a pocketknife and cut out the apple core, make a hole through the side of the apple down to where the core used to be, put a screen there and some pot, and she'll light that sucker up. When the pot's given what she wants it to give, when it's dust, and her eyes, which are gray and weary, take on a serene, fathoms-under glaze, she removes the screen and eats the apple.

"Eating the apple afterwards," she says, "is the way the Indians do it."

A sweet girl, that Karen.

Tuesday and Thursday evenings, she goes to Riverside Elementary School in Menomonee Falls, which is a suburb on the northwest corner of Milwaukee, and attends meetings in an upper-floor classroom that's been converted into the Alcoholics Anonymous Clubhouse. A couple dozen of her fellow teens show up for the meetings, too, and sit for an hour in a semicircle and yap. They're all fucked up because of booze. Booze has made them fuck every*body* and every*thing*. Booze has made them do for-garbage in school. Booze has made them not clean their rooms or mind their parents or basically do anything but want to drink more booze. And after they've discussed their horrible lives, they play cards or foosball or set themselves on stools in the clubhouse, stools that are lined up before a soda-fountain bar. Then they wander back into the temptation-laden quadrants of Menomonee Falls, cured, at least for the moment. Karen's cured, too, but after the meetings she makes pipes out of apples anyway, and she drinks. The cure's one day at a time, and if she's bad one night, she'll surely as cats hack hairballs do her best to be good the next day.

So KAREN'S THE ILLEGAL CHICK or whatever she is. And here's the rundown on Riverside Elementary: It's not an elementary school anymore. It's closed. There aren't enough children in Menomonee Falls to fill it.

Mike's dad, Jack Magnuson, superintendent of the Menomonee Falls Public Schools, he's the village's acknowledged expert on why there aren't enough schoolchildren in Menomonee Falls. Jack will tell you straight out that his school system's imploding: down by two thousand students in less than a decade. He's closed five schools already, Riverside being one of them, and he's contemplating closing some more. This enrollment loss—or this is exactly the way he'll say it: *declining enrollment*—is a textbook-example consequence of the baby boom. See, when the boom was on, when Americans were reproducing themselves as quickly as hamsters can, Menomonee Falls had more children than it knew what to do with. There were three, five, seven children in every family. So the village built enough schools to accommodate them and made by-God sure their education was top-notch.

But look: Kids are kids. They never fully appreciate what their elders have done for them. This is how the schoolchildren reward the

Menomonee Falls Public Schools: They get good grades, graduate from high school on time, and they get their asses the hell out of town. They go away to colleges and technical schools and get good jobs and get settled somewhere else, and if they have their own children, and not many of them do, their children attend school somewhere else. End of story.

Jack Magnuson will tell you that 70 percent of the district's graduates go on like this: to higher education, to resettlement in other towns. The other 30 percent—the fuckups with bad grades who *don't* leave town after they graduate—they go to work in the factories and machine shops of Milwaukee and linger in the Menomonee Falls trailer courts and taverns. They're drunk and stuck working for the Man forever, but they're not stupid enough to bring children into the horrors of the Menomonee Falls life they're leading. They're using birth control, buddy. That's for damn sure.

So Riverside Elementary—it's closed, but that doesn't mean the building's a piece of shit. Check it out: It's practically new, built in 1957, and in perfect condition—L-shaped and fireproofed, made of bright blue-and-white glazed brick and dug into a loping hill that rises from the banks of the Menomonee River—and the school district rents space here to two community organizations: Alcoholics Anonymous, which meets in a room upstairs; and Bright Days Day Care, which occupies six rooms downstairs, the rooms where the kindergartners and the first-graders used to be. Jack Magnuson is officially pleased with this arrangement; renting out the space is the best the district can do under the circumstances. They can't let a first-rate building like this go to waste.

But while the Riverside building may not be a piece of shit, it certainly is located next to a lot of it. The locals call it Sewerside School, and with good reason. Between the school grounds and the Menomonee River stands the five-acre Menomonee Falls sewage-treatment plant. Here, not a hundred yards from a state-of-the-art elementary school, is where the toilets of Menomonee Falls drain. Here is where the Menomonee Falls citizenry's solids settle in three vast brick tanks and where their liquids are sprayed through rotating aluminum noz-zles into a circular rock-filtration bed that's a hundred feet wide. A heady mist rises from the sewage-treatment plant every day of the year; on calm days Riverside Elementary is shrouded in an excrescent fog.

MIKE MAGNUSON has just turned twenty. He stands five feet ten. Goes 230 pounds most days. His hair's red and greasy and curly, prone to sticking out to the side as if he's grabbed a 440-volt cable and can't let go, and he's got a big red beard that he keeps big to cover the zits that grow on his chin like buboes. What else? Oh, and he doesn't give a hoot about much. His personal goals: (1) to be a rock star, (2) to get wasted at kickass parties every day, (3) to get regular hand jobs and stuff from supercool groupie chicks, (4) um, probably more hand jobs after that.

Sure, he's not living the rock star's life just yet, but he's getting around to it. He's just got some things to sort out first.

Like, for one thing: A year ago, he flunked out of the University of Wisconsin at Eau Claire. Really disappointed his parents. But he sure had a great time. He did the music-major thing, went off to college figuring on spending the rest of his life playing drums in bars and get-ting drunk in them, which is a very cool life's goal. And he did get drunk. He went to the dollar-a-pitcher happy hours. He played drums in a couple of jazz combos, played a gig or two. He stayed up late at night listening to Miles Davis records and smoking pot and ponder-ing the wonders of Igor Stravinsky and Anton Webern and Alban Berg. He even *did* get a hand job once; chick named Alice, French horn player, she volunteered for the duty at a party, just before Thanksgiving break. But the going-to-music-classes part of being a music major sucked total ass, in his opinion: all those days sitting there with kids who wanted to become public-school band directors when they grew up. Fuck being a *band* director. What kinda people want to spend the rest of their lives directing the pep band at the bas-ketball game? Not Mike, that's for no-kidding certain.

So he blew off his classes, never turned in his homework, and, presto, he's a full-timer at Custom Products Corporation, Milwaukee. He's machining parts, ten hours a day, six days a week.

But he sure has got something to live for. He's got himself the monster drum set now. Brand-new jet-black Pearl. Double bass. Four tom-toms. Eight-ply maple. Even the snare drum is eight-ply maple. Seven cymbals and boom stands. Six Zildjian cymbals. He's got one eighteen-inch Paiste china-type cymbal, which, when Mike bashes it with a drumstick, lets out a bark like a dog with galloping pneumonia. You get the picture. It's the rock-star kit. It's worth three thousand dollars. Fuckin-A. On the first of every month Mike pays the Farmers and Merchants Bank in Menomonee Falls a hundred dollars for the set. Worth every penny of it.

At Custom Products, he runs a Moog multistation drill press that bores out piston heads for Harley-Davidson Sportsters. Eighty piston heads a day is his quota: That's what the lifers at Custom tell him to do—no more, no less—and that's exactly what he does. The work's easy, basically. Just dirty and dull. But it'll still mess you up. The machine drills into metal, and little sharp chips of metal flash are everywhere around the machine: on the parts themselves, on the press-cycle buttons, on the levers, and so on. Everything Mike touches at work has metal chips on it. Mike's hands are a gridwork of cuts and nicks and tiny embedded metal filings that form pus-seeping sores on his fingers, infections from the oil-based coolant the drill bits require to bore a hole smooth. At night, when he picks up his drumsticks, his hands hurt as if tiny knives poke them, which is true: His hands are full of metal.

Mike's been renting the old music room in Riverside Elementary for thirty-five bucks a month. He doesn't exactly qualify as a community organization, but his father has arranged for Mike to rent the room under the auspices of "an individual engaged in musical study and research." Which is the kind of manure only a superintendent can successfully sling. Mike's supposed to practice his drums here, on the bottom floor of the building, across the hallway from the six rooms of

Bright Days. While Bright Days is open, weekdays, six in the morning till six at night, Mike's not allowed to practice; his drumming freaks out the toddlers and keeps the infants from sleeping. But this doesn't mean squat to Mike. He's never at Riverside during the day.

The north wall of the music room is lined entirely with tall windows that open to a concrete walk-in storm gutter that extends along the length of the building. The gutter is ten feet wide and fifteen feet tall, a waterless moat between the upper playground and the building. On top of the gutter: a series of steel grates put there to prevent children from falling in. A dozen years ago, when Mike was in the second grade, he used to play Hot Wheels on top of the storm gutter. He would push his toy cars along the concrete ledge and make motor-revving sounds. Sometimes he would lose control of a Hot Wheels car, and it would plummet through the grate fifteen feet down to the stones that lined the gutter bottom. Every time this happened, Mike would get weepy because he could see his Hot Wheels car on the stones down there, and the school janitor would never go into the gutter to retrieve it for him. "You should know better," the janitor would say, "than to play with your cars on top of this gutter."

Some nights, when Bright Days is closed and Mike's hands hurt too much for him to play his drums, he looks out at the stones and wonders if some of his Hot Wheels are still there, rusted under the rocks. Mike's still here, after all. He hasn't gone anywhere. In fact, Riverside Elementary is where he lives. This is his home. He sleeps here at night, on the floor, next to his drum set. He's been doing this for five months, since January.

THIS IS THE STORY: In January, Mike hauls his drums into the music room and sets them up on a foot-high carpeted riser that used to be the music room's stage. The carpet's lime green. The walls: lime green. And Mike's drums: jet black and shiny. Mike sees the room, the drums, and experiences the endless-possibilities-of-rhythm-and-truth thing. He's been living at home with his parents since he flunked out of college. A disgrace. But home's been okay: plenty to eat and a comfortable place to sleep. But he's got these drums, got the urge to be with them. And he's twenty. Goddammit, a twenty-year-old man shouldn't be living with his parents anyway. That's fucked *up*. He tells his folks he's moving out. They say, Cool. Go. But they don't know he moves into the school.

And Riverside's a wonderful building, sure enough. Fireproof. Clean. But it's not designed for somebody to live in it for an extended time. For one thing, elementary schools don't have communal showers; they're not in the code. So there's no way for Mike to bathe. And because most of the building's boarded off to save on heat, Mike doesn't have access to the bathrooms. They're here, all right: a boys' and a girls' room upstairs, each adjacent to the Alcoholics Anonymous Clubhouse, and some kindergarten-size ones in the Bright Days' rooms. But he doesn't have the keys. He only has the keys for the lower entrance and the music room. What does a guy expect for thirty-five bucks?

So all that first month he lives in Riverside, he doesn't bathe. He's not shit out of luck; he just doesn't have a place to take one. He pisses in a bubbler in the hallway. Goes outside, into the January cold, to take a dump. Once, when it's supercold, thirty below zero and windy, too cold to drop his ass outside, he squats and takes a crap right there on the hallway linoleum and wipes up the turd with one of his torn flannel shirts. He's got no way to make hot food, no way to wash his clothes, and, let's face it, he fucking stinks. He smells like the cutting fluid that spatters him all day at the factory. Sweat and cigarettes and beer and pot, too. He's not what you call steady-chick material.

But he's a guy. He's cool with living raw. What the fuck. He doesn't care that he shits outside, or on the floor, or that the sewage treatment plant's steaming right near him all the time. He's got the drums, man. They're kick*ass*. He'll clean himself up some *other* time. Besides, his parents' house is, like, three blocks away. He's been in nose range of the sewage treatment plant his whole life.

KAREN NEILSON, she looks at who she was four years ago: She sees herself in the last fifth grade class to attend Riverside Elementary. No pigtails for her even then. She's one of those girls in jeans who sit cross-legged by the fence, pulling grass blades from the ground and pretending to smoke them. She's in high school now, a freshman with a hopeful future. Like, give *her* a *break*. Like, what bullshit the future is. Completely. But over the last four years she's proved herself to be a bad girl. Clinical in her excesses, that's what her father says she's been. A girl for whom teen meetings at the Alcoholics Anonymous Clubhouse are designed. Her raps: Emptied her father's liquor cabinet more times than most children visit the zoo or the museum or the county fair. Slept with high school boys. (Oh, if we *have* to.) Made lewd advances toward her male teachers. (Mr. Hendrickson, do you think my jeans are *too* tight?) She's skipped school or shown up drunk at school enough times that her behavior has been brought to the attention of Jack Magnuson, who has duly noted her transgressions.

Jack in fact takes extra note of Karen Neilson because a couple of years back, just before Christmas, on a gray afternoon, Karen's father put to sleep the Magnuson family dog, a twelve-year-old golden retriever named Ginger. Ginger had a stroke and couldn't walk anymore, which is basically the end for you, if you're a dog.

So Karen's father kills dogs for a living. Mike Magnuson's father superintends a school system that's spiraling down the toilet. Mike sleeps nights on the floor, next to his drum set in Riverside Elementary, on the old music room's stage. And Karen's taking the Cure, a day at a time toward happiness. She's maintaining a C average in school, and everybody's proud of her.

THIS IS MIKE'S boyhood-in-a-nutshell story: When he's in diapers, he stays at home with mom. She's a housewife, which is common for women when Mike's a boy. All the moms are housewives. It's the mid-sixties. The suburbs. The era of June Cleaver. Moms are supposed to bake and smile and worry their asses silly about everybody's troubles but their own. But Mike's mom is what you'd call progressive nevertheless, even though her profession is housework. She keeps up with the current news, reads contemporary literature, gives a damn about politics, votes Democrat, is opposed to the war in Vietnam, and secretly admires hippies. Mom listens to public radio all day: *Morning Concert, Afternoon Concert.* The orchestras of the world accompany her housework.

Mike spends his days rolling on the carpet near the radio, twisting his body with the surge and the rhythm of symphonies and piano sonatas and operas and string quartets. If for some reason mom switches off the radio, Mike hums what he's just heard and waves his arms as if he's Sir Neville Mariner conducting The Orchestra of the Academy of Saint Martin in the Fields. Mom says, "That's right, Michael. That's Sibelius." Or "Now *that's* from *Die Gotterdammerung.*"

Sometimes his mother gives him big picture books to play with, coffee-table art books, and he spends hours making stacks of them and staring at glossy plates of Brueghel and Rembrandt and Kandinsky and Roualt. He pretends he's living inside a triptych of Hieronymus Bosch, standing among the villagers while blackbirds fly in circles around Christ.

So there you go: Deep down, Mike's is a pussy's heart. Trouble is, because he is a lummox, he is incapable of *behaving* like a pussy.

Like this: One June day in 1966, when he's three and potty-trained and ready to mingle with the society of his likes, his mom sends him outside to play with the neighborhood kids. All the families up and down the street have kids—three, four, five of them—and it's routine in the neighborhood for moms to assemble the kids in somebody's front yard to let them play. The older kids supervise the younger, and good wholesome middle-class fun is had by all.

The Magnuson yard, it's as green as can be, a mowed lawn, manicured shrubs. The lilac hedge along the boulevard gives off a pleasant little-old-lady smell. Ten kids play here on the lawn and sidewalk, the older kids messing around with roller skates—the old-fashioned type that you fasten on to tennis shoes—the younger kids dreaming of their roller-skate futures, their bigger days when they can do whatever they please.

Mike stands on the lawn and observes them laughing and poking at each other and having fun the way kids everywhere do. They remind him of an opera he listened to with his mother that morning. *Peter Grimes*. That's a neat name for an opera. *Peter Grimes* sounds dirty. It sounds like trouble. Mom says it's written, both libretto and music, by Benjamin Britten. It's his monument. It's about a fisherman who's having some rotten luck. A real metaphor is what Mom says. There's an awesome moment near the end when a mob gathers and sings "Peter Grimes" at the tops of their lungs. *Peter Grimes!* This is ennobling! *Peter Grimes!* This is something, Mike's thinking, he's got to share with everybody! He toddles to the sidewalk, takes up a position in the middle of the semicircle of kids, drops his trousers, and makes dirt, right there on the sidewalk.

The girls scream. The boys run. Up and down the street, dogs bark.

Mike admires what he's done—a shiny turd steaming on the sidewalk. His heart stirs. "Peter Grimes," he sings. Perfectly in tune.

Mom comes out of the house and sees her son's contribution to the arts, recognizes it immediately as something essentially operatic, and she doesn't startle. She says to the kids, "Watch it."

And they do. They watch it. They surround the turd and stare at it till Mom returns with some newspaper and a wet rag. While she cleans, the kids remain quiet, awestruck, their eyes wide, fixed on the unimaginable. Mike Magnuson's done this to them, created this response in them. Mike Magnuson's done something that none of the neighborhood kids would ever think of doing. He's got special talent. He's an original. Today: *Peter Grimes*. Tomorrow: What a world Mike has before him!

A couple of years later, when he starts kindergarten at Riverside Elementary, he's hefty, off the weight-chart range for a boy his age. The kids call him Fatso. They call him Tub O' Lard. But sticks and stones can break bones and so on, and Mike lets the names slide over him. He *is* chubby. Wears Huskies jeans. Likes seconds at snack. Has a beer gut that isn't one yet but looks like one. *Obese*, Mom says. And he knows it's *wrong* to be *obese*. But he's got other concerns. He wants to be somebody people notice.

One area that engages him: He's mastering the Ancient Art of Class Clown Grab-Ass. Really enjoys himself at it. He can belch like a forty-year-old construction worker and often does so when the classroom's as quiet as a church, at naptime. At lunchtime, he gargles his milk and steals cookies from little girls sitting across the table from him. During art period, he throws crayons at the other kids, sticks crayons in his nose. Performs armpit farts, too. And blow-the-palm-of-the-hand farts. And the stick-out-the-tongue fart, too. He's got an emission for every occasion.

But he's still a pussy. He's got that dainty-deep-down heart. He loves music more than anything in the world. So his parents sign him up for piano lessons. He's not a virtuoso, but he tries to be. In no time, he learns to play Bach in a savage and percussive way and at tempos far faster than J. S. had ever intended. When he's not practicing his two-part inventions or his preludes and fugues, he sits in the basement and listens endlessly to Bach records that Mom procures for him at the public library. How Bach soars in Mike and raises goose bumps on his arms!

Sometimes he has a neighborhood boy over for a visit and takes him down to the basement on the pretext of playing Hot Wheels, but Mike instead tries to enlighten the boy with a Brandenburg Concerto or with Wanda Landowska's recording of the *Well-Tempered Clavier* or with E. Power Biggs performing from *The Art of the Fugue*. Pretty soon, the boy leaves; no normal boy from Menomonee Falls can tolerate sitting still and listening patiently to the ecstasy of Bach.

In 1970, two weeks before the Kent State massacre, Mike's in Mrs. Weber's second-grade classroom, taking the Stanford Achievement Test, a see-what-the-kids-know test with multiple-choice questions that requires a Number Two pencil and that the children in the classroom sit still and concentrate for a period of several days. Mrs. Weber is a short and humorless woman, curly blond hair and cat's-eye glasses and a weak nasal voice. This is her first year teaching in Menomonee Falls, and she takes her job seriously. She's a professional. She's got her work cut out for her, too. She's got the superintendent's son in her classroom, and she thinks, and has ample evidence to support her thinking, that he's a behavior problem.

And Mike thinks the Stanford Achievement Test—and Mrs. Weber—are boring beyond belief. We're talking simple math problems and simple reading-comprehension problems. *Very* boring. Yesterday, the first day of testing, Mike completed each section of the test a full half hour before the rest of his classmates. But he'd been a good boy, sat there at his desk and avoided fiddling with his pencils and being in any way disruptive.

But today Mike's ants-in-the-pantsy. He figures if he can finish his test section quicker than everybody else, he should be allowed to leave the classroom when he's done and maybe go outside to hang out by the fence and pull grass blades from the ground and pretend to smoke them. He asks Mrs. Weber if he may do this, and she says he may not. "There are rules we must follow," she says.

So Mike and the children in Mrs. Weber's class take to their desks quietly at 8:15 A.M., get their test booklets and their answer sheets, and they begin their test that's to last, timed, one hour precisely. This test is about natural science: whether, say, trees grow in annual increments or whether sunshine's in some way connected to the rain or whether the Earth, like Mrs. Weber's head, is round. Mike thinks these questions are needless and obvious and not at all as interesting as the beauty of Bach he's been contemplating lately.

He finishes the test in a half hour, carries his papers and his Number Two pencil to Mrs. Weber's desk, sets these items down there. He looks at her hand, at its gauzy older-person skin. She's holding a Number Two pencil, just like the kids, but she's revising her lesson plans with it. She frowns at Mike and whispers, "Return to your seat quietly, please, and wait for the others to finish." And he does as he's told.

He stares out the window. This classroom's on the upper floor of

Riverside Elementary, and from Mike's vantage point he can see only the sky, which is a boring midmorning blue. He listens to his class-mates fidgeting, sniffling, struggling with their tests, and he recalls in his mind the Partita for Solo Violin he listened to last night with Mom. He remembers the melody, how it weaves with the world and soars over it; then he transforms the violin part he hears in his mind to his fingers, and he begins methodically tapping out the rhythm of the melody on his desk.

The other children keep at their tests. They don't notice that Mike's tapping his fingers in such an artful manner, and this lack of attention depresses Mike. Here these kids are, answering with much agony irrel-evant questions about an irrelevant natural world, and they're not noticing that one child among them has answers to the planet beyond what's on their tests: The glory of Bach! The vision! The perfection!

Mike strains forward in his desk, spreads his butt cheeks as wide as he can, announces in a dramatic voice to the class something he's heard often during the evening television reports of Vietnam—"Fire in the hole!"—and he bursts forth with an earsplitting eruption of gas.

Mrs. Weber drops the pencil she's holding. Two girls sitting next to Mike jump up from their desks and scream. And within seconds such a melee begins in the classroom—boys laughing, girls screaming and running for the door—that Mrs. Weber breaks down and cries.

Eventually the hubbub subsides. Mrs. Weber gets control of herself and of the classroom, and she sends Mike summarily to the office, with a note for the principal, written in a mean and scrawling large-lettered hand, that says, "This boy is a disruptive lummox."

On his way to the office, Mike reads Mrs. Weber's note, and though he's never formally encountered the word *lummox* before, he imme-diately comprehends its meaning. *Lummox* means fat and naughty and rude. *Lummox* means Mike Magnuson. But what Mike and Mrs. Weber and the principal don't know about this disruptive lummox is that he's just posted the highest Stanford Achievement Test scores for all the second-grade classrooms in the entire district that year and that his high scores won't be equaled during the following ten-year period the Stanford Achievement Test is offered in Menomonee Falls. But that's irrelevant. His mental aptitude doesn't endear him to anybody; it never will.

The principal hollers at Mike for a while, gives him a two-week term of detention. Because the principal is in more or less daily contact with Mike's father the superintendent, Mike's father knows about the gas bomb within the hour of its explosion. And, like many times before, when Mike's been apprehended at one shenanigan or another during the school day, Mike goes home that night and receives from his father a long lecture about how to conduct himself like a proper young man, instead of like a barnyard animal.

Two weeks later, the Ohio National Guard fires live ammunition into a crowd of protesting students at Kent State University, killing five students and wounding nine, and while Mike watches the footage of the shooting on the evening news, while he's still in the doghouse for breaking wind during the achievement test, he wonders what it really means to conduct himself like a proper young man. If he behaves properly, does that mean that one day he *won't* get shot? Or if he doesn't behave, does that mean that he will get shot? Certainly those dead students weren't behaving properly. They were supposed to be doing their homework, not smoking dope and waving banners and badgering well-meaning law-enforcement officers on the university quadrangle. They were supposed to be preparing for orderly, proper lives—lives that benefited America, that produced more proper children, like themselves, who could get jobs or go to war or spend their hard-earned dollars in the good old American Gross National Economy. But there they are: as dead as their happiness. And here's Mike: a second-grade lummox who can post high scores on a test.

AND HERE'S MIKE AGAIN, a grown-up lummox who lives in a closed-down elementary school next to a sewer. It's a shitty life, but at least it's the same old shit. He knows the terrain. So he lives like an animal. So what? Most people do. All he has to do is look at his three best buddies for proof.

BUDDY #1

Bob Schaeffer: He's twenty-two. He needs fresh air, exercise, and a new shirt. He's five feet four inches tall. The runt type, basically. Brown hair, wiry and dusty-looking. He wears the traditional Pabst Blue Ribbon cap at all times. His skin: sallow and pasty. He's got the somebody-might-have-punched-him dark circles under his eyes, but nobody's punched him. Too bad. He just doesn't go outside during the day. He subsists exclusively on a diet of pizza and hamburgers and thinks that's excellent. He's proud of himself. He says he's twenty-two years old and has never eaten an apple, not even a piece of apple pie. He also says he's never fucked a girl older than fourteen. "After a girl reaches fourteen," Bob says, "she's downhill from there."

He's telling the truth, too; at least the where-his-brain's-at part is true. Bob's effected to leave his dick in high school, where he figures it will have the cleanest pickings and therefore be happiest and be the most productive. That's very thoughtful of Bob. And back in high school, Bob's was a happy dick. He'd been editor of the school year-book, played the lead in the school play, *A Funny Thing Happened on the Way to the Forum.* He did serious damage in the pretty-young-nerd-girl department, still does. He says it's his duty to America that he test-drives the new ones rolling off the assembly line. Gots to make sure all their parts are in working order.

He lives at his mom's house, in the basement. The whole basement is his room. Pool table. Wall-to-wall red carpeting. Party mirrors. Disco ball. Plush-red sectional pit group. Big-screen TV. VCR. Hundred-watt Pioneer stereo. Refrigerator. Buys all this shit, and he delivers *pizzas* for a living! *And* he's got plenty *extra* cash for cases of Pabst and Miller and bottles of that Boone's Farm Watermelon fizz that makes a dickwarmer of your basic fourteen-year-old, gots-to-get-over-being-tentative nerd girl. Debate-team chick maybe. Maybe the concert-choir type. The future-Ph.D. type. Bob's basement is obviously party central. He invites high school chicks over whenever. The nerdettes. They drink. They give him hand jobs. He fucks one once in a while. It's a cool scene with Bob. He'll tell you that.

BUDDY #2

This is Hammer. A biker dude. He comes to Mike by way of Bob's mom.

She, Bob's mom, is Sally Schaeffer. She's got the pasty skin, the dark under-the-eye circles. She used to be six feet tall and probably gorgeous, but Godzilla stepped on her a long time ago, squashed her to four feet eleven. She goes 200, 210 pounds or so. Wears beige XXL T-shirts with burnholes and bar-burger stains on them. Stretch-polyester pants. Bob once upon a time emerged from Sally's cervix, no doubt of it. She's been separated from Bob's dad for five years. No divorce, though. It's a Catholic thing. Most things are. She gets the house in Menomonee Falls, gets Bob and all his bullshit. Which is bad, but better than his dad's. She works when the mood strikes her: an occasional light-industrial day shift, a couple of days telemarketing, that type of work. She hangs out at the Old Lamp, your regular friendly neighborhood dump. The Old Lampers are photocopies of Sally: If they got jobs they're hoping to get placed on disability or something. They don't *want* to work, either, which is easy enough to understand. Who the hell *does* want to work?

So Hammer knows Sally from the bar, and Mike knows Hammer because they both know Bob. Biblical. Hammer *is*, too: He goes about 275, maybe 290 with boots and leathers. He's twenty-one. Thinks he's forty, Sally's age. He's got the forty-year-old beard anyway. And the beer gut. His brother's name is Wolf, and Wolf is president of the Milwaukee Chapter of ABATE, which Hammer says stands for Associated

Brotherhood Against Territorial Enactments. ABATE's against motor-cycle helmet laws. And some other things. And Hammer's drunk or stoned. Perpetually. Who isn't? He says he can and will kill anybody who crosses him—with his bare hands—but nobody ever does.

Sally's got an empty room upstairs at her place, which she rents out. Hammer moves in, pays a hundred bucks a month. He's not the first man to move in at Sally's; if it was any other woman, he would try to fuck her. But Hammer's got standards. He wouldn't fuck Sally with Mike's dick. He can't believe that beandick Bob's *dad* ever wanted to fuck Sally in the *first place*. Makes a guy want to puke. The man living at Sally's before Hammer—a dude named Steve—he got arrested and sent to prison for stealing a semi-trailerload of frozen turkeys and try-ing to sell them, for two bucks apiece, down at the Old Lamp. Stupid fucker. Hammer will never let it be said otherwise.

"Stupid fucker," Hammer says. "Shoulda put him out of his misery. Saved the cops the trouble of hauling him to the hoosegow."

One night at the Old Lamp, Hammer meets a woman who's wear-ing a gray T-shirt with ROAD AMERICA silkscreened on it. Road America, see, is where they race motorcycles and Formula Ones over in Elkhart Lake. Hammer's been there a few times and has there decided that the roar of superchargers is about the most incredibly kickass thing in the world, and the woman in the T-shirt is your deluxe-edition tall and willowy chick with blond hair and a dirty tan. Could be Miss August in *Iron Horse* magazine. Probably is. And she's friendly with Hammer, looks him in the eye when she talks to him, laughs with him when he cracks on the Milwaukee Outlaws and the Hell's Angels and them people. Then she touches him, once, lightly on the arm before excusing herself to go to the ladies' room. That's what she calls it: *Ladies' room*. Hammer is prepared to eat her pussy break-fast, lunch, and dinner for the next ten years. At least. But somewhere in there Hammer steps outside the bar to look under the hood of somebody's junkbucket Chevy Impala only to discover that it won't start because the goddam distributor cap is loose. Waste of his fuck-ing time. Chevy Impalas are *useless*. Get a *Ford*, asshole. When he gets back inside the bar, the woman's gone. Hammer doesn't know her name, never will. Therefore, she's Road America, that'll have to be her name, and Hammer's in love with Road America, but he'll never see her again. And the big man commences to weeping and pulling his hair over this.

A few weeks later, Mike goes over to Bob's for beers and bowls and high school girls and whatever. In the driveway there's a sorry scene. Sally and Bob and a bunch of people from the bar are standing in the driveway looking put-out and shit-upon. Like usual. They're smoking butts, wringing their chins, shuffling their feet.

Mike says hello to Bob. "What the fuck, Bob? What's wrong with your basement?"

"Hammer's down there," Bob says. "He's got a gun."

This shit would happen in Mike's family, in Mike's neighborhood, somebody would call the police pronto. But here in Schaefferland, they don't call the cops to deal with a man with a gun. Bob keeps dope in the house, plenty of it, and pharmaceuticals. You got to hope tensions defuse naturally under these conditions.

Mike says, "What's he doing with the gun?"

Bob says, "Talking about shooting himself."

Mike doesn't give a damn. He's thirsty. He wants to smoke a bowl. He goes right in the house, goes downstairs, and finds Hammer.

Hammer's mounded in a chair in front of a card table, on which is a .45 Colt semiautomatic, a bottle of Jack Daniel's, and a pack of Marlboros. He rotates his head slowly toward Mike, barely registering him there. He's crying, for chrissakes. A steady extrusion of tears.

"Road America don't love me," Hammer says.

This moment is made for TV. Mike says, "*Everybody* loves you, Hammer." And just like that, Mike picks up the pistol, fumbles out the clip, and puts a concerned-priest expression on his face.

Hammer wipes his eyes, sniffles, jacks a Marlboro from his pack, and ignites. "You think *everybody* loves me?" he says.

"Fuckin-A," Mike says. "Those people upstairs, they're worried about you, man. They wouldn't be worrying if they didn't love you."

"No shit," Hammer says. His eyes clear up. He's over it. "What the fuck's wrong with Road *America*? Why don't *she* love me?"

Mike says, "She's a cunt if she doesn't."

Mike lets this sink in. He feels the heavy pistol in his hand, sees Hammer mulling over the complexities of love and human understanding. He reaches to Hammer's Marlboro pack and takes one.

"You mind, buddy?" Mike says. *Buddy*. Straight off the TV. Best Actor in a Prime-Time Drama, goddammit, goes to *Magnuson*.

Hammer stands, grabs Mike's hand, and gives it a heave. Says, "You can bum a cigarette from me anytime you want." Hammer swears an oath that him and Mike will be brothers forever.

And they do become brothers, in the tavern way. They meet up at the Old Lamp for beers and such a few times a week. Get drunk. Get stupid. They're naturals at it. When Mike gets his job at Custom Products, he puts in the good word in Hammer's behalf, and Hammer joins the crew. They're within earshot of each other all day and most every night at the bar. Hammer and Mike are goddam inseparable, Hammer says.

BUDDY #3

His name is Todd Mitchell. He's gone from Menomonee Falls. He's tall and skinny and dark-haired. He's always got chicks. He's going to be famous. One way or the other. Right now, in fact, he's taking a shot at entering *National Geographic Magazine*'s hall of fame. He's attempting to walk the entire Wisconsin Ice Age Trail in the wintertime. No shit. That's eight hundred miles, deep snow on the trail, night after night tenting it in subzero cold. Pretty awesome, hey? Todd's got a dog along on the hike, too. Roxanne. Alaskan malamute–German shepherd mix. Nine months old. So she's a puppy really. Todd's a man. Really. When Todd took off on the hike, the *Milwaukee Journal* ran an article on him. MAN AND HIS DOG ATTEMPT THE IMPOSSIBLE. That right there: fame. Buddy, Todd's an impressive dude.

He's a drummer, too, when he's not out performing wilderness feats. Way better than Mike, or that's what he tells Mike. When they were in high school, they hung around and listened to records basically constantly. Frank Zappa. Jeff Beck. Stanley Clarke. Dixie Dregs. They dug the tunes with the coolest drummers. The complicated ones. Thing was, though, Todd was the genuine article drumming-wise. *Modern Drummer* was going to write articles about him someday. Smoke a bowl, put on the headphones, and drum along with anything. How many people can do that? Well, Mike can. But Todd says just not good enough for *Modern Drummer*.

BUT MIKE'S NO DUMMY. He lives a shitty month in Riverside and starts adjusting to the circumstances. He's good at adapting to adverse conditions. He doesn't own a car, but every morning Hammer picks him up and takes him to work. Every night after work he goes with Hammer to the Old Lamp or to another tavern and drinks beer and does shots of tequila and maybe eats a hamburger or some fried cheese curds. He's getting his sustenance. Exceeding it. Hey, Magnuson's a fat fuck yet. It ain't like he's *starving*.

Some nights he invites Old Lampers over to see his drum set. He wants them to see how lovely it is, how it's a testament to a man who works in a factory and yet has the inner soul of an artist. Honest of him: to expose his pussified side like that. Cool drums, the Old Lampers say. They're cool people. No shit they are. And the more Old Lampers who come to visit, the more they want to visit again because the music room at Riverside Elementary is about the finest party location anybody's ever seen. There's a whole goddam elementary school here to get fucked up in.

Middle of February, Hammer shows Mike how to break into the other rooms in the school building by sticking a knife into the doorjamb and prying open the latch, and, bango, Mike's got access to the toilets and sinks in Bright Days. He starts sponge-bathing regularly and washing his hair with bar soap. He's one clean motherfucker all of a sudden.

First week of March, Mike and Hammer break into the old cafeteria and find an old floor-model chest cooler, the one that used to hold half pints of milk years ago, and they lug it into the music room and rig it so it can hold a half barrel of beer.

Friday nights and Saturday nights thereafter, Hammer brings the barrel, Bob brings the high school girls over, and the beer flows. They have a secret system to gain access to the parties, too. The lower-entrance door to Riverside is a hundred feet from the doorway to the music room and is always locked, and if there's partying going on in the music room, nobody can hear someone knocking on the door. So folks have to walk all the way around the building to the upper playground and jump up and down on the grate above the storm gutter, producing a thunderous noise that nobody, no matter how stoned or drunk or stupid they are, can possibly miss. Then Mike or whoever goes to the window and looks up through the grate, sees who it is that's here to party, and then Mike or whoever goes to the lower entrance and waits the roughly two minutes it takes for the newcomer to walk all the way back around the building. It's a hassle. It's complicated. But nobody bitches about it, not to Mike, anyway.

THEN TODD REAPPEARS in Menomonee Falls. End of April. Not the cruelest month on record. Weather's been fair. Pleasant. Todd's got his hiking equipment with him. The backpack and the boots and tin pans and that junk. Stuff still looks brand-new. He's got Roxanne with him. She's dog-size now, one hundred pounds probably, but still puppylike. Plays tug-of-war with an old pair of pants, fetches tennis balls, does the cute stuff most of the time. A year-old dog. That's the best age. But she snarls and snaps like a Milwaukee Outlaws bitch whenever anybody gets near Todd's backpack. Trained guard dog, Todd says. But he won't say for-squat about his adventures on the Ice Age

Trail. He looks the same as when he left, acts the same. He doesn't want to talk about it. That's cool with everybody. If he didn't make the hike, that's *his* goddam problem.

Right away, he tries to stay at Bob's because all the good pussy is there and cleaned for his immediate insertion, but Sally would rather smear Alpo over her tits than have that big snarling attack dog in her house. Sally don't have *space* for that bullshit. Fuck *you*. And anyway, Hammer's already there, paying his rent, doing odd jobs around the house, cleaning the gutters, and removing the sludge from the air conditioner and all that. Services everything on the property, that helpful fat bastard. Except Sally.

So Todd surveys his options and does the best he can do. He sits Mike down, gets him drunk, kisses his ass. You're a great drummer, man. Phe-fucking-nomenal. And, like, there's a big party going on *constantly* in the music room, anyway. And who'll ever know if my shit's *living* there or not?

Mike says, "Cool. Move on in."

But the sharp tooth in the blow job of friendship here is this: Mike's got to lay down rules. He's got to watch his *ass*, man. We got his *dad* to contend with, too. It's like this: Five-thirty in the morning, Todd and Roxanne have to split Riverside exactly when Mike splits Riverside for Custom Products because at six o'clock the kiddies show up for Bright Days. If anybody from Bright Days sees that dog, we're talking total disaster. And Todd and Roxanne have to stay vanished till night, like, *dark* night, till Mike gets back from work or from the bar or wherever. Got to be incognito and out of sight, buddy.

Todd says, "I can do that easy."

And he does. He moves in his gear and his dog, leaves on time in the morning, returns in the night on time. Works out great all around. Some nights, Todd and Roxanne don't come back at all, which is cool with Mike.

So okay, okay: Here's your live-action Thursday-night scene in the music room. This is the last day of May. Summer's coming on. Warm and green and dry. It's party time. Always. Tonight's not a keg-ger-type thing. It's just your small-variety, bottled-beer-type warm-up thing *before* the big weekend sessions get under way. Todd's here. And Roxanne the dog. Hammer's here. Bob's here with six nerdettes. The Blues Brothers boom on Mike's boom box, and the girls dance, and everybody's doing *super*awesome. For sure. Slurping beers. Smoking. Playing with Roxanne. It's a Kodak situation. Totally.

And someone jumps up and down on the grating above the storm gutter. Mike goes to the window—good host, hey?—and sees who's jumping. There, in white painter paints and a blue flannel shirt, is Karen Neilson. She squats over the grate, stares down at Mike through her hair, which is hanging fuckably over her eyes.

"I don't feel like going to Drunk Teens tonight," she says.

She's been in the music room a couple of times before. A while back. In March maybe. Mike remembers thinking Karen might be a hand job waiting to happen. Maybe not. He thinks that about all the chicks. But wait: He remembers her because her dad's the veterinarian who put Ginger to sleep four Christmases ago. That shit's hard to forget. The foggy day. Slushy snow on the ground. Mom and dad having a glass of wine in the middle of the afternoon. No Ginger. Her water bowl in the kitchen.

Mike says, "What the hell's wrong with Drunk Teens?" He's being a prick intentionally. You're *supposed* to be a prick because that's what chicks dig.

Karen says, "I'm *bored* is what's wrong with it."

Two minutes later Mike meets Karen at the lower entrance and lets her in. The hallway is dark and spooky-looking. To her.

"This is *really* cool," she says.

In the music room everybody's watching Hammer squaring off with Roxanne. Hammer's touching Todd's backpack. Pisses Roxanne the fuck off. She's snarling and foaming at Hammer. He's brandishing a fist at her.

"Go ahead and try me, you hairy bitch," Hammer says. "Nobody fucks with Hammer and expects to live."

And everybody's laughing their asses off. Really *high*-larious.

Karen's familiar with dogs to the point of finding as much amusement in them as she might find sucking off a senior boy after Drunk Teens. She'll do it. But she'd rather be *done* with it. And get back to smoking pot. She wanders more or less directly to Mike's drum set and sits herself down on the drum stool.

Mike doesn't like this crap. *Ask*, for chrissakes. They're not *your* drums, hey. So he goes over to chew her a new one.

But she's got it together. She's mellow. Doesn't reach for the drumsticks. Doesn't touch the drums at all. Instead she digs into her legside pocket and produces a Golden Delicious apple.

"These drums are *awesome*," she says.

That strokes Mike into a pudding-whipped pussy. "My pride and joy," he says.

She says, "They're *so* beautiful."

Takes out her pocketknife. Slices out the apple core. Cuts a hole in the apple's side. Steady movements. Precise. Mike stares at her hands, how smooth they are, how the veins stand on the tops of them. They'd sure look good on Mike's dick.

When the apple's a perfect pipe, when she's got the screen in and the pot in, she gazes at the people playing with Roxanne on the other side of the room. She frowns. Says, "Let's you and me go somewhere *private* to smoke this."

Private's *ideal*. They go out to the hallway, the darkness. But Karen's a beacon Mike follows. She leads him to the hallway's end, to a staircase on top of which is the plywood barrier to the upstairs, to where the Drunk Teens meeting's in progress. She leans an ear to the plywood and listens.

"They're doing it now," Karen says.

"What's that?"

"Admitting they're drunks."

She nestles on the top stair. The light's dim, only a thin angle of light poking through the plywood. Mike overdrives his eyeballs trying to make out her features, but she's a silhouette, an outline of raggedy hair. But when she flicks her Bic and lights the pot in the apple, there's the narrow nose, the shiny face, the lips as thin as grass blades. She inhales, unthumbs the Bic, passes the apple to Mike. Brushes her finger against Mike's. Makes him about ready to spuzz.

Karen says, "What's your father think about you living here?"

"He doesn't know," Mike says.

"I *under*stand. My father never knows what *I* do, either."

They pass the apple—a ritual at which they are priest-expert—till the pot's dust; then they take turns taking bites out of the apple till all that's left is sticky stuff on their fingers.

"*Your* father," Mike says. Jerky. Too loud. The pot's on its first wave through him. Making him jumpy. And stupid. "He killed our dog."

"He kills *lots* of dogs," Karen says. "That's part of his job."

They don't say anything for a while, sit there thinking. They've talked about this garbanzo before probably, but Mike can't remember when. Stands to reason.

"She was a good dog," Mike says.

"Dead dog now," Karen says.

Through the plywood come the sounds of Drunk Teens laughing and, faintly, a sound like one Drunk Teen crying. From downstairs in the music room: the party's cackle and pop. A metallic echo along the hallway linoleum. Roxanne's yips and yowls. Hammer saying, "I told you I'm tougher than this goddam dog." Nerdettes giggling.

Karen says, "I don't want to go home." Pause. Gives the maybe-you-can-go-ahead-and-fuck-me-if-you-*must* sigh. "I don't want to go home *ever.*"

The enrollment's declining. Mike can't help thinking that. "Where you gonna go?" he says.

"Nowhere," Karen says.

Mike extends his hand to take Karen's. To pull her hand to his lips and kiss it. A soap-opera moment. Corny as fuck-all. But the thing is, it's *real*. To touch her. To make that gentle intertwining of fingers. He believes for a second she will erase everything that's ever been pointless about the world, which is most of it. Too dark in the staircase, though. She can't see his hand reaching for her. His heart.

KAREN DOESN'T GO HOME. When the party breaks up, she stretches out next to Mike beside his drums. Breathes. A wee hissing noise comes from her nose. But she doesn't speak. Doesn't reach her hand to Mike's or turn to him. Another girl, Ellie, who's fifteen and skinny and wears cherry lip gloss, she stays the night, too, on the other side of the room, with Todd. Moans come from over there for twenty minutes or so. Could be *five* for all Mike knows. Could be an *hour*. He's not paying attention. *He's* not moaning, not aloud. He folds his hands over his chest, and recites in his head an imaginary mushy love speech. A profession of his love for Karen. *Somewhere out there*, Mike's pretending to say. And so forth. Maybe they're at a diner having coffee and cigarettes and losing themselves in each other's eyes. This is Mike's vision of love: *Somewhere out there.*

IN THE MORNING, at five-thirty, when Mike's alarm goes off, Todd and Ellie and Roxanne are gone. Mike doesn't know where. Probably Bob's basement. There's a TV over there, and pillows, a shower. And Mike's here on the floor next to Karen.

She doesn't wake up groggy. She's more alert than Mike's ever seen her, eyes wide, glancing about the room.

"So this is your *life*," she says. This is an observation, not a question.

The light in the room's lime green because everything in the room's lime green. All over the carpet: beer bottles and cigarette butts and drum sticks and clumps of dog hair. Mike's life is a trash heap. Pretty funny, he thinks. Because hey: Whose life *isn't* a trash heap?

"I'm gonna quit my job today," Mike says. "That's it. I'm not going in to work ever again."

"Same with me," Karen says. "I'm never going to school again. I'll just stay here with *you.*"

The way she says this—wide smile, perfect teeth, one hand tucking her hair behind her perfect olive ear—produces the only effect it could possibly have on Mike. He loves her absolutely, irrevocably, for all eternity.

AND THE DAY is perfect and sunny and blue. This is the kind of day that should be filmed in slow motion and played back with mushy music tinkling over it.

They leave Riverside before the children from Bright Days arrive. The sky's a goldenrod light growing in the east. Dew on the grass. Robins singing. Chickadees. Wrens. Sparrows. It's the long intro to the overture. They walk to the Piggly Wiggly grocery store a block from Riverside. First customers of the day. Isn't *this* neat? They buy Golden Delicious apples and cigarettes. They go to the woods near the Menomonee River, near the treatment plant and the school building, and they hide themselves in a tag-alder thicket near the water. Make camp. They're going to be here all day. Isn't *this* great? Oh, if we only had a *blanket.*

And maybe the Menomonee River is narrow and polluted, a strip of industrial-stinking water dribbling through town, but in this patch of woods, Mike and Karen only see a fine rush of water tumbling over the limestone rocks, a picture-postcard of water. In the middle distance, there's the sewage treatment plant, the settling tanks, the rock-filtration bed, the slow steam rising. The plant's pretty today. Above it: Riverside Elementary, white and blue, bathed in sun. Gorgeous.

They don't speak much, just take in the river and the world beyond it. They smoke pot out of apples and eat them. They smoke cigarettes. They don't hold hands, but Mike wishes they would.

Somewhere in there Mike guesses it's noon. It's the buzzer at Custom

Products. He should be trudging away from his Moog multistation drill press and joining his co-workers on the picnic table near the tool-crib entrance. Cigarettes and Mountain Dews and Little Debbie Star Crunches: That's what lunch is. Forever and ever. Hammer's there now for sure. Telling everybody he made *twice* his goddam quota and if the cocksuckers in the front office had any sense, they'd make him a foreman of the whole fucking company. Lunch: That shit's gone forever.

Every ten minutes or so, Karen stands from the log where she sits and tiptoes to the river, bends over it and lets her long black hair dangle over the slimy rocks on the shore. Sacagawea. For real.

She says she and Mike are Indians living in the wilds, off the land. The whole world's just her and Mike doing whatever they please. No guidance counselors. No Drunk Teen meetings. No dog-assassin fathers.

Mike listens and smiles. He's thinking nearly the same thing. No time clocks. No foreman. No Moog multistation drill press. No quotas. Just peace and water lazily passing over the rocks.

NIGHT COMES, and Karen and Mike wander back to the school building. They're flush from the long hours in the sun and hungry because they haven't eaten anything but apples all day, and the hallway leading to the music room is as silent as a morgue. Their footsteps tick off the linoleum and reverberate off the cinder-block walls, but that's the only sound. Mike opens the door to the music room, lets Karen in. She halts. Pincers her nose.

"Jesus," she says. "It reeks in here."

It does. Rancid beer. Exhaled cigarette smoke. Pizza crusts. Dog.

Mike says, "Don't know what I can do about the stink."

"There's only one thing," Karen says.

"What's that?"

"Forget the stink's here."

Mike flips the light switch. The fluorescent lime-green hue of the room. His lime green period. The crapola on the carpet, on the walls, everywhere. Now, seems like a million years later, Karen puts her hand over Mike's. Makes their hands into one. Flips the lights back off with her free hand. Nearly pure darkness. Only the Exit light at the end of the hallway shines, almost imperceptibly. The light hums and buzzes.

She presses herself into his chest. She smells like an orchard.

"It's okay, you know," she says. "You don't *have* to be bashful with me."

Mike speaks the truth. For once. "I don't know what to *do* about it," he says. Flowing water and sunshine over the land and whatever.

SOMEBODY JUMPS UP and down on the storm-gutter grating.

Hammer. Of course. "There you are, you fucker," Hammer says. "I thought you *died* on me."

Mike's at the window looking caught and shackled for transport to county lockup. Mike says, "I *am* dead."

"Goddam *right* you're dead," Hammer says. "If you don't let me in, I'm gonna *kill* you."

Mike seeks Karen's advice. She nods happily. "He's your friend," she says. "He's just making sure you're okay."

They meet Hammer at the lower-entrance door. Seventy degrees is the temperature, and Hammer's got the leather jacket on. Unzipped. Black T-shirt. Beer gut hanging. Sweat dripping from his hair and beard. Face sooty.

Mike lets him in, and Hammer does a thorough eyeball meat-assessment of Karen. Nods at the neck parts and the tit parts. Not up to *Iron Horse* magazine standards. But humpable in a pinch.

Blammo, Hammer grabs Mike by the collar and throws him up against the wall. Brings his face in kissing range of Mike's. Mike reels at the tequila-and-beer stink.

Hammer says, "I saved your *ass* today." The treatment plant's a rose compared to Hammer. "I told the foreman you got the goddam *flu*. But you don't come in on Monday: I might kill you just on the principle of the thing."

Hammer maneuvers his head in Karen's direction. Lets her know the law here.

"See how this shit goes, little girl?" Hammer says. "I'll do with this fucker whatever I want. Or with *any* fucker whatever I want."

No startle from Karen. "Absolutely," she says. A life lived around dogs.

But Hammer's got no intention of killing Mike. Fuck *that.* They're *brothers.* He just don't want Mike fucking up his job. He lets him go. Reaches into the leather jacket. Produces three cans of Campbell's Chunky Sirloin Burger Soup. That's the best they make. It's got stick-to-your-gut ability. Here's a plastic bag crammed with strips of venison jerky, too. And you can bet your left nut Hammer shot the deer personally.

Hammer says, "I stopped by to make sure you had something to eat, asshole."

He should be somebody's mother.

He recalculates Karen's performance capacity. Says, "But looks to me like you been eating just fine." Winks at Mike. Gives him an atta-boy elbow to the ribs. Bows then with surprising elegance. He's the impresario of partying. He says, "It's Christmastime, motherfuckers."

He's got a case of Miller and a liter of Cuervo strapped to the bike. And last he's heard from Sally down at the Old Lamp is that Bob and Todd and them are on their way. They'll be here in twenty minutes tops.

So HERE'S THE WHOLE GANG. Beers everywhere. Shots and cigarettes and pot and music booming from the boom box and girls dancing and everyone playing with Roxanne. Karen's mingling tonight, familiarizing herself with the scene. She tells the nerdettes—one of which she points out she is not—about her adventures by the river. What a day! What a way to *live!* She's *never* going to school again.

Mike's discussing the situation with the boys.

Here's Mike having a heart-to-heart with Bob in the hallway:

Bob says, "Karen's really awesome, Mike. I can't believe a guy like *you* can make it with *her.*"

"I need more time alone with her," Mike says. "You know, to figure out who she really *is.*"

"See," Bob says, "you're antisocial. You gotta let her enjoy herself, man. You gotta let her *party*. She'll love you for it later. Trust me."

And here's Mike having a heart-to-heart with Todd beside the drum set:

"You got this fancy drum set," Todd says, "but you'll never be able to play as good as me."

"I guess I got the girl, though."

"She's a dirtmuffin, dude. You'd be better off fucking Roxanne."

Here's Mike having a heart-to-heart with Hammer over shots of Quervo:

"I took over your machine at work today," Hammer says.

Mike says, "Thanks, bud."

"I milled out *twice* the goddam piston heads you usually make. Foreman says he's thinking about putting me on your machine permanent. He says you're *useless.*"

There it is: Mike's *useless.* Like, as if Mike didn't know *that* already. Besides, what's he supposed to do. Be use*ful*? Cut him some slack, man. He's twenty years old. Having a great time, too. Is he supposed to be in law school or doing some shit like running a corporation?

AND IT'S MORNING AGAIN. Everybody's gone again, gone to better places and finer fields. Everybody but Karen, who's next to Mike on the floor near the drum set again.

Today she wakes up confused.

"I'm hungry," she says. Vague eyes. Unfocused.

Mike gives her a piece of Hammer's venison jerky. She wolfs it down, goes back to sleep.

Mike sleeps, too, all day, and he doesn't dream. Never has dreams anymore. He can't remember when he last did.

WHEN HE FINALLY opens his eyes, night's fallen. He doesn't know how long ago. Karen's beside him, breathing softly, sleeping. Somebody's pounding on the lower-entrance door. There's no rhythm to the pounding. Just mean, haphazard blows against the glass. He thinks he hears voices and sees what he's sure are lights. Something's not right. Gets up quietly. Goes to check it out.

He stands outside the music-room door, in the hallway, and sees a flashlight beam probing. Sees the red-and-blue flash of squad-car lights. He tucks himself behind his door, keeps himself hidden from the flashlight beam, and he listens.

"The girl's gotta be in there," a man says. "Why don't you go ahead and call the locksmith already? We can't stand here and pound *all* night."

They're looking for Karen, no doubt about it. Mike doesn't pause to think. He acts on criminal instinct, which works like this: If the police can't find what they're looking for, you can't get in trouble. He clicks closed the music-room door and walks as quietly as he can to where Karen sleeps.

To wake her he places his hand on her stomach. Pliable. Smooth through the flannel shirt. She opens her eyes in a content way, a seasoned way, as if Mike has *always* been placing his hand on her stomach.

"The cops are looking for you, Karen," Mike says.

She doesn't flinch. Never does. "I knew they would," she says. "They've come looking for me *before*."

"We got to sneak you out of here."

"I know," she says. "That's the way it always is."

She rises. Effortless. Languid. Searches the carpet a moment to find her last two apples. Finds them. Pockets them in her painter pants. When the flashlight beam's done probing the hallway, she and Mike leave the music room and hustle down the hallway in the opposite direction of the entrance door.

This is how suddenly Karen's gone: She gets to the doorway on the far end of the school, Mike opens it, and she takes off running, up a small grassy hill, her footsteps not making one sound in the night, not the slightest pitter-patter. That's it. They don't say goodbye. Not *some other time*. Not *it's been fun*. Nothing. She vanishes, and Mike never sees her again.

Breaks your heart in half, thinking about it.

On the way back to the music room, Mike stops at a bubbler and splashes water over his beard. He attempts to make himself presentable. Flicks on the hallway lights, strides to the entrance doorway where the policemen are, and he opens the door. Tries to look happy. Pleased to see them.

Two uniformed cops. They're pleased to see Mike, too. They smile at him.

"You Mike *Magnuson*?" one of them says.

"I am."

"You're Jack Magnuson's *son*, right?

"I am."

"And you're renting—" pauses to examine a notebook he's holding—"rehearsal space here in the school?"

"I am."

"How come it took you so long to answer the door?"

Beyond the squad car, in the moonlight, Mike sees steam rising from the settling tanks. Gorgeous.

"I was listening to music on my headphones," Mike says. "Sorry."

The cop seems to buy this. Nods. Jots something in his notebook. "We received a report that a girl named Karen Neilson might be hiding out in your rehearsal space. This true?"

"I've been here alone all day."

"Mind if we take a look inside?"

Mike does. But what else is he going to do? Tell them they can kiss his ass?

He leads the two cops down the hall. Into the music room. The cops stand there for a time, not saying anything. Beer cans. Cigarettes. All that.

"You *rehearse* here?" one of the cops says.

"I do."

"And you're Jack Magnuson's *son*?"

"I am."

"Look, Mike," the cop says. He smiles in a clenched-jaw way that frightens Mike. "You've obviously been up to *more* than music in here. But we're gonna leave you be for now." Mike's lucky day. "But, buddy, if we find out that you had that girl in here, we're gonna arrest you bigger than shit. That understood?"

Mike says that it is.

Then the cops vanish. Just as quickly as Karen did.

Now Mike's alone in his lime-green room. Sounds kinda poetic, when he thinks about it, which he does, and he decides therefore that he really *isn't* an idiot. He can think things out, man. And *do* something about things. *And* make them beautiful. It's time—like, no kidding it's time—to pull himself together and do what anybody whose shit *is* together would tell him to do: clean up his act. Hell yes. That sounds about perfect.

So he goes to Piggly Wiggly and buys Glad Bags and PineSol and Windex and Brawny paper towels. He's straight from the pages of *Family Circle* magazine. He should buy an apron and rubber gloves while he's at it.

He gets back to Riverside and gets cracking. Picks up beer cans and cigarette butts off the floor. Washes the windows, which takes, like, *two* hours. Dusts his drums, picks his sticks off the floor and arranges them neatly in the little brown briefcase where they belong.

Another two hours, and he's done. There. It's looking sparkly as fuck. Then he breaks into Bright Days and does his thing there.

Washes his clothes in the sink. Gives himself a sponge bath. Washes his hair in the sink. Dries himself off with Brawny towels.

He's squeaky clean. Everything is.

Near dawn, he plops on the floor and sleeps, but still he doesn't dream. And so what? Dreams don't do dick for a guy anyway.

Noon the next day he's awake and everything's clean and spotless and hopeful. He thinks he's traveled backward in time to the day he moved his drums in here five months ago. Good enough then. So he grabs a pair of drumsticks, sits behind his drums, and begins to play.

He bashes the cymbals, all seven of them. He plays rolls and flams, sambas and fatbacks and shuffles and rocks and grooves and hits it hard on the backbeat, and the world's pure and true again, as it once was, when the first humans pounded their first rhythms with broken branches onto fallen logs. He's thinking exactly that. And his hands are saying, *These are the noises my soul makes.* Or something along those lines.

An hour or two later, Mike's sweaty and happy. His ears ring. He should have been doing this all along. Been disciplined about his drumming. That would have been cool.

Todd and Bob jump up and down on the grating. They got Roxanne with them. But no girls. They're very happy, very excited to see Mike.

"Hey, buddy," they say. "We've been missing you."

They're one person today. Two heads. One brain.

They get in the music room, and Todd says, "It's about time you cleaned this place. It was getting to be the rat's ass."

Bob agrees. Says now they can really run some poontang through here. Now that the place is presentable, maybe they can move up from Drunk Teens and get some *cheerleaders* to come by. Then, by God, there'd be *real* action around here.

Mike doesn't tell them about the cops or about Karen vanishing into the night, and Bob and Todd don't ask. And why would they? It's no shit off their asses. And wait: They got something wonderful with them. A piece of happiness. They want to share it. Let's have fun. Just the three of us. For this one time.

Maybe in other places in Menomonee Falls, people gather for a Sunday afternoon meal, to share among them the joys of hearth and family and Christian kindness, but here in the music room of Riverside Elementary, the Sunday meal is three squares of blotter paper saturated with lysergic acid diethylamide #25. On each of the pieces of paper: a tiny blue unicorn wreathed in stars. Blue unicorn, baby. Some of the best. We got to *go* for it. Mike agrees. When Bob and Todd place a unicorn in their mouths, Mike does, too, and leaves it there till it dissolves.

ACID IS *never* uneventful. Anybody who's done the stuff can tell you that. But it never shows a person something that's not really there in the first place; you don't really hallucinate on acid; you just see the stuff in front of you in a different way. And Mike that Sunday afternoon: He doesn't see fancy colors or melting walls or giant giraffes chasing him through the arid wastes of his mind. He shrivels instead. Gets shorter. He gets younger and younger, a second grader, eight years old, a chubby boy wearing Huskies jeans and a western shirt too tight around his middle, sitting in Mrs. Weber's classroom—in row number three, fourth desk, tapping his fingers—upstairs in Riverside Elementary, in the same room where the Alcoholics Anonymous Clubhouse is now. Mrs. Weber's saying, "In Western Civilization." And "In Wisconsin history today." And "A common denominator is." And "Trees, today we will talk about trees." Recess then, outside, pushing Hot Wheels along the concrete edge of the storm gutter, never learning, losing Hot Wheel after Hot Wheel through the grate. The janitors saying, "You can leave those cars rust, buddy." And in the classroom again. Miss Weber saying, "We have a special guest today. This is Dr. Jack Magnuson, Michael's *father*, our superintendent of schools. He's visiting today to tell everybody how our school system works."

Mike still sees real world in front of him, the right-now: Todd playing tug-of-war with Roxanne. Bob saying that if Roxanne were a high school girl they could fuck her and toss her aside like a used Kotex. Todd and Bob busting a gut laughing.

But it's second grade for Mike nevertheless, hours and hours upstairs, in that room where Alcoholics Anonymous meets.

He hears in his mind the music he heard back then, when his fingers could work their way through Bach inventions on the piano, when he would stroll the hallways of Riverside Elementary, chubby and preoccupied, humming strains from the St. Matthew Passion.

He hears Todd saying, "When I was in Madison I met this *chick*."

Bob saying, "I can't wait till the *girls* are off school for the summer."

Todd, "I'm gonna put that fucking *dog* in the hall till my trip is over."

Roxanne barking and barking. A frenzy of barking.

AND IT'S MONDAY morning. Bob's gone home. Todd and Mike, they crashed sometime late. Near dawn. And forgot to set the alarm clock. Roxanne's still out in the hall. It's after six. Toddlers are showing up for Bright Days. Roxanne's got two little boys, four years old, cornered near the entrance door. Roxanne's snarling at them. The boys are crying, and one of them's peeing his pants. Todd's there now, holding Roxanne back. Tells Roxanne to ease the fuck up for once, goddammit. A woman's saying she's calling the police. Got to get the hell out of here. Todd and Mike outside now, running, running. There are police sirens. There's a dog named Roxanne, who weighs 110 pounds, who's about to be sent to the veterinarian's office for an injection.

JACK MAGNUSON writes a regular column in *Menomonee Falls News*, and in it he writes this: "The well-being of our children should be foremost in our minds. In the months ahead it seems important to ask several questions. Can we see beyond the morass of economic and political reality to that fact? Does our concern for their future transcend the myriad of self-interests? Who is going to speak for the child?"

IN THE *Menomonee Falls News,* a reporter writes an article about Riverside Elementary with this headline: "*Man Found Living in School.*"

The reporter writes that the man is Michael John Magnuson, 20, son of Jack Magnuson, superintendent of schools. Michael John Magnuson has been renting the room to teach drum lessons and has reportedly been allowing several of his students to spend the night in the building. The reporter doesn't mention who these students are, or how he's determined that there have been students in the first place, but he implies that the students probably are boys.

Boys, girls, students, Drunk Teens, nerdettes, bikers, drummers, deliverers of pizzas, young lummoxes, what's the difference? They're *all* children.

MIKE'S GONE FROM Menomonee Falls within forty-eight hours of the publication of that article. His father takes the day off work, rents a U-haul trailer, helps Mike load his drums in, and gets him the hell out of town. He drives Mike to Eau Claire, where he's still got friends, a few music majors, other drummers, who live in a big house where Mike can hang out and stow his junk for a while. "You have nearly cost me my job," his father says. Then he drives back to Menomonee Falls. And it's ten years before Mike sets foot in Menomonee Falls again.

Chapter 2

So okay, okay: Mike knows full well he's done something stupid. He knows he's been an embarrassment to his family. He's knows he's been a dick. But your lummox is *supposed* to be a dick, right? He's simply doing what comes natural to him, right? Consequently he begins to think that he not only *is* a dick but his life also *functions* like a dick's; you can beat Mike Magnuson down, but he won't stay down for long.

Get a load of what he's doing now, just a few weeks after leaving Menomonee Falls: He's got himself a job again. This is late June, one o'clock in the afternoon and sunny. He's making four-fifty an hour driving a sixteen-seat Ford Econoline 350 bus through downtown Eau Claire. But he's not a bus driver, like you're thinking. It's *way* more totally ironic than that. He's a child care worker at the Eau Claire Academy, a one-step-before-prison reformatory for teenage boys and girls, and the bus he's driving is loaded with twelve boys from Unit 5, the biggest and oldest residents of the academy, all between fifteen and seventeen years old.

Mike's taking them to Wagner's 66 ½ Lanes for a couple of hours of therapeutic bowling.

The boys are demonstrating first-rate behavior today. They're happy, laughing and joking with each other because they're in the outside world for the afternoon, out on a field trip with the new Unit 5 staff, Mike. He can hear them playing the dozens, the insults escalating, but he keeps his eyes on the road.

"You look like you been slapping that *hammy* again," one of them says, "to see that big grin you having." This is John Smithers, sixteen years old, by far the largest of the boys, six feet tall and weighing 280 pounds. He's lobbing his insult at a boy named Rashon Jackson, who's fifteen and lanky and half John's size.

Rashon says, "*Sheet! My* hammy, it don't need *me* slapping it. I going over to Unit 3 tonight: get my hammy good and slapped proper by *each* streetwalking-bitch LaKenya they got." Unit 3, Mike's learned during his one-week training period, is the teenage-prostitute unit.

"Go right ahead," John Smithers says. "Them Unit 3 LaKenyas get a slap at you ham: You be busted out in herpes disease before morning tomorrow."

"Listen to you biscuitheads jawing," another boy says. This is Clarence Jeter, the oldest boy, seventeen. He's got a grainy, high-pitched voice like an old woman's. "Ain't either one of you gots a hammy, anyhow. You: Born without a hammy, is what you is. *Telling* you."

Mike says, "Keep the insults to a minimum." This is something Mike's been trained to say, for the dozens is a game that frequently leads to violence. "Otherwise we can skip bowling entirely. Doesn't matter to me if we spend the rest of the afternoon on the unit."

Training's a beautiful thing to have. It works. The boys quit their yipping for a while.

Mike's driving the van up a long hill called the Plank Street Hill, and on one side of the road is a steep sandy pitch dotted with jack pine and scrub oak. On top of the pitch is a cemetery where, just last midnight, he sat with his roommate, Joe Murphy, and smoked a couple of doobies. Up there, stoned, they overlooked the entire Chippewa Valley, the night-time town lights a blinking galaxy of pleasant and orderly living, and they named the place Space Mountain because it seemed to them so high, so close to the heavens, they were riding on a spaceship hurtling through the void. Like, wow. Heavy duty.

Clarence Jeter says, "Ain't Mr. Mike the responsible one."

"That's right, Clarence. I'm the responsible one."

"But you don't *look* like a regular Mr. Staff, Mr. Mike."

Mike says, "No, I don't." That's truth: The male staff at the academy sport the jarhead haircuts, wear tucked-in beer-league softball team T-shirts. They're guys in college who want to be cops when they graduate. Whenever that is. They like the words *law enforcement*. And *situation requires the offender be subdued*. And *it sometimes takes violence to prevent violence*. They want to spend their lives ruining other people's days, arresting people and writing them tickets and that kinda shit.

Clarence clarifies himself: "Mike looking like Mr. Just-Come-out-the-Woods *Doper. That* what Mike look like."

Mike's eyes have been fixed on the road, the last long potholed curve at the top of the Plank Street Hill, but now he looks through his rearview mirror to see the face Clarence is making. The kid's smiling, his teeth are showing, but if Mike hadn't been dealing with Clarence for the past few weeks, he'd never know Clarence is smiling. Clarence lost the use of his smile muscles when he was six years old, and along with the smile muscles he lost all the skin on his face. His older sister smeared him with Sterno and set him on fire. Received third-degree burns over most of his body. Now he's got no ears and no hair. Lips and eyelids: indistinguishable. His forehead and scalp: a wafflework of grafts, strips of varying widths and lengths that make Clarence look mummified. Which is basically accurate. He once was.

He says, "I don't mean to fuss with you, Mr. Mike. You go ahead and look like whatever you feel like."

"I'm just trying to make a living, Clarence."

"Something about you ain't like the rest of em," Clarence says. "You ain't all that full of power trip like you *supposed* to be."

All this talk is causing Mike to lose his concentration on the road, and the last thing he wants is to lose concentration and get a ticket or get into an accident or the like. Bitch of it is, he needs the job. So he says, "Give it a rest, Clarence. Let it alone for a bit till I'm done driving."

And Clarence does. He lets it alone. In the rearview mirror Mike locks eyes a moment with Clarence—his eyes: the color of oatmeal sprinkled with brown sugar—then Clarence unlocks, stares off into the trees the bus passes by.

This is the kind of sentimental dipstick Mike is: He doesn't know what Clarence sees in the trees—the stands of jack pine and birch, the lilac hedges, the rows of tall lumberjack houses that were built here in the late 1800s, when Eau Claire was the principal lumber-processing hub in all of western Wisconsin—but he wants to tell Clarence what *he* sees. *Eau Claire,* he wants to say, is French for "Clear Water." And that in *Eau Claire* lies the confluence of the Eau Claire and the Chippewa Rivers. An aesthetic-type place, that's what Mike wants to say.

But fuck aesthetics: Clarence has done two years in the academy already. Raps: stealing three automobiles and robbing two convenience stores and repeatedly getting in fistfights in school. Some other stuff, too. It figures Clarence would be a criminal: A boy with a face like that is like a dog that's got no tail, no way to wag and be cool with other dogs and always having to fight for his piece of the pork chop.

But the other Unit 5 boys, half of them white and half of them black, they got their ways, too, and their rap sheets. Young thugs, every one. John Smithers, for instance, got sent here for raping his eleven-year-old sister at knifepoint. Rashon Jackson's here for attempting to smother his mother in her sleep, six different times, with a pillow. Fistfights break out on Unit 5 every day, and sometimes at night, when the night staff's sleeping in the office, several of the boys set on another boy in his sleep, hold him down, cover his mouth so nobody can hear him cry out for help, and beat the fuck out of him with a pillowcase crammed with bars of soap. They call this a blanket party. A lot of fun. Usually.

WAGNER'S 66½ Lanes really does have sixty-six and a half lanes, the half lane being an ornamental one situated near the east entrance and lined with various trophies the finest Eau Claire bowlers have earned over the years. Wagner's is the largest bowling complex in Wisconsin north of Madison. Plus it's got the billiard-hall room, the video arcade, the *three* full-service bars in it. *And* the kickass rock 'n' roll night club in the basement. Got your AC/DC-type cover bands in there Thursdays through Saturdays. Come to Wagner's on a Saturday night, you might see a thousand people here getting drunk and getting their rocks off on bowling and billiards and heavy metal and some serious whatever-the-fuck.

Today, though, it's about six cars here in the parking-lot sun.

Mike does the cheery leader-of-youth thing when he pulls into the lot. He says, "This *is* great. We got the place to ourselves." Parks the bus in Wagner's lot. Gives himself a good fifty yards between the bus and the entrance. Regulations. Assembles the boys on the asphalt. Checks off each of their names on a checklist. Gives the group the you're-not-going-to-be-assholes look.

Only John Smithers and Clarence Jeter look back at Mike. The rest: staring at their feet or off into the middle distance where there's a highway, a bank, a half-mile stretch of strip mall, telephone poles, and other clutter. To the boy, they appear far older than their age, something dirty and roughshod and worldly about the way they stand in the afternoon sun, begrudging the way they have to be assembled and addressed before they do *anything*. They look like a chain gang in training, which is essentially what they are.

"You guys are going to handle this, right?" Mike says.

"We *always* handle ourselves," John Smithers says.

Clarence cackles. "Speak for yourself, motherfucker. It's a *sin* to be handling yourself."

Mike says, "That's one demerit, Clarence."

"For what?" Clarence says.

"Saying *motherfucker.*"

"*You* just said *motherfucker*, Mr. Mike. How's it come *you* don't get a demerit?"

Mike says, "Because I'm the boss."

Clarence cackles again—"You sure *is*"—but it doesn't matter. Mike's got the situation stable enough.

He boots toward the entrance, and the boys fall into a shuffling line behind him, a couple of them trying to smoke a full cigarette in the thirty seconds it takes to get to the building.

Inside, the sixty-six and a half lanes are shiny and empty, not one lane in use, and the boys follow Mike to the shoe-rental stand, where stands a pale-looking guy Mike's age, maybe a little older. Guy's got the bowling-alley chubby face and a double chin with the Captain-Morgan-and-cokes-nightly stubble trying to grow on it. He's been munching on pretzels he's got in a plastic bar boat, but when he sees Mike and the boys, he sets down the pretzel he's going to eat, brushes his hands on his Wagner's 66 ¹/₂ T-shirt, and tries to appear preoccupied. Guy stares at the cash register to look busy.

"We'd like to bowl," Mike says.

Guy doesn't lift his eyes from the cash register. "You'd like to bowl."

"That's what I said."

On guy's name tag: DIRK. Mike looks at the name carefully, ponders the name Dirk. Guy named Dirk has *got* to be a shithead.

"Well," Dirk says, "you'd like to bowl." Now Dirk does look up, and his eyes, an anemic blue, bug a little. His thick lower lip quivers. He's freaking out here. It's not Mike or the six scruffy white boys that's freaking him, either; it's the six scruffy black boys. Black boys are as indigenous to Eau Claire as blizzards are to Nairobi. Eau Claire's population is so white, in fact, that a white-supremacist group has selected it as the best place to live in America. The group says, *No Negroes here.*

Mike says, "We're from the Eau Claire Academy." He's been trained to identify the group this way. In public.

Dirk says, "I can, uh, see that." Eyes settle on Clarence Jeter. Gives him the standard look of horror.

Clarence says, "We fin to bowl, mister."

"What's that you say?" Dirk says. Obviously Dirk is incapable of translating the Black to the Cheesehead, a capability Mike somehow possesses as if he's been doing it his whole life. Which is pretty fucked up, if you think about it: Mike's more honky than a goose.

"Set us up with shoes, hey," Mike says. "We'll need three lanes."

Dirk indicates with a curl of his fat index finger that he'd like a private word with Mike, and like lawyers approaching the bench, they meet at the far end of the counter, out of earshot of the boys.

Dirk says, "What's up with that one?" He cuts a quick glance at Clarence, who's staring out over the lanes as if he's staring at the ocean for the first time.

"Burnt," Mike says. "When he was six."

"Never seen a burnt nigger before," Dirk says.

Nigger. Mike's not your a social-activist-angry-righteous-liberal type—he's a dude who likes tunes and hanging out, stuff of that nature—but goddammit if he's letting this cocksucker Dirk call Clarence a *nigger.* See, Clarence isn't a nigger; he's a creature burnt *beyond* nigger or anything else. Mike leans into the counter, inhales some Hammer into his chest, and says, "I guess you're seeing a burnt one *now.*"

Dirk keeps an eyeball on Clarence's backside. Gets a chickenshit bead of sweat on his brow. Says, "We've had some of you academy people here before." Mumbly. Sounds like he's about to turd up his undies. Says, after a collect-himself breath, "And they've been *trouble.*" Points past Clarence to the unused lanes, their white pins as still as gravestones. "And I'm having an easy shift, *man.*"

Mike amps up the Hammer thing he's doing, grunts for effect, and pokes his index finger into Dirk's name tag. Raises his voice so the boys can hear him. Says, "What the fuck kinda name is *Dirk?*"

"Give me a break," Dirk says.

"Dirk is a bullshit name if I ever heard one."

"Um," Dirk says. Confusion in the eyes. Pussyface expression in general. "D-Dirk's the name I've always had."

"Change it to Dickhead," Mike says, "because you're acting like one."

Dirk mulls this over, slackens his shoulders, gets even paler. This crap's too much effort for him. "Well," he says, almost apologetically, "I can't help it my name's Dirk."

Mike says, "Set us up with some shoes and some lanes already." Wants to add, *You stupid fuck.* But he doesn't. He's not used to bullying people. Makes him feel good, though. Which is probably *not* good.

So everything's tits-up and ready-to-go. Dirk gets the boys their shoes and assigns them three lanes, and apart from Rashon Jackson complaining about the shoes looking stupid, which everybody has to admit is true, the boys do an appropriate, orderly job of leaving their street shoes away from the lanes and selecting themselves balls from the rack and getting divided into four-man teams for the first game. Mike's impressed as hell with this. Congratulates himself for their good behavior and just for a second thinks maybe his real calling in life isn't music but working with delinquents. The pay's shitola, but fuck you if there isn't honor doing this type of job. Look at these goddam kids for a second: They're having a great time.

True enough, they suck ass at bowling. They throw gutter balls, or knock down, like, just the ten pin, and pretty much they're a bona fide disgrace to all that Wagner's 66½ Lanes stands for. But the boys don't give a fuck, and Mike doesn't either.

Dirk's over there at his counter looking like somebody's driving a railroad spike through his left nut, but fuck *him.*

After the first game, Mike gets the kids each to give him a dollar, and he wanders over the bar and gets everybody sodas and potato chips. The kids laugh and swill their sodas and are having a lovely Christian-variety picnic here. Fuckin-A. It's beautiful to see.

Halfway through the second game, Clarence by some miracle rolls a strike.

"Look at that shit," Clarence says. "I fin to become a bowling *professional.*"

He's bowling in a foursome with John Smithers, who's up to roll after Clarence, and Clarence stands a ways off to the side of John, folds his arms, and with his newfound expertise scrutinizes John's turn.

John launches a purple sixteen-pounder toward the pins, and it thuds into the gutter halfway down the lane.

"John, if you fuck like you bowl," Clarence says, "you pathetic."

"If *I* fuck like *you* fuck, motherfucker," John says, "I play Stick the Dick in the Pillow."

Clarence saunters to the ball return and picks up his ball, rolls out of turn, sends the ball straight down the lane's middle. Smashes the head pin. Dang! It's the seven-ten split.

Clarence says, "See that shit, John? I just turned them pins into a picture of you superstanky, big-enough-to-drive-a-truck-through-it *pussy*."

John takes a look at the seven-ten split, then at Clarence, shakes his head, walks to the scoring table in such a way as to establish that there's at least a dozen feet between him and Clarence. Says to him, "My dick so big, I could slap you upside the head with it from here."

Clarence shrugs. "Proof, motherfucker. I always knew you been wanting me to suck you dick."

"My dick so big, you couldn't get you fat-like-you-mama's-ass *mouth* around it."

"More proof, John. You is *Superfag*."

John says, "You is some burnt-crisp *pussy*, is what you is."

"Least *I* ain't fucked my sister."

And that's it. John angles his body forward and with a running offensive-lineman start dives into Clarence. Knocks him over the ball return. Sends balls rolling everywhere. Clarence gets back to his feet and windmills some punches at John. He's much quicker than John. Smacks him upside the head and in the teeth a good five times. John goes for the high-percentage retaliation: dives into Clarence again. And the two fall to wrestling and punching and biting one another on the floor.

The rest of the kids cheer at this shit, and Mike does as he's trained to do. He dives into the fight without thinking. Sticks his arms between Clarence and John and tries wrenching them apart. Won't budge. It's like separating dogs. Then Mike's right in there with them, elbowing and brawling, trying to gain some leverage, smelling Clarence and John in the process—a mix of cigarettes and sweat and institutional soap. Somewhere in there, in the million years two seconds of a fight seem like, Mike gets a grip of John's arms and maneuvers them into what's known as the baskethold restraint, which is a way of folding someone's arms across themselves, forming the equivalent of a straitjacket. And hey: This shit works. Mike's got John wrapped up and defenseless. Cool.

Mike yells, "Ease up, John."

In the split second that John can't use his arms, Clarence sees the opening and instead of punching him again, he pats him once, gently, on the cheek, and walks behind the scoring table.

John keeps trying to wrestle free, but Mike rides him like a bull, pulls the baskethold as tight as he can make it.

Mike yells, "Ease the *fuck* up, John."

After a moment for two, John does. Relaxes. Says, "I'm cool. It's over."

Mike lets him up, stands there with him, looks him square in his brown eyes, which look empty and beaten. Mike's outmuscled John, and John's taking this hard.

"You sumpin," John says. "You tougher than you look."

Mike's breathing hard, broken into a full sweat, surveying the scene. Bowling balls are scattered about the floor, along with plastic soda cups and potato-chip bags. The boys are standing in their circle, thrilled and happy, and now Clarence comes back from behind the scoring table and starts laughing, and John starts laughing, too.

John says to the boys, "Mr. Mike, he a tough fucker, ain't he?"

Clarence says, "He had your ass in some serious restraint, John."

They approach each other and high-five.

"We just fucking with you, Mr. Mike," Clarence says. "Seeing what you was made of."

Mike's not responding. He's in a dreamy, brawl-induced haze: sweating, replaying the blow-by-blow of it.

Now Dirk arrives on the scene, looking smug and self-satisfied, and he says to Mike, "Have everybody take off their shoes and get out of here. Takes more than a minute, and I'm calling the cops."

The boys know the drill. They hear the word *cops*, and they're ready to split.

A COUPLE OF HOURS LATER, Mike's shift's over, and he's walked a mile in his own shoes, and here it is: 819 Barland Street. Home. A little house, painted blue, with a gravel driveway, a small yard, and a couple of trees. Quaint as hell. Nice neighborhood. There's some other rental houses in the neighborhood, some houses that aren't rental, but nobody here's rich. It's quiet, too, except at 819 sometimes when Mike or his roommate Joe get to banging on their drums and doing the thundering-herd thing or whatever.

Mike comes in the front door, puts the long-day-at-work sag on his face for effect, and he's in the living room. There's a couch, an easy chair, and a coffee table, and Joe perched on the couch-edge, flipping through the pages of *Webster's Ninth*. Loves his *Webster's Ninth*. Regularly.

Joe points to a page and says, "Here's one for you, Mike. *Iconoclast.*"

Joe's got some miles on Mike. Twenty-eight years old, but you'd never know it to look at him: tall and lanky and athletic, has veins as big around as pencils standing on his forearms. His hair is a wiry brown. He's an excitable person, prone to saying whatever's on his mind. He's a guy who blurts.

Joe says, "So what do you think about *iconoclast*?"

Mike smiles a $4.25-an-hour smile. "Can't you ever just say hello?" he says.

"Check out the second definition of *iconoclast*," Joe says. "'One who attacks established beliefs or institutions.'"

"I had a hell of a day," Mike says. Plops himself on the easy chair. Kicks out his feet. Torches a smoke.

"See, Mike, *I* am an iconoclast. *I* attack all things established. I question *everything*!"

"I suppose you do, Joe." Mike exhausts a smoke funnel toward the ceiling and sighs. "One *hell* of a day, I'm telling you."

Joe deposits *Webster's Ninth* on the coffee table and suddenly springs to his feet, a motion so quick it startles Mike, though it shouldn't. Joe's always jumping up like that.

Joe says, "I can see I need to get you up to speed."

Mike says, "You're right. I'm way behind you."

What this exchange means: It's time for the stoner routine to get under way.

Joe's off to his room, where he keeps his Buddy Rich Model Ludwig drum set and his nice constantly-cranking-jazz Pioneer stereo. He digs Miles Davis and John Coltrane, Charlie Parker and Charles Mingus. Anything that's black and has that edge to it. The origin of Joe and jazz: Back when Joe was Mike's age, he met the great drummer Elvin Jones at some cheesy Youth for Chord Progressions festival or whatever it was in Minneapolis. But Elvin was the *real* Elvin. And he told Joe to study the Watusi. And it was something like Elvin Jones said he was a descendant of the Watusi tribe and somewhere in there when Elvin was explaining his tribal heritage he wrapped his arms around Joe and rhino-hugged him and hefted him off the floor. Which Joe's always taken as a sign that he's been anointed by artistic greatness. Not that Joe's ever learned much about the Watusi; he sure listens to a lot of records, though.

The first selection on this afternoon's program: Miles Davis's *Live at the Plugged Nickel.* "Milestones" is first, and way heavy and cool. Of course. It's the modal stuff, the swing lingering on the underside of the beat, digging deep. Dude.

Now Joe's back, wobbling his head in an Egyptian way. He's carrying a three-foot red plastic Graffix bong. Betsy's her name. Called that lovingly because she's about the only pussy Mike and Joe are getting these days. And Betsy's fingerprint-smeared and has got much gunk caked on the lower part of her tube, where her stale water sloshes. Betsy's bowl: a dented French-horn mouthpiece Joe stole from the Music Department storeroom. Enterprising, hey?

This is what Joe always says: "Ah, Betsy."

They pass her back and forth, suck on her, gurgle her, use her till she's spent. And light cigarettes. And all the while Miles and Ron Carter and Tony Williams and Herbie Hancock, they're warping somewhere beyond the world of Betsies.

"This music," Joe says, "is a thing of supreme darkness."

"That it is," Mike says. Because it is.

And Mike sees other darknesses: a rerun of the brawl at Wagner's a few hours ago. Figures on telling Joe about it. And does. But it takes five minutes to get the whole story out because Joe keeps blurting in about the tunes. Listen to the *communication*, man. Syncopated, man. It's *so* intellectual. The *way* their minds work. But Mike gets the story told, at least up to the part when he figures out that the fight's a test of Mike's capabilities. And Joe slaps his knees and busts a sudden gut laughing.

Joe says, "That's ironical as hell."

"The kids've gotta be crazy for real, hey." First time this actually has occurred to Mike. Which is for sure a disgrace it's taken him so long to figure it out.

Now Miles and company groove into "So What," and Joe palms-out his hand to shush Mike, to draw his attention to the keen interplay between Ron Carter playing the theme on the bass and Tony Williams laying way back, popping out the time on the cymbals.

After a bit, Joe's mind drifts to other drummers. "I've told you before," he says, "that Elvin Jones is descended from the great Watusi."

"About a thousand times. Yes."

"In that case—" Joe gazes at the ceiling, searching for the truth up there, and finding it— "you're lucky you fell into your job at the academy."

Mike hoists *Webster's Ninth*, flips through the pages to find the word *Watusi*. It's not in here. Figures.

"*Watusi* isn't in here," Mike says.

But this doesn't matter to Joe. "How many of the kids you work with are black?"

"Half of them."

"A marvelous opportunity."

"If you think it's so great," Mike says, "why don't you go in and work for me tomorrow?"

"I'm serious. Talk to those kids. Listen to them, how they talk, what they have to say. Rhythm, it's intrinsic to them. That job, I'm telling you, Mike, will help you mature as a *percussive artist*."

Joe's standing now, waving his arms about. He does a little Hitler-defeats-Poland victory jig. "Make sense?" he says.

Mike says, "Probably."

Like, whatever. Don't matter what they're talking about. They're just bullshitting, just having fun. And fun's something Mike wants to have without interruption, for all eternity.

And fun is had by them. For sure. There's tunes for a few more hours. There's a Betsy-fondling every twenty minutes or so. There's laughs, words looked up in the dictionary. All that.

WHEN NIGHT FALLS, they walk to the Eau Claire River, near the Uniroyal tire plant, where there's a footbridge, about six feet wide and a hundred feet long, that crosses a gorge the Eau Claire River has carved out of the sandstone. The footbridge connects the Uniroyal plant with its employee parking lot, a few acres of potholed asphalt on the other side of the river. The drop from the bridge to the river is easily a hundred feet, and Mike and Joe stand at the bridge's middle, staring at the river, a dim silvery flow in the night. They try spitting over the edge of the railing, but it's too dark to watch the gobs fall all the way to the water.

Mike says, "Spitting is more satisfying during the day."

"I am *beyond* spitting," Joe says. "I am becoming a black intellectual."

THE NEXT DAY: Gray and cold. Fifty-five degrees. Drizzling. Sharp gusts. But Mike's happy and relaxed. He thinks your regular Wisconsin balmy day is killer indeed, the slate skies, the wet streets. Kinda romantic. Even though he didn't crash last night till some time past three, he feels as crispy as a critter. Superfresh. He walks toward the academy at a strong pace through the drizzle, contemplating his future, which he figures to be comfortable and filled with good music, good dope, and plenty of stimulating conversation.

Precisely 6:30 A.M. he's on Unit 5. On time and ready to have at it. Unit 5's on the third floor of the Eau Claire Academy and occupies what used to be the maternity ward of Sacred Heart Hospital. Which is what the academy used to be: Sacred Heart Hospital. Way back.

Unit 5's your essentially open square area with rooms situated around the perimeter. In the unit's center is a square glass-lined room that was once the nursery but serves as the staff office now. From the office, staff can observe anything that occurs in the unit's commons area, like, kids plopped in front of the TV or hanging near the Ping-Pong table. This kind of staff-office positioning is a precursor to prisons of the future; Unit 5 has pod design.

Keith, the unit manager, sits at his desk and fiddles with some paperwork: reports, plans for the day. He's six feet three, a former University of Eau Claire tight end. But he's got a sweet disposition. Really a friendly type. No kidding.

Next to him there's Tim, the night staff, who's also six feet three and a former football player, but he's no sweetheart. Tim's got the cop-with-a-major-case-of-hemorrhoids demeanor. Which is intentional. Once Tim's got his Law Enforcement degree from the university, he plans on being a major asshole cop. Can't wait to start upsiding folks' heads with his truncheon.

Him and Keith are wearing T-shirts and sweatpants. Tough Love Counseling Clothes.

Mike comes in the office: Tim's looking up from his night-report sheet and frowning and saying, "You look like you slept *outside*, Mike."

Tim's never liked Mike; the long-hair-and-beard situation pisses him off. But fuck *Tim*. It don't matter to Mike what Tim says or does; Tim's never around when Mike's pulling a shift.

But Keith's happier than shit to see Mike. He says, "I'll give you this much, Mike. You come in that door precisely when you're supposed to. I write you down for six-thirty, and by God, there you are at six-thirty, not a minute sooner or later."

Mike pulls up a chair and waits to hear the report, which Tim proceeds to give directly. Tim says nothing unusual's transpired during the night, a state of affairs that puts the mope into him. He likes it better when there's fights and fuckups and all kinds of physical-intervention situations going down all night. He loves to restrain kids, to show them just who the hell is boss around here. Still, Tim does have an item or two of concern. John Smithers was given four demerits for calling the cook in the cafeteria a *cunt*.

"That was really a disgrace," Tim says.

And Rashon Jackson was sent back early from a visit to Unit 3 for offering to reveal his penis to the female staff there.

"The kid has got no control of himself," Tim says.

And Clarence Jeter: Tim figures something's up with him because he was *way* too helpful on the unit during the evening, offering to mop the floors and empty the wastebaskets and in general behaving like a black Eddie Haskell who's got no ears or hair and can't smile.

"Keep your eye on Clarence," Tim says. "I'm figuring him for a Code Green."

Mike says that he will, and Keith jots this information down in his daily planner.

Code Green means "running away." It means that one of the residents has split from the building. A Code Green is one of a series of codes the staff periodically call over the academy's loudspeaker system. The most common of these codes is a *Come To*, which indicates that there's a fight erupting that requires additional staff assistance. For instance, if there's a six-kid brawl on Unit 5, and Mike and Keith can't handle it by themselves, one of them will run to the office, pick up the telephone, dial eight, and say "Come to Unit 5," and this will be broadcast throughout the building. In no time, extra staff from all over the building will appear and assist with restraining and calming down the kids. So a *Come To* is your general call for help, and a more specific call is your *Core Staff Come To*, which indicates that the situation is grave indeed and that not only every available staff should beat feet to the unit where trouble's happening but an elite group of training crisis interventionists, the core staff, will be required to settle the situation. The residents fear the Core Staff as if they are a troupe of professional wrestlers, which is a well-founded fear; that's exactly what the Core Staff looks like, a troupe of goons.

Tim says it again: "Watch Clarence for a Code Green."

Mike says again that he will, but he thinks Tim doesn't have the aggregate intelligence of a box of Wheaties. Clarence would never run. Where would a kid who looks like Clarence hide in Eau Claire, Wisconsin? Where would a kid who looks like Clarence hide anywhere in the world?

When report's over, Mike leaves the office to perform the first of his daily duties—waking up the kids. A nonintrusive procedure, of course. Mike's not to *enter* a boy's room, but instead he's to *stand* in the doorway, turn on the lights, and say, in friendly voice, "Good morning. It's time to begin another day." Ridiculous. Who among these kids cares if another day's dawned? But the goddam rules are the rules, and that's what he's paid to do: follow the rules.

Clarence shares a room with a skinny fifteen-year-old white kid named Paul Schmidt, who's got long stringy hair and fine features and has been committed to the academy for showing the early mental-derangement signs of a serial killer in training. He once, for example, killed and dissected his family's black Labrador. Did the same to several other dogs, too, along with a dozen or so squirrels and rabbits and cats in his South Milwaukee neighborhood. But it figures: He's a handsome boy, popular with the girls from Unit 3, representatives of which are forever obtaining passes to visit Paul on Unit 5 and watch TV with him.

When Mike flicks on the lights, Paul rolls over in the midst of a dream he's having and says, in a daze, "That's good. That's good. Keep touching it like that." Then he dozes off again.

But Clarence ain't dozing. He bolts upright, smiles his muscleless smile that isn't really a smile, and says, "Mr. Mike, I'm so happy to see you today. Knowing you here on the job, that mean today gone be perfect."

Clarence is shirtless, the topography of his grafts intricate—here a strip of skin as thick as a leather belt, here a checkerboard pattern between the raised places, here a small patch of skin with a hair growing from it—but Mike tries not to stare. But then again, who the hell *wouldn't* stare at a sight like this?

Mike says, "What are you so happy about, Clarence?"

"Dunno," Clarence says. Swings his legs over the edge of his bed. His legs don't seem to be grafted as extensively as the rest of him. "You thinking I should be pissed off about something?"

Mike informs Clarence that being pissed off is not an appropriate behavior.

"I *should* be pissed something righteous, though," Clarence says, "listening to this pretty-boy babbling about his hammy *all* night."

Paul hugs his pillow, buries his head in it like he's kissing it.

"Get up, Paul," Mike says. "Your pillow doesn't live on Unit Three."

Clarence lets out a laugh, broad and satisfied; he couldn't have thought of a better line himself.

"I know you *cool*, Mr. Mike. We gone be friends for real."

Mike ponders this, stares at Clarence's arms, thick and a gauzy shade of dark yellow, and doesn't imagine that Clarence's arms are anything remotely like Elvin Jones's arms.

Now Paul's awake, rumpled and yawning. "Both of you can suck my cock," he says.

"That's one demerit, Paul," Mike says.

"Hoo*wee*," Clarence says. "I fin to tell Keith to mark down that demerit right now."

He jumps out of bed, goes to his closet, selects a Milwaukee Bucks T-shirt and a pair of black acetate pants. "Day starting perfect," he says, "if Paul already getting demerits."

Mike says, "Clarence, you should focus on your own behavior, not someone else's."

But Clarence isn't listening. He tugs on his basketball shoes. Doesn't lace them up. Brother don't *need* them laces. And he's out the door in a flash, on his way to see Keith.

Paul says, "He's way into the ass-kissing thing lately."

"As long as he's not literally putting his lips to my ass," Mike says, "I figure I can let him slide." Then he smiles and winks at Paul, who seems to appreciate that a staff's making an inappropriate remark.

AT SEVEN O'CLOCK, Mike and Keith lead the boys downstairs to the cafeteria for their cereal and toast and juice. The cafeteria is small, contained: low ceilings and only enough table space to accommodate two units full of residents and their staff, no more than thirty people. Meals are served therefore in shifts, and each shift of diners is expected to eat their fill in a period not to exceed twenty minutes.

The Unit 5 boys file prison-style into the cafeteria, a shuffling and disinterested line, moving their legs as if they're shackled and chained. Which is close enough to the facts. They pick up trays, plastic utensils, get served their food by two plump white ladies. Norwegian farmwives, Mike thinks, who work to help make the farm payments.

Mike keeps a special eye on John Smithers going through the serving line, John having been just a *tad* abusive to the cafeteria workers last night. But no problem: John was only upset last night because macaroni and cheese was on the menu, and John hates him the fuck out of some macaroni and cheese. This morning the menu features Life Cereal and a banana, a prospect that suits John just fine. He even says "Thank you, ma'am" when he's served his portion.

The boys settle into their seats and set to chowing. The only sounds in the room: crunching and the occasional cough or sniffle.

Then another unit of boys enters the cafeteria. They, too, walk in a shuffling line, their eyes fixed to the floor, but they're grimier than the boys from Unit 5, their eyes vacant and shellshocked. These are kids from EVAL, or the evaluation unit, the new kids, who are undergoing a two-week assessment before being placed on a unit permanently.

Mike doesn't know the names of the two EVAL staff: one's a large butch-looking woman; one's an ashen-colored man with a trimmed beard and aviator glasses.

Because these EVAL kids look very green to the academy—here only a couple of days or so—the Unit 5 boys take it upon themselves to warn them of a few dangers inherent to an institution of this nature.

Rashon Jackson provides the first caution. "Careful you don't bend over too far," he says. "Somebody might be fin to take you for a test drive."

Keith says, "That will be enough, Rashon."

Now John decides he has to add his opinion to the discussion. "Y'all better eat up. My main white-boy Paul likes him some skinny boys like you."

Mike says, "John, *please* be appropriate here."

To which Keith casts an approving look at Mike.

The EVAL boys don't look up, merely go through the line and get their cereal, all except one, the smallest boy among them, a white boy, pale and not weighing more than ninety pounds, who says to the boys from Unit 5, "You niggers don't deserve to eat one of my turds."

As one, the Unit 5 boys rise from their table. Fists, plastic utensils brandished.

John Smithers shouts: "I kill you: you call me *nigger* again!"

Rashon Jackson shouts: "I stuff a turd down you throat, choke you dead, motherfucker!"

Mike's on his feet, too, as is Keith, whose mouth is full of cereal, preventing him from speaking.

Everything's way quiet. Mike can hear the fluorescent lightbulbs overhead buzzing, and somehow he decides to say something. "Think about it, fellows," he says. "You guys get in a fight, and you won't have anything to eat till lunchtime." Stupid, but what else is there to say?

Clarence watches Mike saying this, detects the nervous crack in Mike's voice, and decides now's the time to repay Mike the favor for playing it cool at the bowling alley yesterday.

"Mr. Mike right," Clarence says to the Unit 5 boys. "We gots to eat."

Then Clarence speaks, very calmly, to the skinny boy from EVAL. "Punk," he says. "We deciding to let you slide this one time. We on Unit 5 more worried about eating our breakfast today than teaching you to show us our propers."

With that, Clarence retakes his seat and spoons some cereal into his mouth. The rest of the Unit 5 boys do the same. Cool. Mellow. Totally under control.

By MIDMORNING the rain is falling harder outside, and the wind's blowing hard, angling the rain into gray sheets of misery that batter the windows of Unit 5. Some of the boys are watching TV, some playing Ping-Pong, some sitting in their rooms, on their beds, looking at pictures in comic books. They're bored shitless, is what's happening. Which is always your basic dicey situation on Unit 5. Boredom equals brawl potential, that's the rule. But so far so cool.

Mike's hanging with Keith in the office, and Keith's supergiddy, overjoyed about this morning's turn of events.

Keith says, "That was some masterful conflict-avoidance, Mike."

"Ah, I probably got lucky," Mike says.

"Not at all," Keith says. "You work with these kids like you've been doing the job for years."

Mike's getting embarrassed. Keith's been larding on the compliments for several hours now, which is his way: always stressing the positive, reminding everybody of it whenever there's opportunity. No doubt Keith's look-on-the-bright-side nature is what makes him the perfect man to be manager of Unit 5.

"You know something else?" Keith says. "I think Clarence is taking quite a shine to you."

Mike nods, chews on his thumbnail, hopes Keith moves on to another subject. Pussy, for instance, would be a nice thing to blab about.

But Keith ain't the type to talk about pussy. He says, "Clarence has been on this unit two years now, and he hasn't opened up to *anybody*."

Mike ponders *opening up*, the idea of it, and feels himself coming to the genuinely mushy place where Keith's heart's at. Says, "I feel sorry for Clarence, to tell you the truth."

Keith picks up Clarence's chart from the desk. Gravely flips through a few pages. "Right. Things are never going to be easy for Clarence." Skims several more items in the chart. Cocks his head in a light-bulb's-just-turned-on angle. "I've just come up with a great idea," he says.

Next week he wants to write Clarence a pass for the afternoon. Give him a taste of freedom for a few hours—supervised, of course. Mike being the supervisor. Which is excellent with Mike, provided he doesn't have to do it Monday because he's got an appointment on Monday with the assistant dean to see about getting back into school, which is some major-big important stuff in Mike's life, and Keith can dig that totally.

"Tuesday from noon to five it is," Keith says. He pauses and pats Mike on the shoulder. Father Keith. "And I'll see that you're paid for a full eight-hour shift."

Then a Core Staff Come To EVAL code blasts over the loudspeaker system. The voice calling the code is female, jerky, frightened, behind the voice kids hollering *Cunt* and *Bitch* and *I'll kill you* and chairs clattering.

Keith is Mike's Zen master of codes: "You take this one, Mike." Keith can handle whatever while he's gone.

$4.25 an hour, Mike's on a full run toward EVAL for it.

FIGURES. Mike's never been able to run worth a shit. He's late for the action on EVAL. Ten staff from other units are already there, formed in half-huddle near EVAL's office. Nobody says, like, hello to Mike or anything. They're concentrating on the textbook physical-restraint deployment happening at their feet. A core staff's got a kid pinned to the linoleum. *Immobilize the resident who acts out.* That's the rule.

The core staff's a gigantic jarheaded dude named Henry. He's covering the kid completely. Probably three times the kid's size. Only the kid's tiny fist sticks out from underneath Henry's chest. The fist belongs to the tiny pale boy who called Unit 5 *niggers* at breakfast.

The boy's saying, "Get off of me, you fat motherfucker. You're crushing me."

And the boy ain't lying: It's possible Henry outweighs him by two hundred pounds.

Henry says, "Is it over?"

"Your goddam *armpits* stink like *bacon*," the boy says. "I'm getting crushed by a *smoked pig*!"

Henry says, "I'm asking you again: Is *it* over?"

The kid's no dummy. He folds. "Okay, goddammit. It's over. I give up."

Henry gets to his knees with much caution. Kid might make a sudden move. But when the kid don't do anything, Henry helps him up. The kid's face is as red as a maraschino cherry, a dented-in spot on one cheek where his face got mashed into the floor. And the kid keeps his peace. He's whipped and knows it. A dozen staff versus him: no way. *He'll get even some other time.* That's the kind of sneer he gives everybody when Henry ushers him by the arm a few steps to the butch-looking female staff who Mike saw at breakfast. She's sweaty and flushed, ashamed that she needed core staff help restraining the kid.

Henry says, "Here you go, Jill. He'll behave appropriately now."

Jill eyeballs the kid, fakes a smile at him, and he fakes one back. Jill says, "Let's sit in the office for a while, Marty." Her voice: jerky, weak. She's really fucked this one up. But young Marty follows her into the office, and all the extra staff assembled on EVAL split back to their own units, their own troubles.

WHEN MIKE'S a few hallways down from EVAL, hands in his pockets, taking a nice leisurely stroll back to Keith and his compliments, he feels a big hand on his shoulder. Henry's.

Henry says, "Name's Mike, that correct?"

Mike says that it is and looks into Henry's eyes. Translucent gray, angry pea-size marbles sunk inside Henry's huge head.

Henry says, "How's *Keith* treating you on Unit Five?"

"Fine. I like Keith a lot."

Henry doesn't say anything for a while, merely stands there in the hallway with arms folded in Mussolini fashion. Then this: "I was watching you there on EVAL. You looked unhappy. Why's that?"

"What makes you think," Mike says, "I looked unhappy?"

Henry grunts, picks at his teeth with a pinkynail. "You were frowning there, ace. I'll take that for unhappiness every time."

Rules: *Don't bicker with core staff.* Mike says, "I don't remember frowning."

Henry says, "Buddy, you've hardly been working here a month. I've been working here *six* years."

Mike doesn't move. He pretends to be taking in an important lesson. Smiles. Nods.

"This is the way things are around here," Henry says. "You never know if one of these kids might up and try to kill you. So if a kid needs to be restrained—any kid, I don't give a damn who—I'm taking them down to the floor and putting the hurt to them. That way, they'll know who's running the show, and they'll think twice before acting out in the future."

Mike imagines Henry after work, going to a meathead tavern with his meathead buddies, having a few paramilitary beers and telling everybody how he held the line for solid citizenship today, how he squared off one-on-one with a criminal and put his ass in its place. Mike wonders if Henry's buddies know the criminal in question weighs about the same as a bag of rock salt.

Back on Unit 5, Keith's got Clarence with him in the office— they're jawing the way old buddies do: kneeslapping, yucking it up— and Keith asks Mike to take a seat. Mike's got no problem with that.

"Clarence and I," Keith says, "have been having a conference about the pass I'm going to give him on Tuesday."

Clarence sits in a roller chair next to Keith's desk, his eyes repeatedly glancing toward the paperwork there, trying, Mike can tell, to learn some secrets to share with the other boys.

Keith says, "Now you understand, Clarence, that this pass is not only a big responsibility but an *opportunity*. You will spend the afternoon with Mike, and Mike alone, and if you do well, maybe I can arrange for you to have an afternoon pass that you can use by yourself, some other day."

"I won't mess with Mr. Mike. He got my guarantee on that. Me and him, we friends."

B EFORE M IKE LEAVES work he picks up his paycheck. Awesome. $187 after taxes. A guy can totally get by on that. He goes to the credit union and deposits everything but thirty dollars into his checking account. Hey, that's some responsible-type stuff there: a checking account. One month after living in Riverside, and Mike's gotten himself into personal checking. Ah, the working life!

Mike's roommate, on the other hand, he doesn't have a regular job. Doesn't *need* one. Sure, once or twice a week, Joe thuds on his drums in a jazz combo at the Eau Claire Civic Center. But that's thirty-five bucks a gig. Joe's main money comes from his parents, who live in Minneapolis and are delighted to have their wayward boy finally enrolled in college again. Eight years ago, round about the time Joe met Elvin Jones, Joe barely graduated from a two-year community college, and went listless after that. Worked a bunch of dipshit-style jobs. No-future gigs. To Joe's parents, the fact that Joe's now a full-time music major at a four-year institution, well, that's just so wonderful, Joe. We're so *proud* of you.

So there Joe is when Mike gets home, hanging out in the living room doing nothing. But Joe is especially excited to see Mike today. He says, "I've got a present for you, Mike."

"Bring it on," Mike says. He assumes it's some fancy dope, because that's usually the unsurprising surprise. But it's not dope Joe's talking about today.

Joe reaches to the floor next to the couch and picks up an enormous black box set of record albums, a set so heavy Joe can hardly hold it in the air. "I went to the library today," he says, "and I checked this out in honor of your outing at the bowling alley yesterday."

This enormous box set is Richard Wagner's entire *Ring* cycle, all four operas on something like thirty albums. Joe says, "I'm thinking: Wagner's sixty-six and a half Lanes, Wagner's *Ring* cycle—there must be a connection here."

Mike's got to laugh. Only Joe would make a connection like that, let alone actually go to the library and bring the entire *Ring* cycle home. If Mike were a chick, he couldn't help but thinking Oh, isn't that sweet? But thank God Mike's not a chick.

He plays up the asshole side of his gratitude. "Do we have to listen to *all* that?" Mike says.

To Mike's surprise, Joe says yes. "Should take seventeen hours, if my calculations are correct."

"Joe, you'll never sit *still* for seventeen hours."

"Listen: There's a tradition in jazz of listening to Wagner."

Mike sits and kicks up his feet and prepares to take in Joe's theory. As far as Mike knows, the biggest tradition with Richard Wagner was that he was Hitler's version of Elvis.

"I believe it was Coltrane," Joe says, "or maybe it was Thelonious Monk, or maybe Charlie Parker—somebody very cool, at any rate—once locked himself in a hotel room in Kansas City for a weekend, mainlined heroin, and listened to the *Ring* cycle in its entirety."

"We don't have any heroin, Joe."

Joe doesn't register Mike's dig. Never does. "But I guess this cat—it must have been Charlie Parker; I'm sure of it—this cat apparently discovered something unspeakably beautiful about jazz in the act of listening to all four of these operas consecutively."

Joe's excited. Mike can see there's no changing that. So he tells Joe they should get right to it.

"Bring out Betsy," Mike says, "and let's listen to the goddam opera."

So they gurgle Betsy a few times, and Joe puts on the first record of the thirty, which contains the overture to the first opera of the *Ring* cycle, entitled, obviously enough, *The Ring*.

Mike eases back in his chair and listens to the somber strings gathering together as if out of a mist. It's pretty good shit, no denying that. Pleasant even. But come on: This is 5:30 on a Friday afternoon, and they're here listening to *opera*? That just ain't right.

So after a few minutes, when the singing finally begins, Mike figures it's time to break Joe's concentration. He picks the easiest, redneckiest thing to say, too: "What the fuck, Joe? This shit, it's in *German*."

Joe snaps forward in his chair, wrings his chin. Says, "You're right. Let's listen to Szobel instead." And he's off to change the tunes.

Szobel is Hermann Szobel, a sixteen-year-old Austrian piano prodigy who recorded one album in 1976 and subsequently disappeared from the public eye, if he was ever in it to begin with. This is the story Joe tells: While Szobel was recording his album in New York City he went insane—had a psychotic episode or a nervous breakdown or whatever—and got committed to a mental institution in Salzburg, where he's still housed and is still dashing off avant-garde string quartets and piano concerti between electroshock treatments and monthlong periods of chlorpromazine haze.

On Szobel's album cover is a picture of him standing in front of a tall building in New York City. He's extremely gaunt, has sunken eyes, and is trying to stuff his bony fingers into his pockets, without much luck. Guy can't figure out how to get his hands in a hole. Which is bad, if you're a guy. The photographer clearly means to capture the boy genius coolly surveying the hubbub of the city, but instead what the photographer's captured is a being for whom the machinations of the world are as foreign as a dry riverbed on Mars. He doesn't look lost, exactly; he doesn't even look like he's *there*.

On the album's back cover: more pictures. Hermann playing the piano during the recording session: shirtless, ribs and spine buttons, fingers curled over the keyboard, writhing, appearing almost as if he's playing with his knuckles.

Also on the back cover: A few words of praise provided by, of all people, Roberta Flack, who says only this: "We love you, Hermann."

We love you. People will say that to *anybody*.

This is how the record begins: Hermann plays a distraught and desiccated melody on the piano, no chords, just a series of maudlin tones that he repeats a couple of times as if this melody is so profound and gut-tugging he can't bear moving on to the remaining agony of the tune. Then he chords a pattern, as sad as anything anybody could conjure, in an odd time—9/4—and now there's a tenor sax with him; not wailing, sobbing. Then there's a xylophone and drums and electric bass and a groove that's supposed to be rock, hip and fast and concussive, but which sounds like the requiem vamp for the world's dead children instead.

Mike watches pictures in his mind: a lime-green room and a girl fourteen years old who makes pipes out of apples; a twelve-seat bus moving along the streets of Eau Claire; a bowling alley; a brawl; a tiny white hand sticking out from underneath a three-hundred-pound man's chest; a can of Sterno, a black female hand smearing its contents over a six-year-old black boy; a match lighting; a fire burning; a voice within the flames discording a scream that no one will ever hear; a whole world of irreversible sorrow.

SATURDAY NIGHT at 6:30, Keith calls Mike and asks him if he can come in to work. Not for long. A couple of hours. "It won't be a big deal," Keith says. "Just keep an eye on things till Tim comes in at nine."

Keith explains that all the boys have passes to other units for the evening or are going downstairs to the old chapel to watch *The Fly*, starring Vincent Price. Paul's the only kid staying on the unit. That's it. He's got a Unit 3 girl stopping by for appropriate TV viewing in the commons area.

Mike mulls it and decides on brownnosing. Says, "I sure could use the extra hours on my paycheck."

Keith says, "You're welcome."

So at seven, Mike's sitting in the Unit 5 office, bored and opening up Clarence Jeter's file to keep himself occupied. Clarence is downstairs watching *The Fly*. One of Clarence's favorite flicks. And Mike's thinking, making $4.25 an hour for reading a file: everything's damn good for all concerned. It's a kick-totally-back night here at the academy. Gravy.

True to Keith's word, Paul is sitting on the couch in the commons area, keeping an appropriate distance from a thirteen-year-old Unit 3 girl named Cassie. They're watching *The Dirty Dozen*. Not talking. Not looking at each other. Cassie's got dirt-colored hair, stringy and long, and a homemade tattoo on her forearm that reads BULETS. Mike guesses Cassie doesn't know she'll endure the rest of her life with a misspelled word on her forearm. *Her* problem, though. Not Mike's. All that matters to him: She and Paul aren't doing the spanky-hanky thing in front of the TV.

He fumbles through Clarence's file. Quarterly conduct reports. Demerit summaries. Med charts. He finds at the back of the file several typewritten pages under the heading NARRATIVE CASE HISTORY. Excellent. It's Clarence's life story.

Six-year-old Clarence. When the Sterno thing happens and he somehow lives through that, Clarence spends a full year recovering at St. Luke's Hospital in Milwaukee. Undergoes dozens of grafting operations. Constant agony. But he's remarkably cheery. He's six, looks at life on the bright side. Besides, people are paying attention to him, bustling around him, checking his pulse, bringing his supper on a tray. He's *somebody* for the first time in his life.

And he heals. Goes home to a calm that's never been there for him before. His sister—Amanda's her name—she's not living at home anymore. She's doing an indefinite commitment to the Juvenile Psych

Unit at Winnebago State Mental Hospital in Oshkosh. She's as long gone from Clarence's life as the skin he was born with.

So he has two years of happy recovery at home. His family receives financial assistance from Milwaukee County. He gets private tutors to come to the home. Mrs. Ellingsworth. Miss Gladowski. A physical therapist named Mr. Reginald Witherspoon. Other folks. People who care. Clarence is your typical mangled-freak-with-a-strong-heart type. Smart, too. Of course. Takes the standardized tests the school district sends to his house and scores in the upper percentiles. Has especially strong aptitude in math and natural science. For every freak—this is the way God has designed the universe—there's a silver future. We love you, Clarence.

But if the kid's got aptitude, if the kid's an affable little fellow, he can't stay cloistered forever. He's nine years old. He's got to go to school. Fourth grade is what he's got to do. And irony Number 289: Same week he starts fourth grade in the Milwaukee Public Schools, Amanda gets released from Winnebago. She's adjusted. Clarence is adjusted. They got to live under the same roof. They're family.

So Clarence goes to school. The kids tease him relentlessly. A sideshow freak. They call him Crispy or Cinder or Charcoal or Burnt Weenie. He gets home from school, trying to keep that like-in-the-movies positive-freak-boy outlook, and there, in his living room or on his front porch, sits Amanda.

But she gets hers. That's the way the world works sometimes. On July 8, 1977, sometime after nightfall, Amanda is shot dead while attempting to rob a liquor store on Milwaukee's Polish south side. Her time in Winnebago taught her a thing or two about a life of crime, but apparently she didn't learn enough.

Clarence slides, too. A year after Amanda's death, the cops bust Clarence trying to pawn two hot car stereos. He takes the rap: two stereos ain't shit. Besides, a guy gets caught with two stereos, that means he *didn't* get caught for the other hundred he probably stole. Smart, that Clarence. An upper-percentile person. He's so much smarter than his peaheaded buddies on the street that he becomes their leader in crime: calls the shots, plans the heists, spends the cash. Pulls off this shit for several years till, three years ago, somebody snitches on him. He gets nailed for kiping three cars in three days, and there you go: He's chilling at the academy till he's eighteen.

Mᴵᴷᴱ ᴘᴱᴱᴿˢ ᵁᴾ from the file and notices that Paul Schmidt and Cassie are no longer sitting innocently by the television. They're gone. But Mike doesn't get jumpy and call a Code Green over the loudspeaker just yet. He merely closes Clarence's file, rises calmly, and wanders out of the office and stands near the TV.

The Dirty Dozen is at the point where Lee Marvin has bet Colonel Breed that in the pre-D-Day war games his men can capture his headquarters and his entire staff. The men break some rules to get the job done, but, like, fuck the rules. And Mike can't help digging the part when Ernest Borgnine smiles at Charles Bronson there in Colonel Breed's headquarters; Ernest Borgnine's smile means that he knows Colonel Breed is a useless boob, which is what everybody watching the movie has known all along.

Mike loves *The Dirty Dozen*. His favorite movie, just about. But goddammit if he's not on the job. He's got to find where the kids are at.

No lights in Paul's room, merely a shaft of hallway fluorescence streaming in. When Mike looks in, he sees Paul's bare ass, dim, his pelvis moving. Cassie's legs: up in the air, wobbling. She lets out a tiny moan. Paul's fucking her for all she's worth, and she's loving it.

Mike opens his mouth into an O and sighs. Then he closes Paul's door, walks slowly back to the office, and takes a seat.

A ꜰᴱᵂ ᴹᴵᴺᵁᵀᴱˢ ʟᴀᵀᴱᴿ, Paul and Cassie emerge from Paul's room, rumpled and flushed, holding hands. Cassie glances across the commons area and tries to catch Mike's eye. He sees that she's nervous and guilty, fearing demerits and probably the resulting long conversations with various social workers. She's not seeing what Mike's thinking: He would give anything in the world to sneak off into a bedroom with a skinny tattooed girl and fuck her and have her enjoy it.

On the TV *The Dirty Dozen* are situated *Last Supper*-style around a long table cluttered with half-empty wine bottles and several turkeys eaten down to the bone. The men are smoking cigars and laughing their asses off about that dipshit Colonel Breed and how easy it was to outconnive him. Lee Marvin's saying, "Up till now, it's all been fun and games. Tomorrow, it's the real thing, and my guess is most of you won't be coming back."

This is 8:45. In a few minutes, the rest of the Unit 5 boys will return from their passes or from watching *The Fly*, and Tim will arrive, ready to intervene in whatever crisis may come. This means Mike's got to fill out report for the last two hours' events. He takes out the daily log, thinks for a bit on what he'll write.

Here's his first attempt: *Observed Paul and Cassie fucking at 8:25. At 8:30, they were watching TV.*

Reads that over a couple of times. Decides the wording isn't quite clinical enough for Tim's taste. He crosses out what he wrote and tries it again.

Paul had a visitor from Unit 3. Cassie. At 8:25, I observed them having intercourse.

Ah, that's a little better. A bit more official-report-sounding. But after reading it over for five minutes or so, glancing occasionally up from his desk to see Paul and Cassie sitting on the couch watching the Dirty Dozen parachuting into France on the night before D-Day to kill hundreds of German officers and their wives in a lovely château by a river, he decides that Paul and Cassie are just two souls doing their best to improve the darkness. If he were them, he'd have done exactly the same thing.

He crosses out his second entry and writes this: *Uneventful. Paul had a visitor from Unit 3. They watched* The Dirty Dozen *appropriately.*

MONDAY MORNING AT NINE, Mike enters the assistant dean's office at the university and stands rigidly before the man's desk, wringing his hands, sweating. The dean is Dr. James Woodson, a thin neat man with round glasses who joined the faculty some years ago as a mathematician but eventually wandered over to administration for the increased pay that comes with not having to show nineteen-year-olds how to factor polynomials and how to comprehend the imaginary number. He assesses Mike for an uncomfortable time: Mike's ripped overalls, his ripped shirt, his long hair and beard.

"I take it," Dr. Woodson says, "you didn't think this was a formal occasion." Frowns. Lets out a calculated disappointed sigh.

Mike says, "I apologize for my attire."

Dr. Woodson shakes his head, lets Mike stand there and suffer a moment longer, in which time Mike scans around the room to avoid looking into Dr. Woodson's eyes. His desk is orderly, some files arranged in a neat pile on one side, his name plaque dusted and shiny and perfectly in the middle front. On the wall behind the desk is a framed painting of a sailboat, next to which is a smaller framed photograph of a beautiful tanned high school girl wearing a cheerleader's uniform and sitting on a log surrounded with brown fallen leaves, her legs glossy and her smile as pure and friendly as the air in Eau Claire.

"This is a university," Dr. Woodson says finally, "not a fashion show. I suppose we'll discuss your case on the merits of your mind."

He gestures for Mike to sit on one of the visitor's chairs in front of his desk.

Dr. Woodson picks up a file, Mike's, from the stack on his desk. Opens it. Thumbs through it with further sighing disinterest. "Looks to me," he says, "like you weren't meant for the Music Department."

"But I'm a musician," Mike says. "A drummer."

"Funny. You don't *look* like one."

"People *have* said that to me before."

"I'll bet." Dr. Woodson closes the file and tents his fingers, examines them for a time as if they will provide him with his line of inquiry. He swivels in his chair and gazes with a tired smile upon the picture of the girl in the cheerleader uniform.

"See that girl?"

Mike says he does, but he wants to say, *Sweet Jesus, how could I miss seeing her?*

"That's Jenny. She's my daughter. Does she look like a musician to you?"

Mike stares at her, her eyes stone blue, her skin so blemish-free it's glossy, the kind of girl, in real life, Mike would never be able to look in the eye.

"She looks like a cheerleader, I guess," Mike says. Feels the itch of sweat beginning somewhere in the back of his scalp.

"Well, Jenny *is* a cheerleader. But she's a musician, too. And a fine one. She's first-chair clarinet in the Eau Claire Memorial Band."

Mike imagines young Jenny holding her clarinet, playing earnestly the allegro section from, say, *Brighton Beach* or *American Overture*, her delicate fingers manipulating the keys over runs and trills, her mouth taking the sweet air that passes through her lungs and forming it into a miracle of melody and tone.

"Very talented," Dr. Woodson says. "Exceptionally gifted. But do you know what field she's choosing to enter? Dentistry." He pauses to let this information work into Mike's brain, which it doesn't; if Mike thinks about teeth with respect to Jenny, it only has to do with her biting her clarinet's mouthpiece. "See, she understands the need for clarinetists in this world is not great; but the need for dentists—why, it's inexhaustible, Mike. I'm sure proud of that girl."

Hell, Mike's proud of her, too. She sits on that log applying no more pressure to it than one of the fallen leaves surrounding her might apply to the ground. Her legs, crossed so fuckably comfortably. Mike imagines putting his head in her lap, just for an instant, and breathing in her smell of the forest and of the cork grease she uses to lubricate the joints of her clarinet.

Dr. Woodson says, "Let me ask you, Mike. What did you do—how shall I say?—to expand your horizons this weekend?"

Mike's still thinking of Jenny's reeds and her ligature, the virtuosity of her. But he's still paying attention. He knows what the fuck's going on here. He knows it's time to field the standard recreational-partying question, a question he figured in advance must be put to all students who have flunked out of school and want back in, and he's quick to dodge it with the first thing that comes to mind.

Mike says, "I listened to the *Ring* cycle in its entirety."

"The *Ring* cycle?"

"The *Ring* cycle, as in Wagner." Mike pronounces *Wagner* in the correct German *Vahg-ner* way he heard his mother pronounce it years before.

But Dr. Woodson isn't buying Mike's bullshit. "Oh," he says. Rolls his eyes. "You were hanging out at Wagner's sixty-six and a half lanes this weekend. Very productive use of your time, I should say."

"I mean *Ree-kart Vahg-ner*. The *Ring* cycle. The four operas. I listened to the whole thing."

Dr. Woodson doesn't respond. Examines his fingers instead. Fiddles with his cuticles.

This is going like crap. Horrific. So Mike decides to lay on a different level of horsepucky. "Fourteen hours into it," Mike says, "it hit me that this beautiful music is what inspired Hitler. That was *very* disturbing."

Dr. Woodson levels his eyes at Mike and suddenly laughs through his nose. "Hitler?"

"Hitler," Mike says.

Now Dr. Woodson claps his hands, keeps chuckling. "That's a first: I've *never* heard a kid mention Hitler in a readmission interview."

Mike's not giving up just yet. "It's true," he says. "Hitler was *fascinated* with Wagner."

Abruptly Dr. Woodson stops laughing. "I know that."

Then, snap of the fingers, no further discussion, Dr. Woodson dismisses Mike. Says he'll personally call him later in the week with his decision regarding readmittance. They shake hands before parting, and when they do, Mike takes a long drink-her-in gander at young Jenny's picture and silently wishes her well. *A beautiful girl like you*, he thinks, *you will always have people offering you the world.*

T*UESDAY*, C*LARENCE* J*ETER* steps with Mike into the free world at precisely noon, wearing a clean blue University of North Carolina T-shirt and a pair of white acetate gym pants. Around his neck: the thick silver chain. Around his wrist: the thick silver bracelet. Dude's dappered out today. Looking fine. Which he sees fit to mention to Mike directly.

"Least one of us ain't looking like a bum," Clarence says. "Sometime, Mr. Mike, I gone give you some tips about threads."

Mike says, "You give me all the advice you want. These rags are all I can afford."

"Shit. *You* rich. You got a job."

"You call *this* a job, Clarence?"

"You getting paid, right?"

Mike pats Clarence on the shoulder. Says, "Hell, spending the afternoon with you, I'd say that's a goddam vacation."

Clarence busts a chuckle. "Fuckin-A right," he says. "We on vacation today."

They stroll a bit, talk about this and that. The nice day. How fucked up the academy's insides are. They look at the Roman Catholic church, Sacred Heart Cathedral, that's next to the academy. It's made of the same red brick as the academy, and has two spiring steeples overlooking the Chippewa Valley. A picture of Jesus is carved above the church's narthex entrance. Jesus is looking happy. Jesus says, "You guys go out and have a nice time today."

They reach the steps that descend into the valley and can see the Uniroyal plant, blocks long and chugging a pleasant-looking steam from its stacks. Mike figures he'll play tour guide for a while. Says, "See Uniroyal over there."

Clarence sure the fuck does. Like, he'd have to be blind not to.

Mike says, "Let's go check out the cool footbridge over the river down there."

Clarence nods, and Mike's superencouraged by this. The afternoon's going to be cake for sure.

THEY TAKE MIKE'S usual route home, past the taverns and the lumberjack houses, and Clarence keeps slowing down to scrutinize the sidewalk or the thin grass in somebody's front yard.

He says, "Never seen Eau Claire this way."

"How's that?"

"Slow."

Mike doesn't say anything. Just walks at the pace Clarence sets, stopping and looking at something and starting off again.

Clarence says, "I like seeing the dirt up close. Can't see dirt up close when you riding through Eau Claire in a bus."

He points to a little anthill near the sidewalk. "See that? You can see *ants* when you walking."

A dozen or so ants indeed are bustling about their home, carrying tiny sticks and bee wings. One ant is tugging a hunk of potato chip.

Mike says, "Those bastards sure keep themselves occupied."

"I get tired just looking at em," Clarence says.

Mike says, "But a guy can't help but admire how hard they work."

"Fuck *that*." Clarence makes his fingers into a pistol that he points at his temple and fires. "They wasting they time. They gone die whether they work or don't."

Occasionally a car slows slow down near Mike and Clarence, and a white head peers at Clarence. Wide eyes at the sight of Clarence. Open mouth. Clarence waves; then the car drives on.

Mike says, "Does that piss you off?"

"It don't," Clarence says. "They looking freaky to me, too."

AT UNIROYAL, they stop near a chain-link fence surrounding Uniroyal's receiving area. Pallets are stacked in there, and a broken-down forklift rusts in the sun. The factory is four stories high, with huge windows open and revealing the view of finished tires moving along, suspended on hooks from an overhead conveyor. On the fourth story, a man stands by a window, smoking a cigarette and rubbing his hands vacantly through his hair.

Clarence says, "Bet that sucks dog dick, working in there."

"But I hear the pay's *great*." Mike's heard they make twelve bucks an hour in there.

"*Fuck* the pay." Clarence whiffs the air, its melted-rubber tang. "That shit *stanky*."

"You got a point, Clarence. Work always stinks."

Mike gets a move on. He doesn't want to draw attention by loitering outside Uniroyal's fence, and Clarence is 100 percent down with *that*. He falls in alongside Mike, and they hands-in-their-pockets their way around the plant till they reach the footbridge.

At first Clarence is freaky-deaky about crossing. Don't wanna mess with *that* shit. He can see that the drop's long, the water down there shallow, and the sharp rocks plentiful.

He says, "Let's walk around this shit, Mr. Mike."

"What the hell's wrong with walking across a bridge?"

"Too far down, man. Like looking at dying, a drop that far."

"You're not gonna *jump*, are you?"

"No, Mr. Mike. I ain't the type for jumping."

"Then you got nothing to worry about."

Mike goes to the center of the bridge and waves the this-is-pie wave, the follow-me-and-you'll-be-okay wave, and, after a hesitation, Clarence follows. He joins Mike in the center, peers over the edge, and hangs on to that railing like a motherfucker.

Mike spits over the edge, and the gob spirals for a few seconds downward and touches the rippling water like a hard drop of rain, then disappears. Downstream, the hickories and tag alders are as lush green as leprechauns, leaves ruffling in the breeze.

"A long way down," Clarence says, but he's mellowing. He lets go of the railing, reaches into his pocket, produces his Kools, and lights one. Mike lights a Marlboro.

They smoke for a while without saying anything, and finally Clarence leans over the railing and spits. His gob spirals downward but doesn't hit the water; the breeze guides it to a slagpile on the river's shore.

"If I's Mr. Country Boy like you," Clarence says, "my spit would hit the water."

Mike chuckles your Grade-B philosopher's chuckle. Says, "I guess there's more to life than spitting off bridges."

"Telling you: Two years I been at the academy, and I never knew this place was here."

"I'm happy I could show it to you," Mike says, and he means it. He loves this goddam job. Best job he's ever had.

Clarence says, "Now, Lake Michigan, that shit's *blue*. That's some blue goes for miles, man."

Mike says, "I've always thought Lake Michigan is amazing." And that's the truth: When Mike was boy, his family used to go for picnics at a beach by Lake Michigan—Doctor's Park was the place—and he could never get over how blue the water was and how much of it there was.

Clarence says, "You lying. You ain't never seen Lake Michigan."

"I have, hey. Lots of times."

"But your ass is grown up here. All you gots here is rivers."

"I'm from Menomonee Falls." Menomonee Falls is about twenty-five miles from Clarence's neighborhood. A guy could walk that far in a day, if he had to.

Clarence says, "Where the *fuck* Menomonee Falls at?"

Along the shore below Mike sees a beer can, dreck of the land of the living, next to which is a dead bluegill, dross of what the living have done to the land. Twenty-five miles, that's a continent apart.

THEY'RE QUIET AGAIN, two figures leering over a dizzying drop. Squadrons of blue jays dart from one tree to the next on the river bottom. Small fish nip at the surface in the river shallows.

"Mr. Mike, I gots something to ax you."

"Ask away."

Clarence now flicks his cigarette over the bridge, and it sails for an endless moment outward and downward, hitting the water and drifting lazily downstream.

"There it is," Clarence says. "Hanging with you gone make me country after all."

Mike flicks his cigarette, too, and it doesn't hit the water. It lands next to the beer can and the dead bluegill, and keeps smoldering.

Clarence says, "I been in that academy shithole so long I barely gots memory of what it was before I was there. You dig?"

Mike says that he does. He digs it completely.

Clarence says, "I been thinking you the type of man keeps him some dope in the house. That right?"

Way downriver, at the farthest possible point in Mike's line of sight, he sees a raccoon digging about in the rocks, hunting crawfish.

Clarence says, "Ain't no point lying bout it, Mr. Mike. We *friends*."

Oh, the poor misunderstood fat boy—this has been Mike's general theme since he can remember having a general theme. But he can see right now, at this sunny instant high on the footbridge, that he's really just been full of shit. Mike's life's charmed. He does some stupid shit in Menomonee Falls, gets caught, and he ends up having it twice as good. He's got the way-perfect easy job. He figures Dr. Woodson will let him back into school. Hey, if not for the fall term—sometime. That's the thing: Mike's life is always going to work out. Clarence, though, he's doomed, black and burned and larcenous; life's never going to turn out for *him*.

"I keep dope in the house, Clarence. You're right."

"It good?"

"Good enough."

"Let's go get us some."

Two kids: one of them twenty years old, one of them seventeen. Two fuckups having a nice time on a sunny afternoon.

To MIKE'S HOUSE from the footbridge is a walk of four blocks. Easy. Not far but still long enough to plan out how they're going to get the dope out of the house without Joe thinking something's up. A CIA-type operation, that's what they were thinking will work. We're talking secrecy to the deluxe extreme.

Mike explains Joe, his form and his theory. Says he's older. Says he's a jumpy person. Flighty. Which is no slight to Joe but the truth. Mike says Joe won't be expecting company this time of day.

Clarence says, "I'll keep his shit occupied, Mr. Mike. No problem."

Here's the plan: They'll walk right in, Clarence will tell Joe he loves music, and while Joe's putting on tunes, Mike will surreptitiously roll a fatty. Then they'll leave Joe to his jazz, walk a mile or two to the other side of town, to Carson Park, which stands on the shores of Half Moon Lake. They'll go to the place Mike calls the Stones, a hundred-year-old sawmill, roof gone, floors gone, a pile of crumbling slag in the woods near the water and the weeds out there. Nobody will ever see them smoking dope at the Stones.

MIKE'S FRONT LAWN. There's drumming coming from the house, a series of single-stroke rolls haphazardly battering one drum or another. The china-type cymbal barks.

"That goddam Joe," Mike says. "He's playing my drums."

But Mike plays it cool. Keeps the under-control face on for Clarence. Ushers Clarence inside and leads him up the stairs to where Mike's kit's at.

Joe's got headphones on, is playing along with a tape, but the way he plays—no rhythm, just wild single-strokes flailing everywhere in no particular sequence—there's no way he's correctly jamming along with that tape.

Finally Joe looks up, quits his manic rolling so suddenly he loses the grip on one of his 5A sticks and fumbles with it to keep from dropping it. He rises from the drum stool as if snapping to military attention, takes off the headphones. Face goes way crimson. Mutters something about how he's working on his free playing. But that's not what he's thinking about. He's staring at Clarence.

Clarence is on top of it. Says, "You got you some *fast* hands, man."

Joe can't say anything. For once in his life. Looks at his hands, all popped out in veins after drumming. At his sticks, chipped near the tip from crashing cymbals and hitting rims.

Mike tries to clear things. "Clarence has a day pass, Joe. We're just stopping by to check out my drum set." Does an authority-figure-style smile and self-deprecating chuckle. "Figured I'd prove to him I *actually* own one."

Clarence says, "They *good* drums, too, Mr. Mike."

Joe is very studious about not staring at Clarence. He looks at each drum in Mike's kit individually and finally says, "They certainly *are* nice drums."

Mike cuts a quick glance at Clarence, who does a let's-get-the-fuck-outta-here eye rotation.

Okay, then. Mike executes the plan. He says to Joe, "You want to go downstairs with Clarence here and play some Szobel for him? I've been telling him about Szobel."

It's perfection, hey: Instantly, Joe's out from behind the drums and heading downstairs to his stereo, and Clarence is following him the way he's supposed to. See, this is dream-come-true stuff for Joe: to have a black person in the house and a chance to share jazz with him.

In no time, the first tormented strains of Szobel begin oozing through Joe's stereo speakers. And Mike pops open his dresser, produces his dope, his papers, rolls the largest two-paper fatty his rolling skills will allow, and ponders, just for a second, the extent to which he's fucking the dog here. Baking up one with a resident, that's your get-canned offense, no doubt. But on other hand, who cares? Clarence *deserves* to spend an afternoon stoned. Because who doesn't?

Downstairs, the first Szobel tune winds through its impossibly distraught out-chorus. Hermann weeps the chromatic runs of his suffering-in-hell life into the piano.

Joe's eyes are closed in the suitable Szobel ecstasy, his hands clasped together prayerfully in his lap.

Not Clarence's eyes. He's looking wide open at Mike and nodding. He's waiting on the all-systems-go, and Mike gives it.

When the tune ends and Clarence is on his feet, ready to split, Joe asks him, "So what do you think of that music? It's genius, don't you think?"

Clarence shrugs. Says, "Ain't much beat to it."

Joe is crestfallen. His head tilts forward, and he slumps limply into his chair. Mike can see in Joe's body the collapsing of a thousand corollaries to a theory.

And Mike and Clarence leave him to his collapse without saying good-bye.

Outside, on the sidewalk, Mike says, "Joe figured you for a jazz man."

"He figured wrong," Clarence says.

THE TIME'S GETTING on one o'clock, the sky still a brilliant blue, and on the western horizon a faint jet contrail slices through an odd midday moon. Mike and Clarence walk through the heart of Eau Claire, by its courthouse and Masonic Temple, by its taverns and little shops, and Mike keeps staring at this contrail slicing the moon, thinking that a freak-coincidence sight like this will only be afforded him once in his lifetime, but he doesn't say anything to Clarence, other than to tell him to cross at this intersection or that one. Clarence is too whacked about getting stoned to care about the sky.

But when they cross the Chippewa River on another footbridge, this one not nearly so high over the water as the one at Uniroyal, Mike tugs Clarence's arm and insists they stop and at least take a gander at the river. Clarence is irritated about stopping—who the fuck gives a shit about *rivers?*— but he stops.

They lean over the north rail of the bridge, and from here they can see, a few hundred yards upstream, the confluence of the Eau Claire and the Chippewa Rivers.

"There it is," Mike says. "The confluence."

"Confluence?"

"A confluence, Clarence, is when two rivers combine into one. That's why the Chippewa, the river we're standing over now, is so wide here." It *is* wide, too, 150 yards across, and muscular and deep.

Beyond the confluence, at the crest of the northern ridge of the Chippewa Valley, are the twin church steeples of the Eau Claire Academy, and Mike points them out to Clarence.

Clarence says, "All that bullshit going on up there at the academy— kids getting they ass beat by the staff, kids shitting theyself or shitting the floor—all that going on, and worse, and what the people down here in the valley see is the motherfucking church steeples."

HALF MOON LAKE is an oxbow lake, meaning that it was once a lazy meander of the Chippewa River, but time and the mighty flow of the river cut off the meander, and now it's drying up. A hundred years ago, before Half Moon Lake was cut off, this is where the logs of the great Eau Claire lumber trade were funneled for processing, but now the lumbering is a distant memory, and Half Moon Lake is mostly weeds and lily pads. What's left here is a kind of memorial to lumbering called Carson Park. This is the home of the Paul Bunyan Lumberjack Museum, which features a few old-time lumbering buildings and some old saws and a big wooden table where the men used to eat their flapjacks. Near the museum stands a small minor-league baseball stadium, home of the Eau Claire Bears, the team on which Henry Aaron first played pro ball. Across the way from the stadium is a miniature steam railroad, the kind kids can ride on for a dollar, and its tracks pass through a four-acre stretch of pines. And there are picnic areas here, concrete pavilions with barbecue facilities, and nice grassy areas with picnic tables and freestanding cast-iron grills.

There's a hiking trail, too, that goes through all this, which is what Mike's telling Clarence, along with everything else that crosses his mind about Carson Park, when they stand in full view of Carson Park, preparing to walk the last quarter mile to the Stones.

Clarence says, "Why you playing tour guide, Mr. Mike? Just take us where you taking us."

"I thought you might be interested in some park history, is all."

Now Clarence gently puts a hand on Mike's shoulder. "You okay, Mike. I don't mean to go rushing you. Sound to me, the way you talking, you know all kinda shit you never get to tell anybody about."

Clarence is exactly right, and Mike halfway wants to tell him so, but he doesn't; he shuts up and walks again.

THE STONES ARE PART of a stand of maples and scrub brush that borders the swampiest, shallowest, weediest corner of Half Moon Lake. No official Carson Park trail extends here because the woods are simply too overgrown. The only way in to the Stones is a small deer trail, and Mike leads Clarence down it, making certain not to snap him with twigs and thorny branches.

"Hey, Clarence," Mike says. "Be careful not to fuck up your fancy clothes."

"Now I gots it figgered," Clarence says. "I know why you dress like a bum, Mr. Mike: You coming here to the forest all the time."

Mike likes that: forest. To Mike, this is just overgrowth in a city. To Clarence, this is a wilderness.

And these are the Stones: a hollow sawmill made of sandstone patched together with rocks and mud, the concrete of an unrefined age, and in the middle of it a maple tree grows, its branches extending way beyond the point where the roof used to be. A couple of large doorways remain in the crumbly walls, and on the ground within the walls are rusty beer cans, a fire pit, cigarette butts, empty potato-chip bags, and a few stray unrelated socks. On the walls themselves are several unimaginative spray-paints of graffiti: *Oly and Lena were here. Eau Claire Memorial '79.* There's even one that says *Dirk Gunderson is the King.*

Dirk. That fucker's everywhere.

On the lake side of the sawmill stands a concrete chute, a few feet wide, where the logs used to float in to meet the saw, and Mike sits on one side of the chute and Clarence the other. They're not speaking, just solemnly preparing to pass the joint. Mike gives Clarence the first-toke honors, hands the fatty to him, and lets him light it. Clarence takes a few thoughtful drags, closes his eyes in a destroyed kind of ecstasy, and passes the joint to Mike.

Beyond the Stones, through the foliage, Mike sees the lake, overgrown with weeds. Here and there between the weeds muskrats swim, and not far from them wood ducks and coot forage. High in the maple tree that grows in the center of the Stones, a white-throated sparrow sings its natural pattern over and over: one note high, two notes low. The bird sounds intrinsically rhythmic and happy.

A WHILE LATER Clarence says, "I wanna get right down to the shore. I wanna see this shit for what it is."

Mike's in a dreamy state. How calm this is! What a great way this is to make a living! He wants to sit here like Ferdinand the Bull and smell the flowers of the afternoon.

But dope's got the opposite effect on Clarence. He's—bango—on his feet and crashing awkwardly through the brush to the shore. Twigs snapping. Leaves tearing. Clothes tearing. When Clarence finally gets to the shore, he says, "Shit. Muck. My shoes is ruined for good."

Mike wants to say *That's what you get for wandering off on your own, you stupid fucker.* But he doesn't. He picks through the brush to where Clarence stands, ankle deep in lakeshore mud. Mike finds a safe spot to stand, on a small rock.

"This is how you do it, Clarence. You stand where you won't sink in."

"Fine time to tell me, motherfucker." But Clarence isn't upset. His eyes are wide and bright, the best he can do for a smile. All over his arms, though, Clarence is bleeding in trickles. He looks like he's been scratched up by an alley cat.

"Jesus, Clarence," Mike says. "You're bleeding."

Clarence examines the scratches and doesn't seem to be bothered by them. "I bleed easy," he says. "That what happens when you gots patched-together skin."

"How's about you take it easy, then?"

"Easy? Fuck *that*. I'll get me some easy tonight on Unit Three." He gazes over the weeds, which stretch as far down the lake as he can see. Says, "Lake look like this the whole way around?"

"Mostly," Mike says. "The lake's basically a weed bed. There's some open water on the other side, I guess."

"I fin to walk around the whole lake, Mr. Mike. You with me?"

"I guess it's better than standing here doing nothing."

So they begin bushwhacking their way through the brush toward the official trail. Clarence takes the lead. He gets slashed by vines and thorns. Lets branches whip into Mike. But Mike can't slow Clarence down. If Clarence stops, it's to let his feet sink into the shoreline muck and to regard the weeds and the water.

"The lake," Clarence keeps saying, "it's alive."

And it is. Bluegills boil to the surface between the weeds, and water bugs skitter from one lily pad to the next. Over the weeds dragonflies dart in precise lateral lines, searching for mosquitoes. Along the shore ahead of Mike and Clarence, frogs and toads and muskrats scare up and bolt into the water, and in the trees squirrels chatter, and birds call to each other, warning each other that there are people in the woods.

Clarence says, "Just look at all this shit."

"I'm looking," Mike says. "I'm looking."

Finally they hit the official trail, a groomed one with wood chips covering it. They follow the trail up a hill, emerging into a stand of tall pines, not far from which are the tracks of the miniature steam rail-road. The ground here is reddish brown, matted with pine needles and little pine twigs. After some not-too-close examination of the ground, Clarence and Mike notice that dozens upon dozens of con-dom wrappers are strewn about. At least a hundred couples have left behind the green and red and blue and brown cellophane proof of their indiscretions here.

Clarence says, "So this where the white people come to fuck."

"Good gravy," Mike says. "I never knew all these condoms were here."

"You must not fuck much, Mr. Mike."

Though this is true and a source of sadness for Mike, he makes a joke out of it. "I don't need to, Clarence. Life is always fucking me one way or the other."

"I hear that," Clarence says.

He hears everything. When they resume walking, Clarence hears a bird, and he points to it. If he hears a squirrel in a tree, he says, "There that motherfucker is." He skips sometimes, too, shuffling his feet on the trail's wood chips and saying, "Even my feet sound different in the forest." Clarence is entering a new level of living, with clean air and open spaces and nobody giving him demerits, no fistfights going on around him.

Mike feels he's giving Clarence a kind of Christmas, but not really. Clarence is leading now. Clarence is taking Mike on a tour of Carson Park.

The trail eventually passes through a picnic area on the other side of the lake from the Stones, far up the lake. Mothers are here with their children, supervising their play on the swing set and the jungle gym. On the shoreline, which isn't muddy here, a few old men sit on pickle buckets, fishing for bluegill and bullheads with cane poles. No one seems to notice Mike and Clarence—we're talking *no* one; not an eye Mike can see turned their way—which means to Mike that all these people are actually staring at them. And they look suspicious all right: muddy shoes, scratched all over the arms, Clarence bleeding,

Clarence being, well, Clarence, who always looks like a character in an old monster movie.

But Clarence keeps his eyes on the water: "This ain't no Lake Michigan, but it beautiful. *Dang.* Water: beautiful."

The trail then moves along a series of small fifteen-foot sandstone cliffs that overlook the north end of the lake, the only part of the lake where the water is open and relatively weedless. On the far shore looms a high ridge, below which is an enormous washout, where the dirt's eroding from the hill. Hawks circle over the ridge, and the sky up there, Clarence says it's the bluest he's ever seen.

But the trail doesn't go all the way around the lake. It stops near a cattail swamp that serves as a barrier between Carson Park and the washout ridge.

Mike says, "This is as far as she goes, buddy." He wants to sit down and relax. Since noon, he and Clarence have walked probably six miles. That, plus the dope, have made Mike sleepy.

Clarence says, "You think we can make it across that swamp?"

The water in the cattails is maybe a foot deep, Mike guesses, but factoring in the muck, it's going to feel more like four feet of wet concrete. "We can't walk through that shit, Clarence."

Clarence rubs his hands together and gazes at the high ridge in the distance. "Fuck it. I fin to get up there no matter what."

And off he wades into the cattails.

"Hoowee," he says when he's slogged twenty yards in. The muck's up to his waist, and he's pulling himself forward with the aid of cattail shoots. "This shit like being in Vietnam."

So Mike follows him into the muck. The day is turning out that way. He tugs himself through the muck, too. Breathes hard in its stink of rot and methane gas. The cattails are so thick Mike keeps losing sight of Clarence in front of him. Gets a brief glimpse of his grafted head once in a while, but that's it.

Clarence keeps saying, "Only a little way more, Mr. Mike. We making it."

Mike doesn't respond. Just keeps moving. Feels the mud caking his legs and his underwear and his belly. He starts thinking he's never going to get to the opposite shore, but, after some hard minutes, he does, and there stands Clarence, clothes dripping wet and filthy, eyes happy as a three-year-old with a new tricycle.

Clarence regards the washout slope, which is steep indeed, made of loose-packed sand and small rocks. He says, "One more obstacle, Mr. Mike." At the top of the slope, maybe two hundred feet up, are the branches of a tree that looks like it's going to topple off at any time.

Clarence commences scrambling up the slope, crawling on all fours, keeping solid footing, ascending like somebody who's been scrambling up washout slopes his whole life.

Mike tries scrambling, too, but he's too tired to scramble. He merely moves one limb after another upward. Feels himself rising. Feels the wind getting stronger, the space behind his back getting vaster. He remembers from years ago The Hiker's Prayer: "If you pick em up, O Lord, I'll put em down."

When Clarence's legs vanish over the ridge rim, Mike hears him let out a holler.

Clarence yells, "Sweet motherfucking Jesus!"

Mike all of a sudden finds the strength to clamber quickly upward, kicking and pulling. He yells, "You okay, Clarence?"

Clarence yells again: "Sweet motherfucking Jesus."

So Mike busts ass to the top. When he gets over the rim, there's Clarence, his arms rigid to his side, his hands trembling. Everywhere around Clarence, in a grassy space of several acres: gravestones, maybe three hundred of them. Clarence has climbed into a graveyard.

"Bad shit gonna come from us ending up here," Clarence says.

"It's just a graveyard. Don't sweat it."

"Graveyard: bad. Why didn't you tell me this shit was here?"

"I didn't know there was a graveyard here," Mike says. This is true. He *didn't* know. Not till now. He turns to look over the valley—they're high up, and Half Moon appears very remote, a smear of dull blue—and way out there in the distance, Mike can make out the faint outline of Space Mountain, where he and Joe go late at night to ponder the weight of the sky. Space Mountain is in a cemetery. This place is in a cemetery. An odd thing: two cemeteries on high ridges in one small town.

"You know, Clarence," Mike says, and tries to think of something reassuring to say. "I somehow end up stoned in graveyards all the time."

"Bad things gone come from that," Clarence says.

"I don't know," Mike says. "I feel fine."

A FEW MINUTES LATER, after they leave the cemetery and are on a nice sidewalk, strolling their way back to the academy, Clarence is very happy. He says, "I gots to thank you, Mr. Mike. Today been a lot of fun."

"Fuckin-A, Clarence. It's been an adventure, all right."

Clarence stops to dig a cigarette from his pack and discovers that his cigarettes got ruined in the cattails.

Now Mike looks Clarence up and down. The T-shirt muddy and dotted with brambles and burrs. The acetate pants torn at the knees. The fancy white shoes turned into the color of the ground.

Mike's got to laugh. "Look at your sorry ass, Clarence. You look like you just crawled out of the hog pen."

Clarence regards his attire and his skin, the dried blood and dust, and he's got to laugh, too. Freedom is filthy.

SOMETIME AFTER five o'clock Mike returns to 819 Barland. Joe's hanging for once in his own room. He's in there with the door closed, sticking flam patterns on a rubber practice pad. Joe's way big on patterns, on developing repetitive technique and speed, but he doesn't have much rhythm. That's a major flaw in a drummer, having no rhythm. Mike thinks this is sad; Joe's whole life is music, but he's got no talent at all. He leaves Joe to his flams, gets some clean clothes, takes a shower, and when he's dressed he meets Joe in the living room and takes a seat in the easy chair.

Joe's got the dictionary out again, is locating a word.

"Here it is," Joe says. "This is the word of the day. *Disconsolate.*"

"Disconsolate?"

"Cheerless. Dejected. Downcast."

Mike stretches his legs out; they've gone through a lot today. "Hell, Joe. I'm not disconsolate. I'm just tired."

"Here's another one then." Joe flips back a few pages. "*Dialectic.* That's 'the Hegelian process of change in which a concept or its realization passes over into and is preserved and fulfilled by its opposite.'"

Mike yawns. Maybe he'll go to bed early tonight.

Joe says, "This is definition number six: 'the dialectical tension or opposition between two interacting forces or elements.'"

"I'm having a good life, Joe. I really am."

Joe raises his eyes from the dictionary and appears to be puzzled. "What's that got to do with it, Mike?"

MORNING. Mike's got a few hours to kill before going in to work. His shift starts at 11:30—that's the lunch-through-dinner shift, a pain-in-the-ass one—and he's up early, way ahead of Joe. He's mellowing out, sitting in the living room, smoking a cigarette, cup of coffee at his side, not thinking about anything in particular, just enjoying a blank peaceful moment alone, when the phone rings.

This is Dr. James Woodson calling.

"Michael, I'll get straight to it. I'll readmit you to the university, but I'll only do this on one condition: You must not take any music courses."

Mike doesn't say anything, a pause that Dean Woodson takes to mean he should speak further.

"Let me give you one bit of advice, Michael."

"What's that, Dr. Woodson?"

"Quit living like an animal."

"What do you mean by that?"

"Precisely what I just said: Quit living like an animal, Michael."

And that's that. Mike's back in school. He flushes, feels a full-body smile wash over him. Everything about him is joyous. He wants to dance and holler Fuckin-A and sing songs about victory and freedom and how the world is good to him. He wants to get drunk again, and he figures, Why the fuck not? He will. This last month of clean living has paid off, and by God he deserves to wet his whistle once more.

Then the phone rings again.

This is Keith calling from Unit 5.

"Can you come in early today, Mike? There's a meeting at ten. I'd like you to be there for it."

Mike says that's no problem. Everything's no problem. A few extra bucks, that's sure as shit worth watching a film on the after-effects of domestic violence or whatever's going to be on the agenda for the meeting. The meetings at the academy are always gravy: film, or a presentation, usually accompanied by coffee and cookies or dough-nuts.

EXTRA MONEY TODAY, school in the fall, which means Mike can get the extra money of a student loan—Mike's thinking about this while he makes the trek to the academy. He's triumphant.

He ponders what courses he'll take: maybe Anthropology, maybe History, maybe a course in Religious Studies. He resolves to do all his homework on time and to get an A in every course. He's so pleased with himself he literally begins skipping while he walks. But he doesn't care if anybody sees him skipping. Fuck the people who can't understand what a kickass life Mike Magnuson is having.

NONE OF THE BOYS are on Unit 5. Just Keith's there, sitting at his desk, and when he sees Mike, he smiles a strained smile. Says, "Meeting's not here, Mike. Downstairs. In the core staff office."

"Aren't you coming?"

"Nope. Just you go."

Anthropology in particular interests Mike. He figures his time on the job here makes him qualified to examine cultures other than his own. Okay, he thinks, I'll get an A in an introductory Anthropology class, then become an Anthropology major, then I'll go to graduate school in Anthropology, then take a nice advisory-board position with *National Geographic*. The path seems clear to him, and trouble-free, and he knocks on the core staff office door.

Henry, the jarhead Mike quibbled with last week, he opens the door and allows Mike in, and there in the office, sitting on folding chairs that have been brought in for the occasion, are all fifteen members of the core staff, every unit director except Keith, as well as the head nurse and the head social worker. There are almost thirty people crammed into the office, and each one of them scrutinizes Mike when he enters the room. Nobody smiles. Henry doesn't offer Mike a chair; there isn't one for him.

They've got him. They've found out he got stoned with Clarence. That's all there is to it, and Mike knows this immediately. Something in him sinks, but somehow he doesn't go flush or start sweating. He keeps his cool, which, later in life, Mike will always remember as odd, probably indicating that there's a profoundly sociopathic element to him; he just doesn't give a shit.

Henry does the talking.

"You escorted Clarence Jeter on his day pass yesterday, is that correct?"

"Yes."

"Where did you go?"

"We walked all the way around Half Moon Lake, Henry."

"Clarence says you smoked pot with him yesterday."

Not one flinch from Mike. "Clarence has got an active imagination."

"He says you went to your house and got pot for him."

"We went to Half Moon Lake, Henry."

Henry breathes in a disappointed way, sighs almost angrily.

Around him the people in the office shift their postures, cross and uncross their legs. Mike thinks they might suddenly pounce on him and beat him to death.

"Is that your statement then," Henry says, "that you did not smoke pot with Clarence?"

"That's my statement. We did *not* smoke pot."

"Are you sure?"

"I am."

"Are you aware, Mike, that if you did smoke pot with him, and we can *prove* this, you may be subject to child-abuse charges?"

"I guess I am now, Henry." Mike's tone: insolent. He figures it doesn't matter anymore what he says to this son of a bitch.

Henry stares sadly into a piece of paper he's got in front of him. "This form will constitute your resignation. You may choose to take a leave of absence without pay, in which time you will be under investigation. My advice: quit. In my opinion, Clarence's story is simply too detailed for you to refute. We'll end up firing you eventually, one way or the other."

Mike signs the piece of paper. Hands over his keys. Leaves. That's it. He doesn't go back to Unit 5 to find Keith or to find Clarence and ask him how it came to pass that he'd turned Mike in. He merely walks out the front door and strikes a steady pace toward home, not pausing to gaze back at the building or to look at the stained-glass windows of the church or to admire the view from the steps that descend into the valley or to regard the sky, which this day is partly cloudy.

AT HOME Joe's once again hanging out in the living room, twirling his drumsticks, and he's surprised to see Mike.

"Fuck working at the academy," Mike says. "I just up and quit."

Joe regards Mike for an unnerving time, sets down his sticks, and nods. Joe can tell Mike got fired, of course, and he can probably make a reasonable guess why, but Joe is a fine enough friend that he knows better than to press Mike on the subject. Shit like this, among friends, is best left alone.

Mike picks up the dictionary. Thumbs through it. Closes it. Sets it back down.

"*Disconsolate*," he says. "That's the goddam word all right."

So THEY DRINK that night. They attend happy hour at a tavern on Water Street, near the university, where pitchers of beer cost a buck. The beer tastes as watery to Mike as the name of the street on which they drink. He drinks gallons. And he and Joe have fun. That's what Mike and Joe do best: have fun. And there's never a consequence to their fun.

A COUPLE OF DAYS LATER, Mike gets another job, one that pays *much* better than the Eau Claire Academy. Six-fifty an hour. He works as a yard ape for a landscape company, digging holes in the ground and filling them with shrubs and small trees.

ON THE FOURTH of July, Mike and Joe pick up two women at a tavern on Water Street, escort them to Space Mountain and have their way with them with the lights of Eau Claire flickering below. The woman Mike's with, she's fat and smells of sweat and schnapps, and even though she's born and raised in Eau Claire, she speaks with a bad English accent. She, like, really thinks that Mike, or anyone she meets, is going to believe she hails from a fancy neighborhood in London. She's dumb. And piggish. But Mike's drunk. He doesn't attempt to understand her, or feel sorry for her, how her phony English accent is a way to compensate for who she is, a young unhappy woman with heavy legs and thick hips and breasts as flaccid as the rags Mike uses to wipe excess two-in-one fuel off the Weedwackers at work. Mike's got a new job and a future, and he doesn't care what he does with himself or what he does to other people. Someday, he's thinking, he'll wake up and be a respectable citizen. A few fat chicks along the way, a few beers, some laughs—it won't matter then.

IN THE MIDDLE of August, late on a Tuesday afternoon, three weeks before school begins, Mike gets home from a day's digging and hauling dirt and relaxes in the living room with Joe, splitting a six-pack of Walter's with him. Mike's hands are harder than they ever were at Custom Products and his body stronger; the days operating a shovel are treating Mike well.

And Keith calls Mike from Unit 5. They've not spoken since Mike signed his resignation, and when Mike first hears his voice he figures that somehow the Eau Claire Academy has decided to press charges against him after all. Mike's nervous all of a sudden. He's been so preoccupied with his new beer-and-shovel life he's forgotten he was ever in trouble at the academy. But he needn't be nervous. Keith's voice is grim and withdrawn.

Keith says, "You been okay?"

"Sure, man. I'm digging holes for a living now."

Mike looks over at Joe, who's amusing himself by trying to balance an empty beer can on his head.

Keith says, "Clarence went Code Green this morning. We thought he might have tried to find you, but you weren't home when we called."

"I was working," Mike says. "I guess you could call over there, if you need to know where I was."

"Doesn't matter. We found him. He drowned in Half Moon Lake."

CLARENCE HAD GONE to the Stones, pushed his way through the brush to the shoreline muck, and slogged into the weeds, way out, to where the water was ten feet deep, and he was floating. He must have seen the sun overhead, the fire of life, and felt the tendrils of weeds touching his arms and legs, the water all around him, how cold it was, how it tasted of fish and frogs and muskrats and logs cut into lumber a century ago. He must have been serene when the weeds wrapped around him and pulled him under. He must have thought the weeds loved him and didn't ever want him to leave their lovely home in the water. He loved water. He would not have struggled for the surface. Eleven years ago, this water should have surrounded him, these weeds should have held him, made him immune to burning. It had come too late, but it had come all the same. When the darkness overtook him, when all the world for him was water, he must have had smooth skin again, and ears and eyelids and hair. He must have been able to smile.

Part Two

The Theory
and the Practice

THE FRIDAY OF LABOR
Day weekend, Mike turns in
his shovel and mattock and rake at the landscape company. He quits.
He's moving on. He's got a student loan, plus one of those nifty don't-
have-to-pay-it-back Pell Grants, which means after he takes care of his
fees and shit and buys books for his classes, he'll still have a grand or
two left over. He sure as hell ain't assbusting at a landscape job for one
more second when he's got himself over a grand. No way, buddy. He's
done spending his days moving the earth and walking to and fro with
a wheelbarrow over it. Fuck that forever. So to inaugurate his new life
as an excellent student who's got his future as wide open before him
as a fully dilated cervix, he goes to happy hour after work. On Water
Street, of course. He goes to a cheap-to-get-trashed tavern called the
Brat Kabin.

This is five o'clock when Mike arrives, right when happy hour's
swinging into action. There's university-variety kids everywhere,
hammering beers from plastic cups, refilling the cups from plastic
pitchers. There's major hooting and hollering and beer-spilling going
on. And The Rolling Stones on the stereo. "Start Me Up." The kids call

this place the Brat, after bratwurst, which isn't an item on the Brat's menu. You want something to eat here, you get a bag of chips or a candy bar or you pick up some pussy, take it outside, to the banks of the Chippewa River, and eat it there.

Mike finds a spot at the bar and buys himself a pitcher; that's a buck deposit for the pitcher itself and a buck for its contents. Gets his plastic cup. Fills it. Drains it. Shit's cold, for sure, which is a plus because it's Leinenkugel's, which is your ultimate dog-turd-variety beer. He looks around for a mirror where he can scope chicks or scope himself, put on suave faces for himself—you know, practice in case a snapperette appears and feels like engaging in pre-dick-suck conversation. But no mirror. Fuck. And no snapperette approaching. He wishes for a second that Joe Murphy was hanging with him—that guy's *always* got something to talk about, something to keep the boredom from setting in—but Joe's got a four-hour combo gig at the Civic Center tonight. That's too bad for Joe, Mike guesses. Nobody will be there. Nobody's *ever* there at Joe's gigs.

A few feet from Mike is a big table, around which sit eight or ten clean-cut fraternity boys wearing TKE T-shirts and ball caps.

One says, "I think Reagan is doing a *super* job in the White House."

Another one says, "I think Tina is the hottest chick in the Accounting Department."

Another one says, "God, I'm drunk already."

They're handsome and lean and tanned, no dirt under the nails. They have created an alluvial fan of spilled beer on their table.

Beyond this group: a table surrounded by six hand-job-from-heaven-type chicks. Perfect poufed hair. Painted-red fingernails. Alabaster wrists. Nice tight shirts with those nearly-make-your-nuts-rupture short sleeves that show the shoulders.

One of these perfects says, "I wish Matt would quit calling me. He never talks about *anything* but his Camaro."

Another one says, "This semester, I'm taking *four* Business Management classes."

Another one says, "School gets *so* old."

Same thing at all the tables: handsome, well-adjusted, normal people talking about irrelevant shit. These people's only real worry in life is whether they'll have time to wash tonight's fuck stains off their sheets before tomorrow night's round of romping begins.

THERE YOU GO: Somebody taps Mike on his shoulder, and he's got company. Pete Blommel is his name, a guy who plays tenor sax. This is totally excellent. Mike used to be buddies with this guy back in the music-major days. They used to get along great: got drunk a bunch, stoned a bunch, talked smart about tunes and other suchlike things music majors talk about. Cool. Maybe they can team up and hunt poon *together*. That's for-real about poon: It's always easier to hunt it when you got a buddy out patrolling with you.

"*Mags*," Pete says. "I thought you split this *scene* forever." He's twenty but looks like he's been touring with Steely Dan since "Bodhisattva" was a hit. He's got the shoulder-length black straight hair, the thick photo-gray aviators, the silk shirt unbuttoned to the navel, the fake gold chain. Smokes Vantage: the official *Down Beat* magazine cigarette. Dude *is* hip, is the general idea he's trying to get across.

And Mike's all for that general idea, too. He says, "I'm back from the dead, Pete."

Pete throws his arms out artfully. Mike does, too. And they hug. The genuine-article hug. They're really happy to see each other. When they unclasp, Mike catches that more than a few eyebrows are frowning at the fag thing they just did.

Pete's *super*hip to this. Sure. "Fucking business majors," he says. "They got no soul."

Fucking business majors. It's been a long time since Mike's heard anybody say that. Good. Him and Pete are in tune. Bar's full of eggheads. Fuck em. Mike gets a plastic cup for Pete, orders another pitcher.

Pete says, "Last I heard, you were gigging full-time in a factory somewhere."

Mike eyerolls some exasperation. "What can I say?" he says.

Pete says, "I can dig it."

Looks like a jazzman. Talks like one. But the life—Pete's been home all summer, working at his father's hardware store in Tomah. He's been playing the You'll-Find-the-Flexhose-in-Aisle-Five Blues for the last two months. Humbling himself, he says. Paying his dues. But now he's way ready to do the Music Department groove again. The year's going to be a swing.

Mike says he's all about branching out right now. Expanding. Says he's going to check out Anthropology this year in school.

Paul says, "That is *way* outside." Which is his musician way of saying that Mike's deviating from the standard chord progression and rhythm of living.

ANOTHER BUCK. Another pitcher. They hang long enough and talk about whatever long enough that Pete starts thinking they should do something other than just stand here at the bar and drink. Pete suggests they need to be on a mission.

"We need to catch ourselves a *groove*," he says.

Mike indicates with a sweep of the hand the dozens of deluxe-model chicks scattered about the barroom, whispering into each other's ears, looking like somebody's *looking* at them. "I want to pork one of *those*," Mike says.

Pete runs his hand through his hair. Sighs like a man who's just returned from a forty-city auditorium tour. "Pussy," he says, "is not a groove. Pussy is a tempo."

Mike nods. But come on: *Pussy is a tempo?* Whatever.

"These business majors," Pete says. Points to them and their laughing and their sloshing of beer. "Their brains are cement."

"True enough," Mike says.

"We could light these people on fire, and they wouldn't notice."

Mike winces at this, drills down the contents of his cup, refills it in a hurry. If Mike's touchy about one thing in the world, it's people getting set on fire.

But Pete's already way too on to the next thing to notice Mike's wince.

Here's the program: There's all these tables jammed with drunk kids here, and the kids are completely getting up from their seats all the time to go to the can or go over and talk to Muffy or whoever they're bumping into. Like, oh, my *God*. How *are* you? How was your *summer*? Oh, that's *awesome*!

"You dig it?" Pete says.

Mike does. He can see the sea of drunk Muffies before him. Their smiles to each other. Their smooth shoulders.

And Pete's saying if you watch carefully when the kids get up from their tables, sure as shit they're leaving their empty pitchers unattended. So the situation is to approach the unattended pitcher surreptitiously, snag it, and return it to the bartender for the deposit.

"We drink free," Pete says. "And make a very mellow profit, too."

Mike says, "I'm down with *that*."

Here's Pete's mathematical procedure breakdown: Don't *look* nervous is rule number one, the corollary of which being that when you pick up a stray pitcher you should appear like you're working here and just bussing the tables, the sub-corollary of which being that you should go ahead and dump an ashtray here or there or go ahead and carry empty plastic cups from the tables to the bar, you know, to appear like you're not doing anything unusual.

So complicated, the theory, but so simple. Everything in the world is easy, if you think about it long enough and drink enough beers while you're thinking.

They commence kiping empty pitchers and dumping ashtrays here or there and carrying empty plastic cups to the bar, and the long and the short of it is that after three hours, they each got twelve bucks in their pocket, and they're 100 percent shit-ass drunk. Pete's so drunk, in fact, that he wanders out to the sidewalk and ralphs up a summer's worth of Mom's home cooking. He doubles over by the curb and mutters, "Man, this groove is fucked up."

Mike stands there near him for a minute or two, watching moths bash themselves against the streetlight overhead and the stars prickling their way through the darkness beyond.

"You're right, Pete," Mike says. "This groove is way fucked up."

And he splits the whole Pete scene and starts stumbling home.

NIGHT, THAT DARK BASTARD. Mike doesn't know how long ago it fell. Maybe this is 9:30 now. The air's crisp. The stars twinkle their bullshit. The moon's doing something moonlike. He's striding good, or at least when he's picking up one foot, he's setting the other one down. He's keeping steady time toward home. In his head he's got that drunken mix of feeling sorry for himself and feeling all wonderful about the future at the same time. He's thinking: Tuesday morning at 11:15 he's got Cultural Anthropology, and at 12:45 he's got Introduction to Religious Studies. Maybe those are kickass classes. Maybe not. They're better than working a job, anyway. Or maybe they're about the same. He doesn't know what the hell he wants to do with himself anymore. He's just a goddam drunk kid, is what he is. Fuck *him*. But on the other hand, he's going to find his old buddy Joe, is what he's going to do.

THE EAU CLAIRE Civic Center is a six-story-high Holiday Inn, a blinking checkerboard of lights that are on in the room windows and in the three-story parking garage and shining from streetlight poles over the employee parking lot, which is where Mike's standing, imagining that this is what heaven must look like: plenty of electric light and plenty of clean concrete. He scans the parking lot for Joe's blue Plymouth, sees it there, walks to it, and no shit: Here's Joe himself leaning against the front bumper, wearing gig apparel—white button-down shirt, thin black jazzer's tie—and he's smoking a cigarette with one hand and wringing his chin with the other. He's looking beaten and bummed. He's letting out long groany breaths. Dude's in a killer funk.

Joe sees Mike but doesn't say hello. He stares into his cigarette filter, bites it, and injects himself with his nicotine. Says, "Kirby convention tonight."

Mike says, "Kirby convention?"

"Vacuum-cleaner salesmen." Heavy sigh. The weight of the world's on Joe. "*Hundreds* of them." He grinds his cigarette into the asphalt with his heel and begins making his way back inside, moving slowly, opening and closing his hands as he walks, riffling his fingers, stretching his hands, but he doesn't say anything to Mike, just keeps heading toward the building and goes inside when he gets there.

Mike sits on Joe's bumper and smokes a cigarette on the subject of Joe. The guy ain't acting normal; that's for sure. You know, dude was a total zombie here. And usually Joe's completely a human spring about everything. So something's fucked up, and Mike figures he'd better go see what.

Here's the scene in the lounge: It's a madhouse. Crazy. Everywhere Mike looks—in the chairs around every table, on every stool at the bar, in the aisles and leaning against the lounge's potted fake ficus trees—there's Kirby salesmen. They got the wrinkled tan slacks, the white button-down shirts stretched over the tubs of guts, the name tags on their chests. BUY A KIRBY FOR A LIFETIME. They got their ties loosened, too, buddy. They're partying big-time Kirby-style partying. Sloshing drinks. Buying each other shots. Slapping backs. Telling jokes about the guy who's writing up the complete hose-attachment package for a housewife while she's under the kitchen table sucking his dick.

Yep. This is your refined jazz-aesthete crowd tonight.

On the stage Joe sits behind his drum kit, clutching his sticks the way Christ would have clutched His, if they had made Him play drums at the Eau Claire Civic Center before He was crucified.

This is a quartet gig. A bassist, a pianist, a saxophone player, and Joe. The other musicians have music stands in front of them, and they're rifling through their *Real Books*, trying to find a tune they all know. Music majors.

When they finally start playing a twangy version of "Take the A Train," the Kirby salesmen are not impressed.

Some of the Kirby salesmen boo.

Some yell, "Play 'Freebird,' goddammit!"

Or "Don't you guys know any Van Halen?"

Or "Hey, you with the saxophone. Sounds like a goose died in there."

But Joe and the boys keep playing. They do the head, play the extended solos through the changes, trade fours and eights with each other, but they somehow play quieter and quieter as the tune wears on. Or maybe the Kirby salesmen get louder and louder. But in any case, the musicians wish they weren't playing, and the Kirby salesmen wish they weren't listening.

Music. The noblest of the arts.

MIKE'S OUTSIDE again, walking through the employee parking lot, thinking about the heavenly lights in the room windows and in the parking garage and what vacuum cleaners do to the human soul, and when he gets a couple of parking stalls past where Joe's Plymouth is parked, he turns to regard an empty stall, and he sees the Hand of God sitting there on the asphalt. For real, hey. The Hand of God is about five feet tall, has five enormous fingers extending toward the firmament. It seems to be glowing orange.

The Hand of God. Mike approaches it slowly and discovers that the Hand of God is a giant plastic orange novelty chair in the shape of a hand. A right hand. A man's hand. Of course. God's. With perfectly manicured fingernails. You're supposed to sit on God's palm. Mike touches the index finger, which is as big around as a watermelon. Very smooth. No fingerprints molded in.

He looks to see if anybody's around. Cars reflecting moonlight and streetlight is all he sees. Nobody. A giant plastic orange hand. Think about it: This hand would be about the *coolest* thing he and Joe could *ever* put in their living room. Damn straight. We're talking *major* conversation piece. You'd never run out of shit to say about a giant plastic orange hand.

He wraps his arms around three giant fingers and hoists. Not heavy at all, man. This sucker's no problem. And in fact Mike goes ahead and lifts the hand way high and maneuvers it onto his head. He rests the palm on top of his skull and positions the fingers behind him, so he can see where he's walking. And hey: It's no problem walking. He cruises out of the parking lot, hits the sidewalk that leads toward home. He's walking so smoothly he feels like he's gliding. He imagines that if somebody were watching him from a distance, they wouldn't see him at all. They'd see a giant orange hand floating along a sidewalk in Eau Claire, glowing like the miracle that it is.

When he gets to the top of the Gray Street hill, which is a couple of blocks from home, he sets down the hand and takes a little breather. The hill's steep, and coming up it drunk and toting this giant hand, it's broken Mike into a sweat. But this is okay. From here Mike can overlook downtown, the Civic Center lights. Ah, the lights! Ah, the views a guy can have in a valley town!

And here you go: Two squad cars drive up the Gray Street hill and stop on the road alongside to Mike. Four cops emerge from the squads, and in the split second Mike sees them he reaches to his back pocket, flips out his wallet and pitches it in a lilac hedge near the sidewalk. He's not sure why he's pitching his wallet. Just seems like being an ordinary nameless drunk is the right thing to do.

He smiles at the cops. Big stupid grin.

One of the cops says, "Is *that* your hand?"

Mike raises his right hand as if preparing to testify in court. "Yes, sir. I was *born* with this hand."

One of the cops says, "We got a live one here."

He then tells Mike to please step over to the squad car, and Mike does, and the cop frisks him.

The cop says, "You got any identification, buddy?"

Mike says he doesn't, and the cop produces a notebook and a pencil and gets ready to write down Mike's facts and figures.

"Okay, buddy," the cop says. "Name. Last name first. Spell it."

Off in the distance Eau Claire twinkles, beckons to Mike to do something stupid.

Mike says, "Last name: P-A-Y-T-O-N. First name: Walter."

The cop writes some of this down, and when he realizes Mike's toying with him he clenches his jaw. Says, "You realize you're talking to a police officer?"

Mike says he sure does and proceeds to give the officer his name again.

"Last name: S-T-A-R-R. First name: Bart."

"A comedian," the cop says to the other cops. And just like that, he handcuffs Mike and inserts him in the back of the squad.

The handcuffs dig into Mike's wrist, but he doesn't give a shit. This is *too* funny. The cops have put him in the second squad, giving him a full view of the first squad where three of the cops are trying to stuff the giant plastic orange hand into the trunk, and they aren't able to do it. It won't fit. They try it fingers first, palm first. They try wedging it in thumb first, hoping to curl the hand into the trunk. But nope. They're going to have to drive to the station with the hand hanging out the trunk.

Laughing. Jesus, Mike can't remember laughing this much. All the way to the station he can see the hand protruding from the back end of the squad on the road in front of him, almost as if it's the squad car waving at Mike, and he keeps yelling shit like "It's the giant orange hand caper." And "This is the biggest crime in the annals of Eau Claire history." He's really laughing his ass off.

And he's laughing when the cops take him, *and* the hand, to an interrogation room and convince him to cough up his real name, which he does without hesitation.

And during booking and fingerprinting—the charges: misdemeanor theft and obstruction of justice—he's laughing.

And in the drunk-tank cell—the cot, the beige walls, the toilet, the solid wall with the little metal grate in it—he's still laughing.

He's been needing entertainment like this for a long time.

Toward morning he dreams of water, of weeds, of the silent spaces at the bottoms of dying lakes. He sees Clarence Jeter in his dream, sitting underwater and happily smoking a cigarette. Clarence says, "You acting crazy, Mr. Mike. You fin to fuck up real bad one of these times." Clarence dissolves into a white light, a scraping noise, the drunk tank's doors sliding open.

And Mike's awake. A thin jailer is standing in the cell's doorway, requesting that Mike get on his feet. Mike complies, gets right up, and isn't wobbly one bit. He feels pretty good, all things considered. Says happily to the jailer, "I'm glad *that's* over."

"What's that?" the jailer says.

"Being in jail."

The jailer grins, but not with amusement. Says, "You're not going home, buck. You're here till Tuesday morning."

Mike figures the jailer's giving him shit. "Give me a break, man," he says. "That's three days from now."

The jailer says, "You gotta wait till your arraignment."

Mike doesn't move. "Till Tuesday?"

"Monday, that's Labor Day. No court."

Block c in the Eau Claire County Jail has twelve lock-down cells—one prisoner to a cell—that open to a barred-in holding area with three picnic-type tables in it. One of the tables is covered with books and magazines and board games, and the other two are set up for smoking and watching the TV, which is situated high up, just outside the bars.

Around 8:30 A.M. Mike arrives on Block C. The jailer assigns him to Cell 6. Tells Mike here's the shitter and here's the shower and lunch is at eleven, supper at five and lockdown at nine. And that's that.

Mike's cooling out in the hoosegow. He's looking at three days of hard county time.

The place doesn't seem too intimidating, though. A few inmates are playing Risk at one of the tables, smoking cigarettes, and a guy there with long black hair and aviator glasses waits till the jailer leaves, gets up from his spot on the bench, comes right over to Mike and introduces himself.

Says he's Tom. He hopes Mike will enjoy his stay. "I'm the welcoming committee around here," he says.

He invites Mike to take a seat, which Mike does, then he offers Mike a cigarette, which he takes, then he gives Mike the straight skinny on Block C.

Tom's nine months into a yearlong stretch here for stealing a few car stereos and doing some other stupid shit, and he *would* get out during the week to work on Huber Law, but he can't seem to find himself a job, and, well, it's pretty goddam quiet here during the weekdays. Pretty relaxing. But on the weekends the block fills up with drunks, and that's cool with Tom because the food's a lot better on weekends than it is during the week. Check out the feast for Sunday lunch, hey. We're talking turkey dinner with *all* the trimmings. And there's of course the Risk game here, which on occasion is very competitive, very quality. And there's this fine stack of magazines and books.

"I myself," Tom says, "have read every book in the stack."

"Cool," Mike says.

The other inmates on Block C aren't as talkative as Tom, but they're completely not dangerous-seeming in any way. A couple of them say they're in for bouncing checks. One guy's in for his second DUI. One guy's in for his third. Another guy, a really skinny fellow with sunken eyes, he won't say what he's in for, but Mike doesn't figure it's for anything but being a fuckup.

After a while, Mike tells everybody his story. The getting-drunk-at-the-Brat-Kabin part, the stealing-the-hand, the giving-fake-names-to-the-cops, and everybody busts complete gut about it. They all say they wish they were in for what's Mike in for.

And there you have it: Mike's buddies with everybody.

LUNCH IS sliced roast beef with mashed potatoes, gravy, peas, and a tin cup full of milk. Awesome chow, that's for sure. He'd never be eating this good at home. And after lunch, everybody yawns and wanders off to their cells, and in no time the only sound in Block C is peaceful petty-criminal snoring, but Mike's still awake. He's in jail, man. This ain't something a person should sleep through! He's got to be remembering this so he can tell his grandchildren about it. Or something.

Okay, so there's a stack of books. Maybe he'll find something to read till his fellow inmates wake up. He's never actually enjoyed reading, and in fact he hasn't read a book cover to cover since he was ten. Some Hardy Boys book, he thinks it was. Or maybe a book about airplanes. But here on Block C: Hell, it's so quiet, basically a boredom situation while everybody's napping, he figures reading is the perfectly natural thing to do.

So there's piles of *Sports Afield* and *Outdoor Life*, all raggedy and with pages torn or missing. And there's some books with sociological-type titles: *Rehabilitation of the Thief. The Social Animal. A Case Against Recidivism.* And so forth.

Finally, he finds a thin black paperback, a movie tie-in book for the film *Rollerball*. Mike didn't see *Rollerball* when it came out, must have been ten years ago, but he remembers that it was about a sort of futuristic roller derby to the death or whatever. The more he thinks about it, he remembers *Rollerball* because there were ads on TV for it and somebody was playing the beginning of Bach's Toccata and Fugue in D Minor on the organ. Toccata and Fugue in D Minor. One of Mike's all-time favorites. If *Rollerball* is about *that*, it's going to be kickass.

He takes the book to his cell, stretches out, opens it up. He's expecting music, sure, or at least a novel about roller derby, but this book isn't either of those things, not really. *Rollerball* is a book of short stories by some guy named William Harrison, a guy who's seen fit to write a preface to his book, a few pages in which he talks about all sorts of things Mike doesn't remotely understand.

William Harrison writes this:

Nowadays a well-documented Cultural Decline has befallen us and the students in the universities are too depraved to listen to talk of standards and so, I insist, am I.

He also writes this:

The author of the story knows this and derives considerable pleasure from this fact; he is a miniaturist—with all the minor and subversive enjoyments of that role—and he sets a small hieroglyph against the armor of the body politic.

Mike reads this whatever-it-is five or six times, grows bewildered, and promptly falls asleep.

When he wakes, the book's still balanced on his chest. Outside his cell a few inmates are gathered around one of the picnic tables, playing Risk with Tom, who seems to be winning. Tom's saying, "Strategy, I'm telling you. The game is about strategy." The inmates are playing Risk for cigarettes, betting one smoke for one country occupied, two smokes for a continent.

Mike reopens *Rollerball*, rereads that sentence about body politic. Like, what in the hell is *that*? And he decides to move forward in the book and maybe find something he can understand there. He sees a story listed on the contents page called "Rollerball Murder." The movie story. He finds it, begins to read. The story's fifteen pages long, mostly explaining the rules of roller derby to the death, and also talking about some other junk like corporations replacing governments and people being all miserable and ignorant and bloodthirsty as a result.

As far as Mike can tell, ain't no Toccata and Fugue in D Minor *anywhere* in this story. He reads the entire story three times, slowly and carefully, and the only thing he reads about music is a one-line reference to corporate hymns and brass bands on the last page. But the thing is, by the time he's read the story three times, he doesn't care if there's a Toccata in there. There's people fucking each other and getting fucked over and fucking other people over. There's action: motorcycles, dudes getting killed. And somewhere near the end of the story the main character, a fellow name of Jonathan E., realizes that playing roller derby to the death is a pretty horseshit thing to do. And Mike finds himself saying, aloud, "No kidding, it's horseshit."

SUPPERTIME COMES. Another nice meal: fried chicken and green beans and potato salad and apple cobbler. Exceptional.

And during the evening Mike joins his fellow offenders in a television film festival. The movie is your made-for-TV type about a grizzly bear loose somewhere in the Northwest, terrorizing folks renting cabins on their summer vacations. Great flick, everybody's thinking. They're cheering for the bear, hoping he rips every one of them vacationers to shreds. And the bear rips up a few, too. And everybody applauds and whistles. But near the end of the movie, when an enterprising young forest ranger manages finally to kill the bear and everything in the movie is happily-ever-after, the skinny inmate with the sunken eyes falls to pieces, breaks down and weeps. The skinny guy can't endure a happy ending on Block C.

IN THE MORNING, after pancakes and sausage, Mike resolves to spend his whole day reading. He's slept well. Sure, he stinks bad because he worked landscaping all yesterday and then got drunk and still hasn't changed his clothes or showered or brushed his teeth. But he's feeling fresh in the physical and spiritual way. This incarceration thing, he's thinking, and the solitude thing in Cell 6, it's exactly the kind of mental preparation he needs before commencing the fall term. He can pull his shit together in here.

Now, you've probably heard that people's lives can sometimes change in one moment, that somebody is one person for a long time, then they experience something incredible, and they are thereafter altered. Folks who go for Christ, they'll for sure tell you that. For He comes to touch you once. And you must be ready to accept Him. And for sure, hey: Damn near every rock 'n' roll musician you've ever heard about says something like: "After I saw the Beatles on *Ed Sullivan,* I knew I wanted to play." Or "When I heard Hendrix in London." All people do this shit; it's easier for them to say *Right here, at this very instant, that's when I knew,* than to say, *Well, I kinda poked along in life and eventually I knew what I wanted to do with myself.*

But on this Sunday morning in the Eau Claire County Jail, on Cell Block C, in cell number 6, Mike's moment comes to him, the instant where everything in his life has been pointing in this direction and everything in his life will be different afterwards.

He reads a story in *Rollerball* called "A Cook's Tale."

It's about a middle-aged man with a job. He's the head cook at the University of Minnesota Hospital. He's large and gruff and is known as the Swede. And unbeknownst to any of his coworkers in the hospital kitchen, he's read the entire Modern Library, four hundred books, in alphabetical order, over a period of eight years. The Swede's name is John Olaf, and the story is about him finally letting his secret life slip.

A woman named Emma works in the hospital kitchen, and on the day the story begins, she's weepy as fuck-all because her husband, who's a graduate student, has just failed a major examination. She can't work worth a hoot as a result, is defensive about her husband, saying that he's not dumb and that he's been studying very hard to pass that test, and it's the Swede's job, it's what he gets paid for, to convince her to pull herself together. He's got a kitchen to run here. And he treats Emma hard, jokes about her husband, but when he sees her weeping there before her industrial dishwasher, his heart gets meat-tenderized for her. He feels sorry for her. So he tries comforting her, and the only words that come to him are a few words from Proust. "Pain she was capable of causing me; joy, never; pain alone kept the tedious attachment alive."

This perks her up all right. She wants to know where the quote comes from, and the Swede, he tells Emma he's just heard it some-where; he can't remember where.

They have an affair, of course, because in stories, Mike supposes, that's one of things people do. The Swede's married to a woman who can't understand why he's spent all that money and all that time read-ing the four hundred books of the Modern Library. Emma is married to a man who's more interested in his studies than in her. Therefore, it's natural that they should come together. But the Swede never lets on to Emma that he's read all those books. He's large, coarse, and oafish, hardly the educated-looking type, and he figures that even if he tells Emma he's read all those books, she won't believe him. To Emma, the Swede is a fresh breath of uneducated air. To the Swede, Emma is everything his wife is not. They picnic. They hang around together. They talk and all that stuff.

Near the end of the story, Emma invites the Swede to a party at her apartment, a party where her husband's friends and professors are chatting about intellectual things. The Swede gets horrifically drunk at the party. At one point, an intellectual accuses the Swede of being a Classicist, and the Swede punches him. The Swede—and Mike knows this is the point of the story—is just as smart as these intellectuals, but he doesn't know how to *behave* like them. He's a large, coarse, oafish dude, and nothing's going to change that.

At the very end of the story, the Swede makes love to Emma, qui-etly, in Emma's bedroom, while the party rages outside the door, and then he goes home to his wife, carrying a loaf of fresh-baked bread under his arm.

Lovely.

Here's the math of it, folks. Mike reads this story and can't help thinking that the Swede equals Mike Magnuson. "A Cook's Tale" is exactly the story of Mike's life—well, except for the lovemaking part and the book-reading part. But there's the Swede: large, ungainly, loud. And there's Mike: same. Which is, in Mike's view, cause for joy. In the story, see, the Swede triumphs in a small way over the world. He can't socialize properly with intellectuals? So what? The Swede *is* an intellectual, and that's all that matters about being an intellectual: being one. So Mike resolves right then and there that he's going to do something grand like the Swede's done. He's going to read four hundred books or something like that. He's going to fill his mind with ideas and beauty, and even if nobody thinks Mike's capable of knowing this shit, knowing about beauty and truth and art and all that, by God Mike can know about it anyway.

And Mike goes ahead and does school the right way. He gets his shit together. He goes to court on Tuesday morning, gets some laughs in the courtroom when the judge reads selected excerpts from the arresting officer's report aloud: "The suspect identified himself as Bart Starr. This court hasn't heard *that* one before." But the judge releases Mike to his own recognizance. And Mike walks home. On the way, he stops by the lilac where he pitched his wallet, and sure enough, the wallet's there. Nobody's touched it. This is a nice town. This is a place where nobody will steal your wallet.

And Mike cleans himself up and gets to his first class on time, and to his next class and to his next class and so on. And he does his homework. He gets some good grades on tests and papers and presentations. He speaks up in class, tries to say intelligent things and sometimes even does, and when he's not in class he's sitting at a study carrel in the library or hanging out in the Student Union, smoking cigarettes and drinking coffee with folks from his classes and discussing with them the meaning of the universe and so forth, and by God he starts making the best kinds of friends a person could have at college: the smart ones, the crazy ones, the ones with goofy haircuts and who wear goofy clothes, the ones with alternative worldviews and alternative ways of living, the ones who know they're brilliant and have every intention of overthrowing the world when they get the chance.

You add it all up: Looks like Mike's turning out okay after all.

Chapter 4

NEARLY A YEAR PASSES.
Mike may not be excelling in
college by, like, Harvard standards, but compared to the historical
Mike Magnuson standard, he's functioning in the Nobel Prize range.
He's maintaining a B+ average, man. Can you believe it? And if it's
true, which it is, that what you take with you from college is determined by the intellectual and social atmosphere of the college itself,
then Mike's education at the University of Wisconsin at Eau Claire is
determined by women.

The ratio of females to males at Eau Claire, depending who's telling
you, is round about 7:3. There's a big nursing program at Eau Claire,
and a big Education Department, which means there's legions of
women taking classes. And it follows therefore that Eau Claire's general curriculum caters to the female majority of the student body.
Here you simply can't get through a course in, say, English or History
or Religious Studies or any other Liberal Artsy type of class without
receiving mind-altering doses of women's issues, of feminism. You
learn here what women have suffered through, and you learn that
society must not allow it ever to happen again. And by extension you

have lots of young women at Eau Claire who are, well, they're liberated, is what they are. They smoke and drink and don't shave their legs. They wear whatever clothes they please and fuck whomever they please whenever they please. They fuck men. They fuck each other. They don't fuck, if they don't feel like fucking. They cuss and argue about literature and philosophy. And these are the women who Mike hangs out with in the Student Union and after classes. These are who become Mike's best friends.

So August comes again, the kind of Eau Claire August where the mornings begin sunny and blue, and at noon, when the heat rises its way toward ninety degrees, cumulus clouds begin dotting the sky, and later on in the afternoon, toward evening, giant thunderheads rise on the western horizon, somewhere over the plains of Minnesota, and after dark, huge thunderstorms slash through the Chippewa Valley and scour it clean for another sunny morning to begin again.

This is the time of year to go ahead and play the theme song from *National Geographic,* folks. For these are the last days of Mike's lesbian summer.

HERE WE FIND HIM: sitting on a porch rail of a big yellow lumberjack house on Main Street, two blocks from downtown Eau Claire. He's chewing the ice cubes from a glass of iced tea he's just drained, and he's doing his best to feel cool in the shade. Main Street here is a steep hill rising from the valley floor, up and down which the sputtering hubbub of Eau Claire's Friday evening rush-hour moves. This is five o'clock maybe. Somewhere around there. The porch is wide and long and has a slatted floor, and in some ratty lawn chairs on the porch sit a group of women.

Here's Eileen and Leila: both of them tiny people, hardly five feet tall. They're wearing wifebeater T-shirts and army BDU shorts and work boots and wool socks pulled partway over their hairy calves. They have bushy, troll-style hair. They've been best friends since they were kids in the little town of Augusta, Wisconsin. Like sisters, they say. They grew up across the street from each other. Now they're twenty-one. Eileen's in Philosophy and Religious Studies. Leila's in English. They're seniors. And lovers.

Eileen says, "This fucking heat." She likes to swear, says that's important for women to do.

Leila says, "I've always *hated* heat."

Another woman, Carol, a plain woman in a sundress who's got hair the color of used straw, she says, "We can gain *strength* from the heat."

Eileen and Leila nod, for they consider Carol to be a woman of exceptional character and power. All the women who come in and out of this house on Main Street consider Carol to be exceptional.

"That's right," Carol says. "Heat *is* something women can overcome."

Eileen says, "Well, if you put it that way—"

Leila says, "I'll go inside and get blankets."

Carol laughs in she's-realizing-something-profound nods. Says, *"Exactly."*

The story on Carol: She was raised in the woods outside Rhinelander, Wisconsin, by inordinately strict Evangelical Lutherans, the kind who rise early to pray and who know the Bible better than they know themselves. She got married when she was seventeen, under shadowy circumstances she says were arranged by the Church, to a man fifteen years older than she. And the sex acts thereunto appertaining to the marriage, she says, can only be classified as rape. Her husband had apparently demanded she jerk him off or suck his dick or spread her legs at all hours of the day, even stopping the car on the way home from church to escort Carol into the roadside pines for a mounting. So she considers it a miracle that she never became pregnant. God, it's her belief—or, more accurately, the Goddess—must have disabled her husband's sperm. But because of the marriage, she says, she developed a heart condition that made her frail and dependent upon daily doses of Darvon, and only through inner strength did she manage to break free of her marriage and receive a degree in Social Work at UW—Eau Claire. These days she's a committed activist lesbian who makes her living doing date-rape counseling for Eau Claire County, speaking in various schools in the county about the horrors of men and their muscles and hard hands and how their hard hearts turned her heart into a muscle that will never tick correctly again.

Carol is twenty-three years old.

She says, "What's the male view of the heat, Mike?"

No breeze blows, only the stir of air the passing cars make, and Mike can smell, rising from the porch enclosure in the late-afternoon heat, the heady scent of patchouli oil and garlic the women let off.

Mike says, "I wouldn't know *anything* about being in heat."

No smile from Carol. "Very funny," she says. "But true. You wouldn't know."

Mike's accustomed to patchouli. Since June he's lived with the stink of it the way a penned pig lives in shit. He's been renting out the basement here for seventy-five bucks a month, which is excellently cheap, but he's neither grown to appreciate patchouli nor learned how to act around it.

Carol says, "There's a man for you, always making a suggestive remark."

Eileen says, "Pigs on all levels."

Leila says, "Animals."

Carol smiles now at Mike, makes an attempt at tolerating the loin-driven community Mike represents. She has lovely lips: thin and moist and not cracked. "But we like you anyway, Mike."

Mike does a big-volume pig snort. "I even *sound* like a pig," he says.

"You do at that," Carol says, and she is amused.

On the porch rail opposite from Mike sits a nineteen-year-old skinny girl named Mary, who is not at all amused. She puts her hands under her legs and stares at her knees, knobby protrusions on gangly, pubescent-looking legs. Mary is a theoretical lesbian, a doctor's daughter from Madison who is conflicted about her sexuality the way she's conflicted about whether she should take a course in Renaissance Literature in the fall term or a course in United States Congressional

History. She's had the identical number of sexual experiences with women as she's had with men: four apiece. But last spring, while taking a course entitled The History of Women, she decided that the correct political stance to take, the best stance in support of women throughout the world, was to declare herself a lesbian, to live among lesbians, and to believe in the feminist slogan that hangs on the refrigerator inside this house on Main Street, which says this: FEMINISM IS THE THEORY; LESBIANISM IS THE PRACTICE.

And from somewhere in the house, from a point nearabouts to the refrigerator, comes the sound of somebody shuffling pots and pans, then loud words from a small throat: "I'll make a rice dish! We'll have people over for *wine!*"

This is Petra Jaworski, the oldest person living in the house—she's thirty—and now she appears on the porch and repeats what everybody's already heard her say.

"Rice dish," she says, and claps her hands together. "Wine party!"

Eileen says, "Great. Rice dish."

Leila says, "Wine party. Perfect."

Mike lights another cigarette, lets his eyes follow a Schwan's Ice Cream Truck grinding heavily up the long hill before him. The guy in the truck is running his hands through his hair; he looks cashed out.

"Let's get ourselves organized," Petra says. "We *really* need something to do other than just sit here."

Petra is short like Eileen and Leila are, maybe even a bit shorter, and she's got perfectly straight hair the color of maple sugar. Near her, which Mike is, it's clear her face has wrinkled a bit and that she's got the tiredness in her eyes that comes with turning thirty years old, but from the street-view, from forty yards or so away, a person seeing Petra night think she's a freshman in high school, so straight's her hair and so tiny are her hands and legs.

She says to Mike, "How much money you got?"

Mike shakes his head. He doesn't know.

"Come on, Mike. You're the *man* here," Petra says. "You gotta have at *least* ten bucks somewhere."

"I might," Mike says.

Petra claps her hands again and then waves her arms. "Get it," she says to Mike. Then to everybody: "Mike and I are going to the Bottle and Barrel for wine." Then she's got instructions: Somebody's got to call people on the phone and invite them over; somebody maybe's got to get after the dishes and the floor and stuff in the kitchen; and so on.

Mike goes down to the basement, down to his room, finds the twenty-dollar bill he's been using for the last few days as a bookmark in the second volume of *Remembrance of Things Past*, which he's been reading, looking at the words but not quite understanding, all summer. He's got the C. K. Scott Moncrieff translation, the big beige Random House hardcover with all seven books in two volumes. That's almost three thousand pages, baby. Small print, too. He paid fifty cents for each volume at a rummage sale. A real value. He's got some other books, all used under-a-buck books—a couple of Faulkners; a moldy library copy of *Moby-Dick*; a book by William Saroyan called *One Day in the Afternoon of the World*—and he's been trying to read them this summer, too. He's turning into a regular goddam bookworm. He's thinking: Okay, you give a guy a year to grow into something better. You let him go to college and resolve himself to study like nobody has ever studied before. You give him some fancy books to read, and you give him some people to hang with, people who like to talk smart and drink lots and all that shit, and then you let him start hanging out with these people at a tavern on Water Street called the Joynt, where the atmosphere is jazz on the jukebox and art majors and philosophy majors and English majors and their professors drinking too much and filing out the door in pairs, sometimes a man and a woman, sometimes a man and a man, sometimes a woman and a woman. You let a guy loosen up a little in life, see the ways other people are living and try some other ways of living, and see what you get.

And you get a cool life, is what you get in a year. The books: cheap. The rent: cheap. *Everything's* been cheap this summer. So what if he blows twenty bucks on wine? He'll be getting another student loan in a couple of weeks.

So MIKE'S WALKING with Petra. It's eight blocks to the Bottle and Barrel, and Mike and Petra are walking them the way they walk everywhere they go together. Petra's waving her arms and talking constantly, and Mike's lumbering along, not saying much and looking at the ground.

Petra's talking about the party. Of course. She's saying, "I feel like Mrs. Dalloway. She was preparing for a party once, you know."

Mike doesn't know, and he says as much. He's never heard of anybody named Mrs. Dalloway.

Petra shrugs. Says, "You're *goofy*."

Goofy is a good thing. It means that Petra has found amusement in somebody or something, in this case Mike's uneducated innocence.

Now she says, "I hope Al will come tonight. Everybody really likes Al."

Al is Al Thompson or Cosmic Al, depending on who you're talking to about him. He's a forty-year-old dude: ex-hippie drifter type from California who appeared one day in Eau Claire and correctly surmised that if he befriended Eau Claire's lesbian and spiritualist community—the vegetarians and handlers of crystals and keepers of dry goods in Number Ten glass jars—he could get laid more than he did in 1969, which, he often reports, was a lot, but *a lot* in a healthy, share-each-other way that did not take advantage of women.

"Al is a very interesting man," Petra says. "He says he's directed a few short films." And, "Al is going to open an espresso shop in Eau Claire. He's going to have art shows in there."

The espresso-shop part is true. Al is currently in the process of opening an espresso shop called Vincent's Ear, which will be the first espresso shop Eau Claire has ever had. And concerning the films he's directed, he doesn't have copies of them with him; they're somewhere in San Francisco, in a storage locker, and the first chance he gets, he's going back there—hell, maybe he'll take some Eau Claire people with him—and get those films, along with the rest of his belongings, and then he'll return to Eau Claire to stay forever.

But it's the art-show-in-the-coffeehouse part of Al that intrigues Petra the most. Petra, you see, is majoring in art. A mere label: art major. For Petra says she is not an Art *Major* but an Art*ist*. She's forever involved in one art project or another, or putting together one group-art activity or another. She's orchestrated several what she calls "happenings" in town over the last year, one of which, about a month ago, involved going with a group of twenty people to the shores of Half Moon Lake, to the very swampy place where Clarence Jeter drowned, and convincing a local derelict known as Acid Andy to appear suddenly from the water riding a bicycle. Another time about a year ago, she organized the same twenty people to rent an unoccupied storefront on Water Street and hold a three-day wrapping there, meaning that she and her art friends literally wrapped in brown paper various objects: mannequins, vacuum cleaners, framed pictures of Mom, refrigerators, and so on. Everybody had a lovely time at the wrapping, got drunk before, during and after, and some people even got laid, which is the highest compliment that can be paid to a group-art activity: People get laid as a result of it.

The trouble with Petra, though, is that she doesn't possess the technical gifts her art friends do, which is to say she possesses the *spirit* of an artist, but she can't, like, sketch a pine tree and have it end up looking like a pine tree, which is to say, folks, that she can't draw worth a shit. But she makes drawings anyway and makes a point of showing them to everybody. She even goes ahead and silk-screens her drawings on T-shirts and sells them all over town. Her big seller—a hundred shirts or something like that—is a white T-shirt with a crude picture of a dead dog, upside down on a not-quite-rectangular grave, Xs for eyes, and this handwritten caption: *poor dead spot.*

It's funny, if you think about it, even if it does look stupid, which is Petra's general theory about art; it can look stupid but still be good art.

Which is probably the reason Petra hangs with Mike: He's one of Petra's goofy art projects. Petra knows Mike is trapped in a lummox body but has a mind for the world beyond the lummox world;

therefore, he's a living and breathing and eating-too-much piece of performance art. They met when Mike was a music major, and he was hanging regularly with a drummer named Barry, and Petra at the time had it big in the love way for Barry, who was Petra's age and who was studying music because he couldn't think of anything else to do with his life. But Barry didn't want anything to do with Petra, and somehow that left Mike.

And Mike has played slap-and-tickle with Petra on occasion, which has been cool, but, like, nothing too intense, which is how Petra has wanted it. She thinks the ideal boyfriend-girlfriend situation is noncommittal, figures people can sleep together on occasion without being in love, and she's probably right. Mike and Petra get along, is all, and understand each other, Petra understanding Mike far more than Mike understands Petra. It was Petra's idea that Mike move in 511 Main Street for the summer. She figured he could discover himself here.

THE BOTTLE AND BARREL is divided into three parts: the bar, the liquor store, and the pool room. The floors are wooden, the ceiling high and covered with ornate copper, a lumber-era barroom, and when Mike and Petra walk in, not a soul seated on the stools along the bar looks up from their drinks. Music plays on the juke, Merle Haggard singing "Back when a woman could cook and still would," but nobody's listening, and nobody's saying much. Happy hour's just started, and nobody's drunk enough yet to put out the effort conversing requires.

Petra says, "It's goofy in here."

You got it: She wants to stay and have a few beers.

Mike grinds his palms together. "If we stay here, Petra, you'll never get your rice dish cooked in time for the party."

Petra laughs through her nose. "That's what I like about you, Mike. You think just like a woman."

Mike thinks about that a moment and isn't sure he appreciates what Petra's just said about him. But what the hell: Beers would be cool. He says, "You buy the first round then."

She reaches into her little gray rummage-sale purse, produces a five-dollar bill and buys a pitcher. Tells Mike to carry it and the glasses to the pool room. And no, we're not going to play pool, Mike. Just find a table and wait for her a minute. She's got a duty to do.

So MIKE'S IN the pool room—three pool tables, a game going on each one. He's slouching in a booth against the wall and politely not pouring the beers till Petra returns. He watches the lines of bubbles rising from the bottom of the pitcher to the top, how they form perfectly straight lines except when somebody walks by the booth, in which case the lines of bubbles curve, but they keep rising all the same. Wow.

Two babes are playing at one of the pool tables. They're lean and tanned, suntan-oil slick. Halter tops. Daisy Dukes. Shaven legs, waxed and shiny. Painted fingernails. They're *smooth* women. It strikes Mike that this summer he's forgotten women like this exist.

He thinks about Proust and the reason he's trying to read *Remembrance of Things Past*, which is to find "Pain she was capable of causing me; joy, never; pain alone kept the tedious attachment alive." But he hasn't found the line yet. All those books: *Swann's Way, Within a Budding Grove, The Guermantes Way, Cities of the Plain, The Captive.* He's just about finished with *The Sweet Cheat Gone.* That leaves only *The Past Recaptured* to go. But "Pain she was capable . . ."—he hasn't seen it anywhere. Or maybe he did see it and just doesn't remember seeing it. But "Pain"—he knows the line applies to women like these shiny magazine-picture women playing pool. He'll never fuck a woman who looks like that.

WHEN PETRA comes back to the table, it's clear she's done at least one duty. She's washed her face, and her eyelashes are engorged with water droplets. She's tied her hair back, making her face seem even smaller than it normally does. And more wizened. Chicken feet extend from her eyes to her ears, and her lips, though they're stretched into a let's-get-down-to-drinking smile, are creased and chapped and look more like a puckered anus than a happy mouth.

She says, "I'd like to have an art show in here." She stares at the young women playing pool, notes with some annoyance that Mike's staring at them, too. "I'd start by wrapping the pool tables in clear plastic; then I'd papier-mâché the cues. Wouldn't that be great?"

Mike says that it would, and pours a beer for Petra and one for himself.

"What a gentleman," Petra says, and becomes instantly bored. She examines her fingers a second. "Or maybe we could make a movie in here. Wouldn't that be something?"

And before Mike can agree with her again, there, standing before the table, wearing a pink Hawaiian shirt and surfer shorts and sandals and grinning like a man who's just won a twenty-dollar bet, is Al Thompson.

He says, "If it isn't the dynamic duo of Main Street." And almost before the words come out, Petra leaps up from her seat and hugs him with such intensity it's like she hasn't seen Al in decades.

When Petra releases Al, she turns to Mike. Says, "Be a dear, will you? Go to the bar and get Al a glass."

Be a dear. This doesn't rankle Mike, not now. He rises with the proper obedience, saunters to the bar, and requests the glass the way a good boy should.

At the bar he hears two men talking, guys with dirty hands and dirty T-shirts and sunburned necks.

One of them says, "I can't wait till the goddam winter. A guy lives a better life when he's on unemployment."

The other says, "Fuckin-A. Tired of baking on a rooftop all day."

Mike remembers the interminable hours at Custom Products, his hands moving in the same patterns from seven to five, the metal chips digging into his fingertips, the pus that came thereafter, and the nights at the bar with Hammer, the nights passed out on the hard floor at Riverside Elementary. Mike's escaped that kind of living, and these fellows never will.

P ETRA AND AL sit on the same booth-side, shoulders touching, and Al's holding forth on the joys of cinema.

"It's the cinematography," Al says, "that makes *Ran* such a masterpiece."

"Oh, I agree," Petra says. "I couldn't agree more."

Mike sets Al's glass on the table and sits down across from them, and Al doesn't look at Mike or reach for the glass. Al's got curly hair, red with a few white strands near his ears, large ears dangling pewter earrings from each lobe. His face and neck have taken serious sun over the years, the effect of which is to blotch his freckles into a uniform leather. The skin on Al's chest, Mike notices, approaches the moosehide-texture range.

Al says, "The first time I saw *Ran* was a defining moment in my life."

Mike understands absolutely that Al's talking about a movie, not a person, but he plays the dipshit routine anyway. He says, "Who the fuck would name a movie *Ron*? That the story of Reagan or something?"

Petra rolls her eyes. Says, "*Mi*-ike. *Pull*-ease."

"*Regan*, actually," Al says. "And Goneril and Cordelia." He says "Akira Kurosawa" in a machine-gun voice, with his teeth bared, trying to make the pronunciation of the name sound as Japanese as possible. And he says "His adaptation of *King Lear*" slowly, with a roll of his eyes, like he's an English gentleman saying it.

Petra says to Mike, "You could learn a *lot* from Al."

Mike sneers a bit. Says, "Would you like me to pour your beer for you, Al?"

But Al's not wearing his Sneer Detector. He says, "Sure, Mike. Pour me a beer."

And Mike pours Al a good one. But he's thinking a guy who acts like Al: asshole.

Petra says, "And you actually met Akira Kurosawa?"

Al takes a long swig from his beer, closes his eyes reverently, and says, in a long breathy exhale, "Yes."

Lengthy pause. Of course.

He puts his hands together now and touches his index fingertips to his nose. "We met ten years ago, on the island of Honshu, where he was conducting a seminar on *The Battleship Potemkin*." He looks at the ceiling, at the copperwork up there, for the words he needs. "His analysis of the Odessa Steps sequence was *masterful*."

Petra put her hands together, too. Says, "Was he a nice man?"

"A magnificent person," Al says. "Humble. Ethereal."

"I met Robert Rauschenberg once," Petra says. "The artist. He spoke here at the university. He really enjoyed the potluck the Art Department threw for him."

Al says, "I met Rauschenberg once, too. In New York. I went to an opening of his in Soho."

And so the conversation goes. Al's been everywhere, met everybody, knows so much about everything that Mike figures Encyclopedia Britannica should give him a call and put him on staff.

AFTER A WHILE, the pitcher's empty, and Mike's finally figured a way to get Al to shut up.

"Rice dish," Mike says. "Wine party. We're going to be late."

It works excellent. Petra says, "Oh, my God." Al says, "Oh, my God." And they effect to split and get some wine and get directly to the party.

Al buys two magnums, a California wine he says is wonderful and he personally knows the vintner, and Mike buys two magnums of a French table wine called Père Patriarche, the wine his parents drink.

GETTING DARK OUT. Must be nine o'clock or so. There's twentysome people milling on the porch at 511 Main. They're chicks, mostly. Women, that is to say. There's a couple of men, too. Friends of The Cause. Everybody's got the wine thing going strong. There's bottles uncorked all over the place, and everybody's drinking from juice glasses and coffee cups and whatever else is handy. A mellow affair. Clove cigarettes. A doobie or two passing around. Cool party.

Mike and Petra and Cosmic Al walk up to the porch, and everybody digs that Petra's finally arrived. There's cheers and shit like that.

"*Awesome,*" everybody's saying. "Petra's here!"

Petra raises her hands to cast aside praise. "I know it," she says. "I'll start cooking." She opens the screen door and pauses to reflect on the great task ahead. "I'll start cooking already."

Al goes with her, says something to her about wanting to be of assistance in the kitchen, about how in Japan he had acquired some highly specialized knowledge of rice dishes, and Mike lingers for a moment on the porch, holding his two magnums of Père Patriarche, one in each hand, like dumbbells.

Carol's standing next to Mike, not drinking, because alcohol conflicts with her Darvon, and she bends toward Mike's waist and grunts, which makes Mike nervous and, well, just a little bit excited. Carol's beautiful in her way, piercing intelligent blue eyes and pale skin that's luminous to Mike in the porch light.

Mike says, "Are you having a nice time, Carol?"

She shakes her head, curls her lips into themselves. Says, "I was just reading your wine bottle."

Mike brings a magnum to his eyes. It's got a beige label, in the center of which is a bearded monk examining a bottle of wine in earnest. The monk kinda looks like Mike.

Mike says, "Doesn't look like much to read here."

"The wine's *name,*" Carol says. "Père Patriarche."

"It's good stuff," Mike says. "My parents have been drinking this stuff for as long as I can remember."

"Well, I think it's offensive."

Mike checks out his magnum again, the bearded man on the label looking content, friendly, thoughtful, the type of person Mike wishes he was inside.

Carol says, "A wine like that promotes the dominant patriarchal paradigm. I would think you'd know better by now—after living here for how many months?—"

"A couple," Mike says.

"—than to bring a wine with a name like that to party here."

She makes a power-type fist-raise gesture toward the people on the porch—women in sundresses or shirts purchased at the Salvation Army store, with their raggedy hair and hairy armpits and their *soupçon du patchouli*—and among the women stands an isolated man or two, hand cupped to his chin, listening intently to what the women are saying about whatever.

Carol says, "Do you see a patriarchy functioning here?"

Mike has to admit that he doesn't; there aren't enough men here for there to *be* one. But he can dig what Carol's saying well enough. He can see that the world can function just fine without a bunch of men hanging around and wanting to fuck everybody in it. And hey: Carol—she *does* have a certain lusciousness to her, something creamy and vulnerable despite the show of strength she always makes.

He allows her a concession. Says, "You're right, Carol. I can *completely* dig what you're saying about this wine. But what am I gonna do? It's the only wine I have."

She smiles then, a lovely perfect-white-teeth smile, extends a hand to Mike's face, and gently fingertips his beard.

"When I was a girl," Carol says, "I would have gone for a man like you." She gazes in the direction of the street and lets out a sigh Mike can hardly hear over the other conversations around him. He feels the primordial beginnings of a hard-on.

Carol says, "I used to love beards on a man." Another faint sigh. "But that's impossible now." And she turns and takes up a conversation with some other women.

Ah, there's Mike's summer in a nutshell: hanging here on the porch where people banter about paradigms and institutionalized patriarchal oppression and the life without red meat or heterosexual sex. You got to love it, buddy.

MIKE HEADS for the kitchen. He's needing a corkscrew and a glass. And you bet: There's Petra and Al cooking their asses silly. A rusty wok's on the stove, a puddle of brownish oil in it. Al holds a cleaver and stands before a wooden cutting board on which he's placed a dozen unpeeled garlic cloves.

"The Japanese principle," he's saying, "is not to *slice* the garlic but to *crush* it."

He places a flat cleaver side over a clove and bashes it with the soft butt of his fist.

Petra leans toward the cutting board, examines the bashed clove, notices how it's spread into the shape of a pressed flower. "It kinda looks like a flower," she says.

"The Japanese way," Al says, "is to concern yourself equally with the visual appearance of the food as with its taste."

Al gets busy with some more cloves, Petra keeps admiring, and Mike uncorks a magnum, finds a coffee cup in the cupboard, and fills it to the brim. He swigs straightaway, doesn't pause to savor the wine's bouquet or appreciate its color. Père Patriarche doesn't taste like a horrific history of oppression; it tastes exactly like red wine.

SOMEBODY'S SET a boom box on the porch and is playing a tape of the English Beat, peppy ska dance music. The party's catching a good groove. Everybody's swaying their hips and hair and talking and smoking and having a great time. There's more folks here now. More men. One of the men is this returning-adult-type student in the Art Department, a guy about Petra's age. Name's Doug Washburn, and he's six feet, probably, and wiry-built and has got a major-league mountain-man beard and some serious hippie hair ponytailed halfway down his back. Doug's thing is pottery, and everybody says he's a wonderful potter, and he's holding a can of beer and holding forth to three short-haired butch dykes in jeans on the true nature of throwing pots.

"Pottery is not just an art," Doug's saying. "It's an act of the *body*."

He sets his beer can on the porch rail and cups his hands around it, pretending the can's a lump of clay. Says, "Imagine that you are connecting with the clay, using your body, every ounce of it. You are using your body to change the clay from what it *is* to what you want it to *become*."

The three dykes nod enthusiastic approval.

"The body *is* the art," he says. He uncups his hands from the beer can, takes a quick glance at his audience, bows nobly, and right then and there he gets naked. Pulls off his T-shirt, his shorts, and his underwear.

There you are: *Nude Potter with Beer Can and Sandals.*

Nobody on the porch gasps or anything. They couldn't care less. To them, a man getting naked to prove a point about pottery seems perfectly natural, as natural as seeking shelter in a thunderstorm or drinking coffee in the morning or eating garlic tablets to prevent the common cold.

Now Doug cups his hands around the can again and slides his palms up and down the can, in the process swaying his hips. Mike can't for the life of him help but admire the way Doug's ass doesn't jiggle when his hips move and how the buttons of Doug's spine stick out and how his legs and arms and torso are lean. Doug's the type of dude chicks want to fuck. Hats off to you, Doug. But no: It ain't right to have a naked dude on the front porch. This is on *Main Street*, for chrissakes. Somebody's for *sure* going to drive by and see this and complain to the cops.

MIKE HEADS for the kitchen to tell Petra what's up, and she's in front of the stove, stirring rice in the wok while Al's behind her massaging her shoulders.

Mike says, "Petra, we got trouble."

She keeps stirring her rice dish. Al keeps kneading her. She says, "What's the difficulty, Mike?"

"We're gonna get arrested."

She says, "What's going on? Somebody get you *stoned*?"

"Doug Washburn, he's naked out there. He's pretending to throw a pot or something."

She digs a small spoonful of rice from the wok, turns smiling to Al, and feeds it to him. He makes an ecstasy-laden humming noise like he's just blown his wad. "Marvelous," he says. "We should cook together more often."

Mike says, "Doug Washburn is *naked* on the front porch."

Now Petra levels her eyes at Mike. Her eyes are slitted: a well-petted cat's on catnip. "That's what Doug *does*," she says. "He *always* gets naked."

Al says, "People need to get naked on occasion, Mike."

"Jesus," Mike says.

Al says, "We're talking about something spiritually *beyond* Jesus."

Mike says, "Whatever."

They couldn't care less; neither will he.

HE MINGLES with four women talking about Simone de Beauvoir, and one of them's saying something like "*The Second Sex* is a major key to our emancipation."

Mike's poked around in a book or two by now and has discovered that Simone de Beauvoir was Jean-Paul Sartre's lover. He says, "Do you guys know why Jean-Paul Sartre had a walleye?"

The women say that *walleye* is a terribly offensive way to put it, but seriously: What's the connection between Sartre's *eye* and Simone de Beauvoir, anyway?

Mike says, "Before Sartre started fucking de Beauvoir, his eye was perfectly normal."

The women don't laugh at this, but Mike thinks he's just made a first-rate gut-buster. He sure is busting *his*. He tries explaining that, ha-ha, de Beauvoir must have fucked one of Sartre's eyeballs loose.

"Now that's some *seriously* emancipated fucking," Mike says.

HE MINGLES with the group of people who are watching Doug Washburn, who's gotten more and more comfortable being naked. Doug's doing a hippity-skippy dance to the B-52's tape on the boom box. Art is a naked thing, and everybody's thinks this is as delightful as shit.

Mike says, "Look at him: He's got a bone-on."

And Doug *does* have a bone-on. Not a full ready-to-go-tunneling bone-on, but his dog's higher than half-mast, for sure.

How wonderful, that's what everybody's thinking.

Mike says, "Well, I think it's a goddam disgrace."

Carol's here, and she's thinking *Mike* is the disgrace here. She says to him, "Doug is *not* having an erotic erection. And believe me: I can identify an erotic erection when I see one."

Mike says, "What kinda erection is it, then?"

"Perhaps Doug needs to urinate."

"Oh," Mike says. "Perhaps."

EVENTUALLY the rice dish is served, a blob of congealed brownish matter on a paper plate, and everybody raves about it.

"Petra and Al," people say, "have really outdone themselves."

Or "This is *fantastic*."

Or "If Al serves *this* at his espresso shop, he'll make a fortune."

Mike takes one bite of the glop—an unmistakable taste of vagina to it—and tosses his paper plate underneath a stunted juniper next to the porch.

"A squirrel nibbles on this shit," he says, "and it'll kill him."

Nobody laughs.

Nobody appreciates a litterbug, either, but Mike refuses to go pick up his plate.

H<small>E</small> <small>DRAINS THE</small> first magnum of Père Patriarche and uncorks the second and begins stumbling around the porch, carrying the magnum by the bottleneck, pointing out the label to everyone, saying, "I'll surely go to hell, drinking a wine with a name like this."

Nobody disagrees.

Mike's getting out of control, and he knows it. He figures he should mellow out, which he tries for a while. He takes up a position on the porch rail and talks with a painter named Mark, who's neither a fag nor a pro-lesbian, just a guy who works as a graphic artist for a local Styrofoam packaging company, and who sometimes works in abstract oils.

Mike says, "Don't you think this party is fucked up?"

"Yep," Mark says. "I do. But these are the only friends I have."

This enervates Mike, makes him feel like he's not alone in the world after all. He talks with Mark for a while about normal stuff guys talk about: beer, chicks who look good in bikinis, the Green Bay Packers, et cetera. Mike tells Mark that someday, years from now, he's going to write a book about this party and how fucked-in-the-head all these people are.

"You go right ahead," Mark says. "But I'm not gonna do a painting of it. Why waste time painting Doug Washburn's dick?"

Carol's milling nearby, hears what they're saying and scoffs. She says, "Will you two *please* mind your conversation?" She's raised her voice so everyone can hear her and be reminded of living's essential seriousness. "There are women here who have been *raped*."

Conversation lulls a moment. Heads nod. Two dozen disappointed eyes glare at Mike and his new buddy Mark.

Mike's head spins: a mix of Père Patriarche and the factory he used to work in and the school he used to live in and the group home where he used to work: a lifetime of being a big ungainly man and ending up in the wrong places because he was a big ungainly man. But here he's arrived, among intellectuals, people who read books and talk about them and sometimes even know what they *mean*. This is the life Mike's been dreaming of, but there you have it: He's got to talk about something else.

MIKE HEARS hilarity in the house, a happy little commotion in the living room, people enjoying themselves, and he goes inside to investigate.

Doug Washburn's in the center of the living room, a few people surrounding him, and he's still naked, and Cosmic Al's there, and Petra's there, and she's lightly paddling Doug's penis with her wooden rice-dish-stirring spoon. Each time Petra paddles Doug's penis it becomes a bit harder, till, after a succession of tips and taps, Doug's got himself a six-inch lovelog that bobs and ticks with each beat of his heart.

Cosmic Al says, "That's wonderful."

"Goofy," Petra says.

"Involuntary," Doug Washburn says.

"But isn't it true," Al says, "that the body's involuntary functions are synonymous with our spiritual functions?"

Doug tugs his beard, and his dick droops a bit. "You might be right."

"Listen," Al says. "I'd like to put you into a trance, and perhaps we could discover who you were in your past *lives*."

Now Doug's dick completely disengorges, shrinks like a toy football with a needle hole in it might. He says, "I've been a potter in *all* my past lives."

Petra's face sags at the same rate as does Doug's dick. She stares at the floor a moment, at her tiny feet there, then looks at Mike with his wine bottle, and when she does she gets supersmiley again.

"Mike!" Petra says. "Al should put *you* into a trance."

Mike raises his magnum and swigs. "In each of *my* past lives," he says, "I've been an asshole."

Al says, "I won't argue with *that.*"

General chuckling. And the Devil talks to Mike. *Petra's right, Mike. You're the perfect candidate to go into a trance. If you go ahead with it, buddy, you might even get laid, which in this crowd would be tougher than climbing Mount Everest in your skivvies.*

"Fuckin-A," Mike says. "Let's do it."

THE LIVING-ROOM lights are off, and Mike's stretched out on the floor, in the middle of a circle of people.

Petra lifts Mike's head gently, as a nurse would an invalid, and places a pillow under his neck. Says, "You'll do fine, Mike. I'm very interested to see how this turns out."

The pillow's comfortable. The floor: comfortable enough, even though it's wooden. Mike stares at the ceiling, a faint gray screen of peeling paint reflecting the distant streetlight glow. His eyes spin, but his mind doesn't race. Everybody's watching him, which is no problem, man. He's thinking he's finally doing something right.

Al makes an announcement: "While I'm taking him under, I'll need all of you to be absolutely silent and still. I want you to concentrate on Mike's spirit. We need our consciousnesses to become one, if we want to release what's in him."

Folks murmur that they will be quiet and will for sure concentrate.

Mike hears Carol Sanderson's voice among the voices: separatist and pure.

Al asks Mike to close his eyes.

No problem, dude. They're already closed.

Al begins talking softly, saying something about streams and hayfields and mountains looming on the horizon.

He's saying, "You are finding who you are now."

And "You can see yourself long ago."

And "This was who you used to be."

And "Open your heart to your old body."

This goes on for a time—five minutes, maybe ten—and Mike keeps his eyes closed. He hears people breathing around him, hears the occasional car driving up the hill outside, and somewhere in there he thinks he hears children laughing and a cat screeching.

He senses Al standing over him, can hear him saying, "Okay, he's under now. We can talk to his spirit now."

But Mike's not under. If he can hear and feel and taste and smell and know for a fact that a roomful of people are watching him, he's *not* in a goddam trance. He's drunk, is what he is.

"Now," Al says, "tell us where you are."

Mike knows he can't say the truth: that's he's in Eau Claire, on a living-room floor, girdled in a fog of patchouli and clove-cigarette smoke. He's not sure anybody here would *believe* him.

Al says, "Nobody is going to hurt you. You are safe with us."

Mike grunts, the best he can do to suggest the void state Al wants him in. A grunt, Mike figures, is what a zombie is supposed to say under these conditions.

"He's under for sure," Al says. "Did you hear him grunt?"

Several female voices whisper that they did.

Al says, "Tell us where you are."

"Woods," Mike says. Flat: pure zombie.

"Tell us about the woods."

"Trees," Mike says.

"How many trees?"

"Lots and lots of trees." It's come to Mike now. He'll go with the little-girl routine, the little Laura Ingalls Wilder settler-type girl. He can see in his mind the woods a little settler girl might see: a vast stand of pines, a log cabin on the edge of the woods, a clearing covered in tall grass wavering in the breeze. In the middle distance, a man approaches on a buckboard, one horse pulling it. The man's wearing a black felt hat.

Al says, "Who are you?"

Mike thinks, remembers stories his mom used to tell him years ago about Lydia the Ladybug, a bug always forthright and ready to save the day and whatever. That'll work.

Mike says, "I'm Lydia." He can feel his voice box tightening, can feel himself becoming a child.

Al says, "How old are you?"

"Six."

"Where are you?"

"A man is coming. He's got a big horse pulling his buckboard."

"What color is the horse?"

"Brown."

"Who is the man?"

"He's wearing a hat."

"What are you wearing?"

"My dress."

"What is the man doing?"

Mike imagines the man, his black felt hat, a rumpled coat and pants, a face withdrawn and withered from hardscrabble living. Mike sees him stopping by a small tree near the cabin, getting off the buckboard, and tying his horse to the tree with a strip of leather. He brushes off his pants, very dusty pants, clouds of dust, and approaches.

"Lydia," Al says. "Can you hear me?"

"I think I can," Mike says.

"Tell me about the man."

"He wants to know where my daddy is."

"Where *is* your daddy?"

"I don't know," Mike says. "He's been gone for hours."

"Where is your mother?"

"I don't have a mother anymore."

"What happened to her?"

"Died when I was born. That's what my daddy says."

"Do you know the man who's talking to you now?"

"Can't remember seeing him before," Mike says. "But he says he knows *me*."

Mike's watching a movie in his head: the man talking, explaining he's got something important to do. *Come with me, Lydia. I've got something to show you in the woods.* He sees columns of sunlight in the woods, blue jays flying from tree to tree. He hears the midmorning breeze rustling the treetops. He sees the man's pants, held up with a string and frayed at the fly.

Mike says "We're in the woods now."

Al says, "What are you doing in the woods?"

"He says he wants to play a game."

"What game?"

Mike puts on a whiny voice. "Do we *have* to play?"

Al says, "What *game*?"

"I've never played Milk the Cow before. We don't have a cow. Only two goats."

"How do you play Milk the Cow?"

"The man says he has an udder. He says he wants me to squeeze it till it gives milk."

Carol Sanderson lets out a screech, a sudden and loud one, which has a gunshot-style effect on everybody in the living room: People gasp, and Mike hears them shifting position and breathing in a distraught way.

Al says, "*Please* keep concentrating. We're getting somewhere here."

Mike lets out a yell. "That's not how you milk a cow!"

Carol can't stand it any longer. Which is what she shouts: "I can't stand it any longer!" And she grabs Mike by the shoulders and shakes him, and when he opens his eyes, she slips an arm around his neck, a soft arm, and Mike smells something soapy on her skin. She brings her face close to Mike's. Hers is wide, with strong high cheekbones, the skin over which seems to shine in the dim light there is.

"It's all over now," she says. She runs a hand through Mike's hair, strokes his beard, leans into his forehead and kisses it. "Somebody," she says, "turn on the lights!"

And there is light.

Mike squints, allows his eyes to adjust to the room. People bend over him, the women: teary-eyed.

"Go," Carol says. "Leave us for a moment."

A MOMENT. Everybody's back on the porch with refilled wine cups. There's new tunes on the boom box: Laurie Anderson intoning a line that goes upward: "The sun's coming up like a big bald head." And Mike's alone with Carol.

"It's *all* over," she says. She brushes her hand through Mike's hair again, running her fingertips over Mike's ear. Such soft fingertips, and she puts off a pleasant Ivory-soap smell, nothing like the other lesbians.

Carol says, "You'll be *all* right."

Mike wants to tell Carol the truth, that he was faking the trance thing, but then again he's not certain that's the case. He's tired. His eyes hurt: When they were closed he did see the woods. For real. The trees. The blue jays darting among them. The man and his buckboard and his black felt hat. That's some vivid shit, Mike's imagination.

Carol helps him to his feet with an ease that surprises him: She's a small person, and she hoists Mike without the slightest strain or grit of the teeth. Her hand is long-fingered and exquisite-feeling, and she takes Mike with it and guides him from the living room and down the staircase to Mike's basement room. She doesn't turn the lights on. She merely leads Mike to his bed, a box spring and mattress resting on the concrete floor, and she helps him stretch out.

"You'll feel better," she says. "Eventually."

The only light in the basement comes through a one-by-two-foot crystal-block window on the opposite end of the room, and the light it lets in is a dark yellow, streetlight filtered by old dust and dirt. Carol sits on the bed's edge, her hair hanging forward from her shoulders and eclipsing Mike's view of her face. With one hand she holds Mike's and works her thumb in back-and-forth patterns over Mike's palm. With the other hand she tucks her hair behind her ears, angling her head with each motion in a way, and in this light, and with the quantity of wine Mike has in him, that makes Mike think Carol is impossibly beautiful. That's what Mike wants to tell her: *You are impossibly beautiful.* But he can't say a word.

Now she stretches out with Mike and holds his head to her breast, a smell of clean living, of a life dedicated to ideals and helping people, and she holds on tight. Mike slides his hands over her lower back: tight, muscular, wide, capable of bearing great burdens. Were he to drop his hands a few inches, he could massage the globes of her lesbian zone. But he doesn't. He can't seem to do anything. He closes his eyes, sees the woods again. The clearing. The fine sunny day. This time the person approaching from the middle distance is Carol, smiling. She's leading Mike away from the clearing, to the heavier forest, where the columns of sunlight are golden and pure, and Mike's spinning here, making a top of himself, getting dizzy over the pine needles, and fading away from the lesbian way of living he knows is unforgiving and will always be.

IN THE MORNING, Carol's gone, and Mike's sitting on his one teetery chair, trying to read onward in *Remembrance of Things Past.* He doesn't have a long ways to go, only a few hundred pages till the end, a pamphlet compared to the nearly two thousand pages he's read so far. But he's having problems concentrating.

He keeps reading the same two sentences:

I could have drawn the rectangle of light which the sun cast beneath the hawthorns, the trowel which the little girl was holding in her hand, the slow gaze that she fastened on myself. Only I had supposed, because of the coarse gesture that accompanied it, that it was a contemptuous gaze, because what I longed for it to mean seemed to me to be a thing that little girls did not know about and did only in my imagination, during my hours of solitary desire.

And he keeps lifting his eyes from the book and staring at his bed, its emptiness, the sheets he hasn't washed in weeks, the torn sleeping bag he uses for a blanket, when the air in the basement is cold, which it often is, near daybreak, which is when he awoke this morning, extending an arm for Carol and discovering that she wasn't there.

He smells his hands, trying to find a faint trace of Carol, her soapy skin, her earnest heart, and he smells cigarette tar and something tangy, a residue of wine he spilled on himself. He rises from his chair and steps to a bulletin board he's hung on the wall, in the center of which is a small picture of Proust he tore from a book at the university library. Proust's eyes are sad and dark and liquid, his hair greased slick, his frail hand to his chin, a fingertip touching the edge of his thin mustache.

"Pain she was capable of causing me; joy, never; pain alone kept the tedious attachment alive."

Proust: a moment come and gone, an instant, a glance, a touch, a view of the sunlight filtering through the bushes, an agony of memory.

Mike fell asleep in Carol's arms; that's all there is to it. He hadn't passed out, hadn't been drunk enough to, merely was tired and sad and worn out from wine and theatrics, and he hadn't torn off her dress and held her legs skyward and pounded into her cervix the hard truth of his unhappiness and his longing to find not love but a woman with whom he could feel like a handsome young man in his twenties rather than a drunk kid with a beer gut who acts like an asshole at parties.

He should have fucked her.

THE FLOOR CREAKS upstairs, and Mike's spirits do the five-stage-rocket thing. He's pumped, buddy. That's Carol up there probably. Pacing. Or maybe standing by the living-room window, gazing out the window at another dull day much the same way Mike's been gazing at his picture of Proust.

Mike goes for it: He heads upstairs, opens the basement door, and *Jesus:* Major garlic-and-patchouli reek up here. Major cigarette reek, too. And no sign of Carol. In the kitchen there's stacks of empty coffee cups and wine bottles and beer cans, and there's crap on the floor like corks and smashed blobs of rice dish and cigarette butts and plastic forks. A housefly circles over the stove, over the wok with a mound of rice dish left in it, but the fly doesn't land, which Mike figures is a wise move.

He regards the slogan on the refrigerator: FEMINISM IS THE THE-ORY; LESBIANISM IS THE PRACTICE.

He doesn't know why he himself has neither a theory nor a practice, but he *does* know the slogan that should hang on the refrigerator of his life: LUMMOX IS THE THEORY; LUMMOX IS THE PRACTICE.

He wanders to the living room and looks out the front window into the front yard and wouldn't you know it? There's Cosmic Al. He's shirtless, wearing a thin pair of shorts. He's barefoot, too. He points an arm at the sun and with his free hand he appears to be gripping his buttocks. Holds this pose for a half a minute or so. Then he's out-stretching his arms crucifixion-style and lifting one leg at the knee. The crucified flamingo pose.

Too funny, man. Mike's got to go outside and hear what this all's about.

There's a pack of Camel Filters and a pack of matches sitting on the windowsill. Could be Mike's. Who cares? He gets a smoke going, busts open the porch door, and saunters down to Al.

Al's eyes are shut, and he's pressing his fingertips into his nose, tak-ing long inhales and making slow exhales.

Mike says, "Whatcha doing there, buddy?"

Al doesn't open his eyes. "I am aware of your presence near me."

"Geez, I'd hope so, Al. I only slammed the shit out of the screen door when I came outside."

Now Al does open his eyes, but he doesn't turn them Mike's way. He strikes another pose: one palm fixed over his heart, the other palm extending toward the road, which thank God doesn't have any traffic on it.

Al says, "This is called tai chi. It's a martial art." He cleaves hands into a fighting stance, moves a leg slow-motion forward and plants a foot in the grass. "I've been practicing tai chi for two decades." Tremendous release of air. Then he relaxes, drops his hands to his sides, and stands there like a regular human being.

Mike chews on this Al situation a second and determines that Al's fucking with him, and this completely pisses Mike instantly the fuck off because hey: What's this dude doing here anyway this time of day? Al don't live here. Mike says, "You look like a flamingo when you're doing that shit."

Al does a serene smile and looks like he's about to say *Grasshopper*, which is essentially what he *does* say: "Mike, your point of view is very Western."

Mike says, "It's the correct point of view, is what it is."

Al stares into his hands, flexes them, makes cleavers of them. They're not very big and are covered in blotchy freckles, but Al sure thinks they're great. He says, "Let me assure you, if you were to try something on me, make a sudden move—"

"—so you're telling me you're a badass."

"I consider myself a spiritualist first and foremost."

"But you could kick my ass at any time, right?"

"I do literally possess the skills to kill you with these hands."

And what do you expect: Mike goes for the sudden move. He grabs one of Al's hands, yanks the arm toward him. Blammo! He hits Al with a flying fireman's carry. Shoots both legs underneath Al and flips him over. Gets on top of him and jacks the arm behind his back. Presses Al's nose into the dirt.

Mike brings his face close to Al's ear. Says, "So much for sudden moves, buck."

Goddam, this feels good.

But oh for chrissakes, look at this now: Al's crying. Sobbing himself shitless. Shoulders shuddering and everything.

Okay, okay: So Mike doesn't like Cosmic Al, not what he says or what he thinks or the way the son of a bitch looks. Nothing about him. But goddam if Mike doesn't get to feeling terrible about making the guy cry. You can fuck with people a little bit. You can give them, you know, some *guidance* when they need it. But making folks cry, that just ain't right.

He releases Al's arm, gets up, and gives Al a wide berth while Al reels to his feet and wipes the grass from his chest and face. He's thinking Al's going to make a sudden move of his own, and he's ready for it.

But Al lets it alone. He does a teeth-grit and shakes his head. "I am too advanced," he says, "to exact revenge for this." And he stalks toward the house and up the porch steps.

Mike watches the door slam behind Al, a puff of dust from the door frame, and hears him moving around in the house, coughing.

Played it stupid again, Mike's thinking. He shouldn't have dumped Al to the ground like that. Really dumb. But he doesn't figure Al will tell anybody about this. Al might be spiritually advanced, but he's still a man, and no man worth his salt will run around telling people he's just had his ass handed to him on a platter.

Across the street stand a couple of small boys, maybe eight years old, and they're watching Mike with O-gaped awe; they must have witnessed the whole thing. Mike shrugs at them. Says, "That's what he gets for lipping off, hey." But he doesn't think the boys can hear him.

He's struck with the urge to find Carol, to knock on her door and talk with her, tell her the truth, that something inexplicably male is wrong with him, that he's a liar and a horndog and a lout, just like all men for all eternity will always be, but you know: *Maybe you can see beyond that shit. Maybe you and me can find a way to work it out.*

MIKE'S IN the basement again, in his teetery chair again, making another attempt at reading.

> In short Gilberte embodied everything that I had desired upon my walks, even my inability to make up my mind to return

home, when I thought I could see tree-trunks part asunder, take human form. The things for which at that time I so feverishly longed, she had been ready, if only I had had the sense to understand and to meet her again, to let me taste in my boyhood.

Proust: Mike digs this guy completely.

You bet: Mike should go talk to Petra, is what he should do. She knows what's what with these things. She'll give him the rundown on Carol and help him pull himself together.

He mounts the stairs again, goes through the living room, and climbs the next set of stairs to the upper floor of the house. Petra's door is closed, but this doesn't matter. Mike's gone ahead and walked in to her room before without knocking; she doesn't care. So he opens the door, and go figure: On Petra's tiny futon, the same futon where Mike's slept many a night over the last few months, there's Al, completely naked, on all fours. And Petra's underneath him, her eyes closed, her torso bucking in time with the thrusts Al makes into her.

Mike watches them the way he might watch leaves fluttering in a tree, not feeling anything, not wanting to say anything, just taking in the scenery. But Mike does make a noise. He lets out a squeaky wheeze, and Petra hears it. She opens her eyes, sees Mike, and she raises a hand, not to shoo Mike away but to allow Al to finish, which, after a few more thrusts, he does. He mutters something oriental-sounding, then collapses into Petra's arms, and Mike, all he can do is close the door and get the hell out.

Sometime in the middle of the afternoon, Mike's napping on his mattress, and he awakes to see Petra standing over him, looking stern, and she settles herself Indian-style on the floor next to Mike.

She says, "You really tapped into something last night, didn't you?"

"I guess so."

"Where'd you come up with that Lydia stuff?"

"Don't know," Mike says. "It was just there."

"There, huh? Interesting."

Petra has showered, her hair's still wet at the roots, and Mike knows she has that just-fucked freshness, that glow she's talked about having when Mike's fucked her, which has been pretty regular, now that Mike gets to thinking about it. She's more or less been his girlfriend for the last five months, notwithstanding Petra's whole noncommittal boyfriend-girlfriend terminology thing, which means Petra's not his *real* girlfriend, which must mean Mike's supposed to be cool that Petra has just allowed Cosmic Al to stick his vegetarian egg roll into her. But here's the thing: Mike really *doesn't* care. Look at Petra a second: her cracked lips, her crow's feet, her little gnarly hands. Mike's always considered her old, just maybe not *this* old.

She says, "Anyway, I'd appreciate it if you didn't go tackling Al anymore."

"He told you about that?"

"He did."

"Jesus."

"Al was hurt tremendously by it."

"Petra, the guy was, like, *daring* me to do it."

"You should have known better. That's all I'm saying."

Mike feels himself flushing. Says, "Got other things on my mind, I guess."

Petra says, "*Carol* should have known better, too." Now she stands abruptly and rubs her hands together. Says, "We're leaving for the beach in ten minutes. If you promise to behave, you can come along."

"Who's all going?"

"Everybody," Petra says.

"Carol, too?"

Petra shakes her head and frowns the worst kind of disappointment. "You'll have to live without her, Mike."

Mike figures she's right: He'll have to live.

Aʜ, ғᴏʀ ᴀ ᴄʟᴏɪsᴛᴇʀᴇᴅ ʙᴏʏ to be out in the sun! How many times has the consumptive young Marcel longed to wander among Combray's hedges and regard the birds and the celestine sky, blue beyond blue, blue beyond memory and time? What power in the wide-open air! What beauty in the delicate crystals of light reflecting off the fountain water's ripples! Such is Mike's mood when he's at the beach this afternoon: a mind for all that's exquisite in the August sunshine and in the way the cumulonimbus clouds far in the western distance are towering and taking the shapes of rabbits and bears and busts of King Charles V.

This is a river beach, a secluded sandbar bend on the Eau Claire River about ten miles from town, in the middle of the Eau Claire County forest, a beach where you park your car on one side of the river and float your stuff across and party with a six hundred-acre wilderness-like tag-alder swamp behind you. Remote partying: the best kind. The purest.

Mike's out here on the sandbar with the same twentysome people from last night, even Doug Washburn, who not only has his privates covered today—he's wearing cut-off jeans—but he's also doing something very commendable: Doug is floating a keg of Leinenkugel's across the river to the sandbar. The water's up to Doug's chest, and the keg's full, but he's keeping it afloat. To Mike, the keg is a diamond among diamonds in the sparkly river.

Mike's going to get fucked up today. Everybody is. Everybody has floated their party supplies across the river to the sandbar: coolers, lawn chairs, Frisbees. There's plenty of pot and plenty of magic mushrooms and sun and good cheer, and everybody is totally mellow about everything. Nobody thinks Mike is an asshole, and Mike thinks that nobody, not even Cosmic Al, is an asshole, either.

Mike's mingling and milling and smoking doobies and chomping magic mushrooms and speaking his mind on whatever, saying stuff like, "Real *art* should be like those clouds over there: sometimes looking like one thing, and a moment later looking like another thing. See how those clouds are alive?"

And people are telling Mike, "You're right. Those clouds *are* alive." Which they are: rising and expanding and shifting shapes and becoming what is simultaneously sad and happy about the world.

And Mike's saying, "Just look at that river, man. That is a sheet of *steel*. That is a *muscle* of water."

"You're right," people are saying. "That's a *muscle*."

Because it is. Because everything is. Because the principal cause of sadness in humans is lack of beer and pot and magic mushrooms and days at the beach. Because the people here are believing that's a fact, and that the central deficiency in the world's churches is not being able to get naked and fuck each other blue in the aisles. Because that's *absolutely* the way God would want it. Because if this afternoon and these magnificent clouds towering in the west were a piece of music, Wagner would have written it. Because the river and the sandbar and the tag-alder swamp and the endless sun is what heaven is and will always be.

"This really *is* heaven," is what Mike's saying.

And Petra and Cosmic Al and Doug Washburn and all the lesbians are digging that completely.

Mike is so happy he could die.

AT DUSK, everybody's so drunk and baked by the sun and stoned and mushroomed up that they're staggering or have retreated to the tag alders to exchange fluids with somebody or have plopped themselves on the sand, grasping handfuls of it like they're toddlers bewildered by a long day of play, and the river is dark slick of truth and night coming on.

So sure, this is when the first forks of lightning appear in the west: bursts of light somewhere out there, followed by tympanic rumblings that echo a long time down the corridor of the river. Some lightning. Some thunder. No hassle. The storm's far off, as remote as this beach is from the world. But a few folks do begin gathering their supplies, blankets and coolers and beach chairs, and begin fording them across the river to their cars. No rush, though. There's no point in rushing away from a fine day like this.

Mike hangs by the keg, watches the lightning and the folks packing up, and he tips the keg a bit by the tapper, to see how much is left in it. About half gone, he's thinking. But that's about all he's thinking anymore.

In the next ten minutes or so, the wind picks up and makes a rush of the trees along the river. The lightning: more frequent, more spectacular, great venous arcs of blue slicing through the sky, flashings of daylight on everybody packing up and fording the river.

Soon rain begins falling thick and heavy, hard splats on the river, and something in the wind becomes harsh, and everybody starts panicking, going as fast as they can across the river to load their stuff in the trunks of their cars, yelling for one another in the rain. And Mike follows the flow, wades across the river and peers back whence he came into the darkness and the wind and the pounding the heavens are dropping down.

Somebody's turned on the radio in their car. A tornado's been sighted in Eau Claire. It's heading this way along the river. People are screaming now. Bolting for the cars. Headlights shine into the rain, over the river, and there's a close shot of lightning, and there, forty yards across the river, on the sandbar, Mike can see the keg.

He doesn't know what drives him, what makes his mind work or not work, but he wades back into the river to go after the keg.

Nobody stops him. Nobody says he's going to get struck by lightning. But he knows everybody can see him. The headlights of a dozen cars are shining on him. And the water of the river and the water of the rain become one, and he feels neither of them on his skin, only the floating feeling of wading of water up to his chest, the jagged blue interruptions the flashing lightning makes. He emerges from the river onto the sandbar, seizes the keg, and hoists it high over his head, a feat of strength, he's thinking, a feat of courage, and he shouts to God: "Strike me dead now! I'm ready for You!"

To die like this: perfect. Twentysome people watching him. Tornadoes somewhere near. The wind blasting. If he gets zapped right now, nobody here will ever forget it.

He enters the river with the keg, floats it, sees the car lights shining on him, the rain battering the river, lightning cracking somewhere near, over the tag alders. He should be killed now—he wants to be killed now—but he's not going to get killed. He'll make it across alive, and later tonight everybody will say to him that it sure was dumb for him to go across the river, but hey: It sure is nice to have all this beer yet. The truth is, Mike doesn't need to be killed by lightning in the Eau Claire River tonight. In a month, Cosmic Al's going to tell Petra that tai chi's given him such spiritual control over his body that he literally can deactivate his sperm, and she's going to believe him, and he'll get her pregnant, and she'll have an abortion, and when word gets out that Cosmic Al has convinced several *other* women that he can deactivate his sperm and has gotten *them* pregnant, too, he'll get run out of Eau Claire and never return again. And eventually most of the lesbians at 511 Main Street will give up being lesbians. In ten years, most of them, even Carol, will have husbands and kids and minivans and nice alcohol-free homes in nice neighborhoods. And somewhere in there Mike's going to start dating a woman named Caryn, an art chick, and he'll fall in love with her and move in to her little duplex on the shores of Half Moon Lake in Eau Claire, and he'll end up running out of money and selling his drums and then getting a job in a plastics factory and doing for-shit in college, and he'll end up working for the next five years in that plastics factory, turning into a mean factory-type drunk and falling out of love with Caryn and cheating on her and treating her like a human turd, and all his lousy hopes and dreams will turn out in exactly the opposite way he's configured them in his mind. If he only knew all this, he wouldn't bother trying to get zapped tonight.

Part Three
The Phantom

Chapter 5

O NE SUNNY JULY SATURDAY morning, five years later, Mike is driving his yellow 1977 Ford Pinto hatchback to Kerm's Super Foods on Water Street for a quart of buttermilk. He's passing the lumberjack houses under a cloudless sky. Seventy degrees: The morning couldn't be any prettier. And he likes buttermilk on Saturday mornings. He likes bacon, too. And wheat bread and tomatoes. And he figures he'll get all that stuff at Kerm's. See, he's got money these days. He's an assistant technician at Jennico Industries in Eau Claire. Makes seven bucks an hour. Plus time-and-a-half for overtime. Plus a week's paid vacation. Plus paid holidays, buddy.

Here's the gig situation: Jennico is a small polebarn-type factory on the north side of town, in the flatland near the airport, which ain't much of an airport, a puddle-jumper stop but a famous one for being the next-to-the-last airport from which Buddy Holly took off before flying to Cedar Rapids down in Iowa or wherever it was and crashing in a snowstorm with Richie Valens and them. Jennico makes generic detergents—pine oil, dish soap, laundry soap, window cleaner—and Mike works in the part of the plant that makes the plastic bottles for the generic detergents. He works on machines, is what he does, which are called extrusion blowmolders. His official occupation: Extrusion Blowmolder Mechanic.

He's been working at Jennico five years now, maybe not that long—seems to him he's been working there his whole life—and it's not, like, a complicated situation or a series of fuckups that led him to working at Jennico. He didn't have much money somewhere in there, and he started dating Caryn, who knew the lesbians on Main Street but wasn't obviously one of them and who was in a mood to cohabitate with Mike because, truth be told, there weren't any other men who wanted to cohabitate with her. So you don't have any money and you're planning on moving in with your girlfriend? You go out and get your ass a job, is what you do, and you buy a 1977 Ford Pinto, and you pay your life's dues without complaint. Fuckin-A. And Mike's original deal at Jennico was he would work a few nights a week, and they'd accommodate his school schedule, which was cool. But you've had part-time jobs. You know what happens. One day, they're short on people and they give you a call and they're, like, can you come in for an extra shift just this once? And you do it. And your check is bigger for that pay period. And you like that. And pretty soon you're pulling extra shifts all the time, and coming in on weekends, and all of a sudden you're a full-time lifer with a pension plan. So Mike works forty, sometimes fifty hours a week in the factory, and he's still living with Caryn, who works as a graphic artist for a lumber company, and somewhere along the line, despite the job and living with the chick and going to the tavern all the time, he's managed to take enough classes to finish his degree. He's got that most useless of all college degrees, too: English Literature. Which is essentially a degree in book appreciation. A guy can't make a living appreciating books now, can he? That would be like getting paid to have a supermodel suck your dick. But what the hell: A degree's a degree. Mike figures it's something not everybody has, and he feels good about that.

Okay. Buttermilk. This is Saturday morning, and he got off work last night at midnight and went and pounded some beers and shots with his second-shift buddies at Hobbsie's Bar, which is a tavern that's actually a brown double-wide trailer home that's been converted into a getting-drunk establishment. The regulars sometimes call it the Shithole because both outside and inside that's what it is. He got home from Hobbsie's and crashed at three or so, and he's a little hung-out-to-dry just now. Groggy. Dry-mouthed. Guts feeling like he drank gasoline the night before, which he may well have. And buttermilk, as any doctor will tell you this, is the cure for the two major symptoms of a hangover: gastritis and dehydration. So there you go: Mike needs the cure pronto.

He parks his Pinto next to a minivan full of children in Kerm's parking lot and stands for a moment collecting himself in the sun. Kerm's. It's an IGA, your small version of one. Your overpriced-for-college-students-style grocery store. The kids partying in the taverns on Water Street have for years called Kerm's Super Foods *Sperm's*, the kind of joke that's funny every time, and Mike's laughing about it now, thinking about Sperm's. Ha! Going to Sperm's for buttermilk. Classic.

The children in the minivan are pointing at the back of his car, and they're laughing just as much as Mike is. They're very amused with Mike's car. Mike's never thought much of his car; it's got the standard Wisconsin road-salt Swiss Cheese of rust on the fenders and quarter-panels; but the son of a bitch runs, most of the time. It's a car, hey. It ain't *funny*.

But the kids keep laughing, pointing at the car's back bumper, and Mike hears one of the kids saying, distinctly, "Turd."

Mike investigates, and sure enough, nestled in the yellow crook between the bumper and back end of his Pinto, there lies a large shiny turd, eight inches or so long. It's got peanuts and peas in it, and above it, in the dust of the Pinto's small hatch, there's the unmistakable imprint of bare human buttocks. This turd's point of origin was *not* the intestines of a dog.

Mike certainly has changed over the last five years. It used to be, if such a thing would happen to him, if somebody were to shit on his car or otherwise to shit metaphorically on his person, he would shrug it off, would feel nothing and essentially think nothing but a form of sad pussy withdrawal, but now that he's a grown man with a job and money and a real-life *turd* steaming on his back bumper, Mike blows a stack.

"God-fucking-*dammit!*" he shouts. "Somebody took a *shit* on my car."

The kids go wild busting their little guts laughing, and the more they laugh the more pissed off Mike becomes.

He shouts, "Somebody dropped their *ass* on *my* car. Fuck, fuck, fuck."

No sooner has Mike gotten the third *fuck* out than a woman, thin and blond and maybe in her middle thirties, touches Mike on the shoulder and says, "*Please.* You don't need to be using that kind of language. Can't you see there are children here?"

The turd shines like the Devil's beacon, and a bluebottle fly buzzes on in for a fresh morning snack on it.

Mike says, "For the love of Christ."

The woman now notices the source of Mike's anger. She puts a small hand to her mouth. "For the love of Christ," she says.

Mike doesn't go into Kerm's to buy his buttermilk and bacon. He leaves the goddam turd on his bumper and drives home.

Mike's house is your ratty paint-peeling gray two-story lumberjacker that's been converted into a duplex. The City of Eau Claire owns the building, along with the other six converted-into-duplex lumberjackers on this road, Lake Drive, which is basically a rutted alley that's near the shores of Half Moon Lake. The city's going to tear down all these houses someday and build an elementary school here in their place.

Mike bumps his Pinto up Lake Drive and pulls into his short dirt-and-pebble driveway and thinks: A guy's living in condemned public housing, but what the hell: The rent's $175 a month, the place is on the lakefront. The only catch to the place is that he's been living here for five years with his old lady. Caryn. She's, well, she's whatever she is. Mike can't stand thinking about her.

He gets out of his Pinto, goes to the back bumper and reaffirms the existence of turd. It exists. This life: You never know what happens next. He's been living here on Lake Drive for five years now, living under this big maple tree with branches shading the driveway, living with Caryn's dog, a female Irish setter named Maroon, and with Maroon's plywood doghouse at the base of the maple and the dirt where her chain rubs the ground, and with the minefield of Maroon-do in the tall grass extending into the yard and down to the lakeshore, the weedy water beyond, where mallards swim in circles and large-mouth bass lurk in the darkness below. Jesus. What kind of person would *shit* on somebody's car?

MIKE STEPS to the front stoop, opens the screen door, and slams it behind him to announce his return home.

"Caryn!" he hollers. "Wait till you see what happened *this* time."

The apartment's quiet, just like it was when he left fifteen minutes ago, and Caryn's still in bed with the dog. Mike doesn't have to walk all the way to the bedroom to know this; on Saturday mornings Caryn *always* sleeps in. Lazy. Pisses Mike off. Most everything about Caryn does. But he figures that's normal for couples doing the five-year-cohabitation thing. You live with somebody for five years, and you get irritated with just about everything they do.

And if you want to get irritated, go ahead and take a look at this place, starting from where Mike's standing in the kitchen: Here we have your tiny room with dingy green walls and a rickety old gas stove and an ancient sink with rusty spigots and a heap of dirty plates in it. The cupboards sag with rot. On the counters and on the kitchen table and hanging from hooks on the ceiling there's junk like bins for flour and noodles and cereal, wire racks for fruit and onions, spice racks (there are three), pepper grinders (at last count: five of them), all this stuff dusty and rusty and mismatched and looking like the garbage it is. Caryn comes from a white-trash family of junk collectors and passers along of used household goods, and she's forever coming back from a visit to her mother or one of her three sisters with a new piece of junk everybody in her family is sure will make her life better once and for all.

Junk everywhere: He heads toward the bedroom and walks first through Caryn's art studio, literally having to pick his steps carefully to avoid tripping over all her boxes of art supplies and other art-related bullshit: two garbage bags full of pinecones that Caryn intends to turn into sculpture some fine day; a light table that her sister gave her last Christmas but that Caryn's never assembled; one garbage bag full of real lobster tails that she got from Red Lobster a week ago and that are making the studio smell like a midsummer day's Dumpster about now. Fucking stinks.

The living room: the same. Heaps of garbage. Knitting projects abandoned. Hunks of driftwood in wicker baskets. Et fucking cetera. And there's a fish tank that holds three syphilitic-looking guppies, bulgy eyes and fins too weak to hold a steady hover in their greenwater home. And for your creature comfort there's a rat's-ass futon stuffed against one wall with a beat up leather trunk in front of it. The trunk's covered with old *TV Guides* and back issues of *Art in America* and *National Wildlife*. Between the windows that overlook Half Moon Lake there's a particleboard entertainment center supporting a 12-inch TV that's tuned to the Weather Channel with the sound off. The forecast is for clear skies, a high in the mid-seventies, a breeze light and variable.

And in the bedroom, on the same noisy waterbed where Mike first laid pipe into Caryn five years ago, there lies the love of Mike's lousy life: She's sprawled with the dog, sleeping with her nose snuggled into the dog's ear.

Mike grabs Caryn's foot, its buniony big toe, and shakes it. Says, "Wake up, hey. I got something to tell you."

Caryn rolls over, opens her eyes, which are a dirty blue, and she doesn't smile, merely stares at Mike and another day of horror here with him on Lake Drive.

"I thought you'd like to know," Mike says, "that the gods have finally gotten even with me for being an asshole."

"What are you talking about?" Caryn says.

Now the dog opens her eyes and makes a feeble attempt at wagging her tail: one slight thump.

Mike says, "If you'd get your ass out of bed and go look at my car, *honey*"—pincers her big toe again, shakes it—"you'd know *exactly* what I'm talking about."

She lets out some long air, closes her eyes, and rolls her face away from Mike. She says, "It's *Saturday.* I'm *sleeping.*"

"Sleep then," Mike says. "I don't give a fuck."

"Good," Caryn says.

Mıke's outside again, standing alongside the house in the clean lake-breeze air. He's got the garden hose hooked up with the blaster nozzle, and he stretches the hose to the back end of his Pinto and begins blasting the turd off the bumper.

He gets to thinking about a guy at Jennico named Boner Hobart. Boner's real name is Jeff, and he's the third-generation member of the Hobart clan to bear the name Boner. Jeff's dad is a Boner. Jeff's grand-father is a Boner. The story: Nobody Mike knows at Jennico has ever seen Jeff Hobart's dick, but Jeff has assured all interested parties that the name Boner refers to the enormous wangs one man in every Hobart generation is blessed to wield. Jeff's always saying shit like "You should see *Grandpa* Boner. He's packing a *monster.*"

Boner the grandson has just gotten divorced. He fucked up his marriage, the way he tells it, when he went camping near Spooner, Wisconsin, on opening weekend of fishing season, on Mother's Day, to be exact. See, Boner and his old lady were sharing their camper with another dude and *his* old lady, and the four of them got cham-pionship drunk on Saturday night, and on Sunday morning, when they were waking up *way* too goddam late to go fishing, when they were groaning and hungover in their bunks, Boner said to his wife, "Don't just lie there and stink, bitch. Get up and make breakfast." That was it for Boner's marriage, right then and there: over.

Mike watches the turd dissolve into a memory on the driveway dirt. He thinks the obvious: He treats Caryn no better than Boner used to treat his old lady. Every man who works at Jennico treats his old lady like shit. Or at least that's what all the dudes *say* they do.

"Don't just lie there and stink."

That's about the truth of it, all right.

Aн, нigн learning! A while later Mike's sitting on the stoop, thumbing through *The Brothers Karamazov*, trying to find the page where he left off yesterday before work. He thinks this book kicks ass. He likes Ivan. That guy doesn't give a fuck about anything.

But here's Caryn behind him pushing at the screen door. He rises and gets out of the way, and she comes outside to chain the dog.

She says, "I'm going to Mom's for the weekend." She's wearing a pair of white painter-pant cutoffs and a blue T-shirt, and she's bathed. Her hair's still wet. Her mother lives a two-and-a-half-hour drive away, in a small town near Madison. "I'm taking Maroon with me."

Mike says, "For chrissakes, don't bring back another carload of junk."

Caryn doesn't frown, doesn't react a bit; she's beyond arguing about her family with Mike; she and Mike have bickered *that* to death too many times.

She says, "What were you all excited about before?"

"Some shit happened," Mike says, "but I took care of it."

Iн нalf an нour, Caryn and the dog are long gone. Mike didn't help her load up her car, didn't kiss her on the cheek or wave good-bye or any of that. She just up and split. Cool with Mike. Besides, she splits every weekend, anyway. What's the point fussing over her taking off?

Mike's lounging on the stoop with a cup of coffee. He's found his spot in *The Brothers Karamazov*. He's at the part when Father Zozima dies and his corpse lets off the stink of death, which totally freaks out young Alyosha and makes him wonder if he will be overtaken by evil and then start partying and brawling and whoring around like his brother Ivan's always doing. It's *heavy*, man. Guaranteed.

A NEW MAN. An older man. Twenty-six years old. He's no timid and taciturn fellow. He can get pissed off and by God *stay* pissed off. He's a big lummox yet, even bigger than he's ever been: goes about 250 in the winter and 230 in the summer. But he doesn't mope so much about being a big lummox anymore. For one thing, he's covered forty hours a week head to toe with plastic dust and machine grime and sweat, so he doesn't give a damn what he looks like. Or *smells* like. Vanity is something a guy who works full-time in a plastics factory loses forever, dude. And for another thing, he completely busts *ass* at work, hangs hundred-pound supercooled molds in machines, carries around ten-gallon pails full of hydraulic oil and whatever. Jennico work has turned Mike into one tough motherfucker. He'll kick your ass, if he wants to. He's strong enough to tear your head clean off.

But here's Mike's major discovery: Being a big factory-stinking, kick-your-ass-type lummox, chicks *dig* that. They do, man. Sure, he's been doing the Caryn thing for five years, but fuck: He never hangs around with her. She's never there when he goes down to the Joynt and gets himself tangled in all sorts of hand-holdings and alley wrestlings and backseat-of-the-car romps on Saturday nights or Monday nights or any old night after bartime. Mike's been hound-dogging in the Joynt for *years*. His modus operandi is to make sure he takes a shower and puts on a clean T-shirt before going out, and if the female opportunity arises—which it seems to do a couple-three times a month, sometimes a couple-three times a week, what the hell: Mike takes it. He figures he's finally been getting all the pussy he used to be too chickenshit to go after when he was a young pup out of high school.

His problem when he was a young pup: He wanted to be loved. But he got over that. He got himself an education instead.

Here's your scorecard:

The school year after the lesbian summer, he took a course with a professor from Rutgers, a professor who all the lesbians said Mike should never take because Professor Rutgers was constantly at the Joynt getting drunk and seducing his female students and of course encouraging the furtherance of the male power structure in the process. But Mike thought Professor Rutgers was cool. The guy would be superwild in class, shouting at people about the importance of art and poetry, and he'd draw insane algebra-looking diagrams about sonnets and villanelles and sestinas on the blackboard, and after class he'd hold court at a corner table at the Joynt, surrounded by students, mostly chicks, who loved it whenever he would talk about Ezra Pound or Paul Valéry or Robert Frost or would mention the Yale Series of Younger Poets Prize and say how he only had two years left of eligibility to win it, but he still *can* win it.

Mike got an A. He wrote little poems and little stories about living without hot running water and about fourteen-year-old girls who would disappear into the night and never see Mike again, and Professor Rutgers said he was on to something.

So Mike got big-time into trying to be the kind of person Professor Rutgers was: started hanging at the Joynt constantly and trying to be artsy and trying to get laid, and somewhere in there Mike started bumping into Caryn at the Joynt, and though he never really had much to say to her, he was attracted to her way of touching him on the forearm when she spoke to him, her way of saying that she was an *artist*, and sure enough, one night late, when he was drunk and she was drunk, which figures, he went to her duplex on Half Moon Lake, and with her Irish setter sprawled on the floor near her waterbed, a drama of diaphragms and spermicidal jelly began that would last another six years.

The morning after, he rose naked and wandered to Caryn's bathroom to relieve himself. When he returned, he stood at the end of the waterbed, admiring Caryn's nakedness and admiring her fine polished wood floors. And he decided to cut a fart, figuring it would impress her. A class guy: Mike. But when he tightened his abdomen and squeezed off a round, he didn't fart; he power-sprayed liquid shit all over the floor.

Caryn screamed. She was horrified.

But after she cleaned up the mess, she went ahead and let Mike fuck her again.

These days, Mike figures Caryn should have known from the beginning what she was getting into, when she fell in love with a guy with the class to shit on her floor.

So we're talking a perfect July Saturday with the old lady out of town. At one o'clock or so, Mike puts down his *Brothers Karamazov*, puts on his cycling shorts, and goes for a thirty-mile cruise in the country, a nice flat route, an easy crank of the pedals through a landscape wide-open and July-beautiful and junk-free, and at five o'clock he drifts over to Fred Lester's house.

Fred is a fellow Mike met years ago in Professor Rutgers's class, and Mike and Fred are buddies because when they get drunk together they can convince themselves that they're better young poets than any other young poets in Eau Claire. Which isn't saying much. They might be the only two in town. They're basically full of themselves, but they're having fun, anyway. Good for them. Fred's a tall guy and extremely bony and has a mustache and wears T. S. Eliot glasses and is the kind of person who has really *correct* politics but somehow ends up fucking up his good intentions no matter what he does. At one time, for instance, Fred was the president of the Eau Claire Feminist

Alliance. President! In fact, Fred was one of the *founding members* of the Eau Claire Feminist Alliance, and while he was president he did a fine job coordinating the various Eau Claire feminist constituencies, getting them formally to identify their goals—their platforms for gender tolerance and the like—and doing all the little painstaking things necessary to get a feminist political organization up and running. But somewhere along the line Fred made the mistake of noodling a few select representatives of the membership, and he got tossed out of the Feminist Alliance on his ear. Fred's never admitted to Mike that it was worth it, noodling the membership, but Mike's always figured that Fred thinks it probably was.

Fred and his wife Patricia own a three-story Victorian house that's situated directly kitty-corner from the Uniroyal plant and one door down from the Elbow Room Bar. They live on the bottom floor of their house, which is way massive and has three porches, plus a big patio out back, and they rent out the upper two floors to make some side income, which they definitely are *not* in need of. Patricia's father invented something technical for the military—Patricia never has said what—and got paid major millions for it and retired at forty. So Patricia's father coughed up the money for the house. He's coughed up for *everything*, still does. She doesn't need a job. She doesn't need to do *anything*, just cash the monthly stipend-style checks from her father and send her father her credit-card receipts each month, a monthly total, Mike figures, that probably exceeds what he makes in four months.

Thirty yards from the house, across a rutted stretch of Galloway Street, the land falls away into the gorge of the Eau Claire River, and when Mike gets out of his Pinto and stands there enjoying the shade the tall house provides, he can hear the river gurgling and churning its way toward the Mississippi: America's vagina.

"Rich people," Mike says.

He reaches into the car and produces an unopened bottle of George Dickel that he picked up at the Bottle and Barrel on the way over, and he walks across Fred's lawn and around back to the patio and the screen door that opens to Fred's kitchen, and he can hear Patricia inside, hollering in her low alto voice, "No, the stone tiles *won't* work. I've been saying for a month now that stone tiles won't work. Or maybe not *those* stone tiles. I don't know anything. I'm going crazy here."

Mike looks through the screen door and sees Fred standing near the cupboard, slumped against the antique-quality stained oak, smoking, so Mike doesn't bother knocking. He pulls open the door, and the door squeaks on its hinges, and Patricia says, "Oh, my God. It's *him* again." Mike can't see her, though. She's probably in the living room or maybe sitting on the john or something.

Fred rolls his eyes toward Mike, and through Fred's glasses and the deep sink of Fred's eye sockets, Mike can detect a wince. Fred's known in advance Mike was coming over, but he's neglected to inform his wife.

"*Him, him,*" Patricia says. "*Every* Saturday night it's *him.*" Mike hears her feet stomping a polished hardwood floor in the living room, and, hard thereafter, her rump assaulting the rattan sofa chair she purchased a few weeks ago at Pier 1 Imports, which is where she purchases a great many of her household amenities.

Mike addresses Fred in code. "You know what Sylvia Plath would do under these conditions?"

Fred says, "Put her head in the oven."

This code means "Let's get drunk immediately."

Mike brandishes his bottle of George Dickel and tries to laugh. "You got *ice* for this?" Says this in a big voice, so Patricia will for damn sure hear him from the other room.

"My *God,*" Patricia says. "He brought a bottle *again.*"

Mike says, "Hey, Patricia. You mind if I take your new Waterford bourbon glasses for a test drive?"

"Not the Waterford, Fred. Please! He'll ruin it *all.*"

"Of course, dear." Fred says this without the remotest tinge of sarcasm; Patricia is right—keep Magnuson away from the Waterford. Fred eyes Mike again and opens the refrigerator and indicates to Mike that he does indeed have eight fine ice trays—fancy metal ones—

loaded and ready to go. Mike winks at him: the hey sign, the you're-cool sign. And Fred winks back.

Ah, the joys of having a buddy!

So while Fred cracks open a tray and puts a few large cubes in the wells of three antique Ball preserve jars, Fred asks Mike if anything's new. Mike says that not enough is or will ever be and you know how it's the same-old same-old whatever you do, but when Mike's got his half-full Ball jar in his hand and is following Fred down the short hall-way to the living room, he remembers that something in fact *is* new.

He says, "Somebody took a shit on my car last night."

Patricia hears Mike saying this but hasn't yet noticed Mike in the living room. She says, "Every time he's here he talks about shit! Can't he—"

She stops when she sees Mike, accepts the Ball jar he hands her, and she softens and attempts to be hospitable.

She's smoking a cigarette—maybe her thirtieth so far today—like it's the first one she's ever smoked and hasn't the faintest idea how to hold it. She's got stubby fingers, and she's pincering and repincering the filter, never getting a comfortable grip. She says, "You look like you spent time outside today, Mike."

Mike says, "Rode my bike."

Momentary confusion. "Oh yes," she says. Now she does take a drag, a massive draw and sudden through-the-mouth-sides exhale upward; then she fumbles with the cigarette again.

Mike says, "Sorry about mentioning shit, Patricia." He looks at Fred, who's attempting an encouraging smile. "But this time, hey, somebody actually took a shit on my car."

A light, a dim one, glimmers inside Patricia, and her eyes brighten as much as is possible with her. She's got very brown eyes, so brown that when she's indoors, which most of the time she is, it's difficult to distinguish what's pupil and what isn't. "Come *on*," she says. "No one would do *that*."

"Seriously," Mike says. "Went to Kerm's this morning, and some kids found a turd on my back bumper. Had peanuts in it, too."

"Stop," Patricia says, but she's major into a belly-and-body laugh, and she's so much in hysterics that the fat under her chin doubles and rolls. Fred often says of Patricia, before going on to enumerate her superior artistic and conversational qualities, that she's beautiful, that he can't hardly take his eyes off her.

Then the phone rings, and exactly when it does, Patricia quits laughing and screws her face into such a serious look that she appears as if laughter's as foreign to her as bacon is to the Ayatollah Khomeini. She greets her caller with a low voice, flat and professional.

"Oh," she says. A higher voice. Girly almost. "It's *you*." She stands, a clumsy rising, cigarette ash floating from her shirt, a splash of her Dickel escaping over the lip of her Ball jar. She says to Fred, "It's Griffin. I gotta take this *privately*. Could you guys hang out on the patio or something?"

Griffin is a Patricia, too. Patricia Griffin. But to avoid confusion between her and Patricia Nelson, everybody calls her Griffin. Besides, if anybody were ever a Griffin in this world, Patricia Griffin would be it. She stands five feet nine on a short day and weighs, on a rare light day, somewhere in the range of 275. She's a blues singer by trade, and a bottlenecker on the Fender Telecaster, and she sings the blues nasty and with muscle and with a growl. She plays gigs all over town, and most folks think she's great, which, to give her her due, she is. She's the best 275-pound female blues singer in Eau Claire. And she's recently embarked on a musical enterprise with Patricia Nelson, an all-girl folk group called Second Sister, and they're completely either rehearsing Second Sister or talking about Second Sister all the time. Mike hasn't seen any proof that Griffin and Patricia have gone beyond Second Sister and commenced playing the rib-tickle blues, but he suspects something unseemly is up between them two.

Patricia says into the phone, "I'd *love* to go have drinks somewhere. *Magnuson's* here. I won't be able to get Fred's attention till *tomorrow*."

When Mike passes Patricia he pats her on the shoulder and smiles, a smile she returns in a brush-off-an-annoyance way that Mike doesn't let irritate him. He's close enough to Patricia that he can smell her, a rich sandalwood-oil aroma that somehow, every time he gets near Patricia, puts Mike in the mood to sprawl out on a couch with her and sniff her for an hour or two.

THE PATIO'S under construction: ground torn up and flattened but not tiled yet; a pile of cedar slats that will end up being a fence, whenever Fred gets around to making it; but there's a decent metal garden-style table-and-chair set with a bright blue Miller Lite cabana umbrella opened over it. This is a comfortable enough place to relax.

Mike and Fred sit at the table, swig drinks, and light smokes, and Fred says, "We're going to put down tile out here maybe next week, once Patricia decides what type."

Mike says, "Lovely." Mike couldn't care less about the fucking patio arrangements, and Fred knows it.

Fred sighs, stares into the bones of his hands. "Patricia is very *concerned* about the patio."

Mike says, "She should get a job—then she'd sure as hell have something else to be concerned with."

"You know," Fred says, "you and Patricia would get along *much* better if you'd quit bitching about her."

SHE EMERGES from the house, proudly carrying her Ovation acoustic guitar in one hand and her drink in the other.

"Fred, honey," she says, "I wanna play a tune for Mike. Could you go inside and get my cigarettes for me?"

Fred rises dutifully. Says, "Your new tune?"

She nods and smiles likes she's just received a Grammy.

Fred says, "Oh, that's a great one, Patricia. That's a *great* tune." And he heads at a brisk clip toward the house.

Patricia hoists her Ovation into playing position, an awkward process, since the Ovation has a rounded back and Patricia has a rounded front, a combination that doesn't provide for any points of guitar-to-human leverage. She makes a couple of tuning adjustments, tweaks the machine heads, and pinkies harmonics and screws her face into a profundity apropos of a sold-out performance at Carnegie Hall. Now she fumbles her fingers over the fretboard to find her first chord, a three-finger chord, a G major with half the strings unfingered, absolutely the simplest-to-finger chord there is, yet her fingers' stubbiness and the stumbly way her tendons react to what her brain's telling them to do, this makes it look as if this simple strum is a feat of concentrated virtuosity equivalent to shredding double-time through a Bach fugue transcription.

Alas, she strums and sings: "I drank cinnamon tea this morning under apricot skies."

Or Mike thinks that's what she sings. He's too horrified by her playing style to catch the exact words. The way her fingers clunk over that guitar neck, each repositioning an agony of fingers flailing—this is flat-out too much for Mike to bear. Mike closes his eyes, puts his palms over his eye sockets to keep the world out.

When the agony's over with, Fred is back outside with Patricia's cigarettes. He sets them gently on the table before her. Says, "That tune's your winner, Patricia."

Mike sees Fred staring lovingly into Patricia's Wilma-Flintstone eyes, and he remembers what Professor Rutgers always says at the Joynt: *If something is bad and you tell a person it's great, you might as well be slapping them in the face.*

Mike puts Professor Rutgers's theory into play: "Patricia, you gotta start practicing that guitar. I'm talking at *least* five hours a day."

Patricia instantly snaps into a rage, thrusts the Ovation at Fred so quickly that he nearly drops it in the exchange, and then she bolts from her seat, shaking the cabana table.

"There he goes again," Patricia shouts. "He *always* bitches about my playing."

And she literally stamps her feet on the untiled patio ground. "He makes me so *mad.*"

Then she's serene again. Mike figures she has a switch inside her and can go from complete hysterics to absolute calm at will. She stares into Mike's eyes, retakes her seat, jerks a cigarette into her lips, pauses reflectively while Fred lights it for her with his Zippo. Says, "Oh, well, Magnuson. Just because *you* don't like it doesn't mean it isn't good. Everybody *else* who's heard my song likes it."

From somewhere in Uniroyal comes a hissing sound, something thumping then, maybe a forklift driver accidentally dumping a skid. Mike waits for the inevitable sound to come next, which it does: "Goddammit!" a worker hollers. "Cocksucker!"

Mike says, "Hear that shit? Now *that's* what I call music."

Patricia says, "He's hopelessly scatological, Fred."

A CAR DOOR SLAMS close by, and heavy footsteps crunch on the driveway gravel, and now Griffin herself appears on the patio. She's wearing a thin blue T-shirt, tight on her body, revealing the rolls of fat under her tits and revealing way too much leg-size expanses of upper arms, and she's stuffing her big hands into her blue-jeans pockets without much success and trying to shrug her shoulders into a hello, but her shoulders are too massive to form a noticeable shrug.

"Soft you now," Mike says, "the fair Ophelia!"

Griffin says, "Fuck you, too, Magnuson."

Patricia says, "Griffin! You've come to *save* me."

Mike locks on Griffin's eyes, her globby blues caged behind a pair of wire aviators. Holds the stare beyond the point when comfort goes. He's thinking him and Griffin are staring each other down like pit bulls from rival junkyards might: ready to pounce on the other and tear out the throat.

Griffin's head: shaking. She's got broad ruddy jowls and unmuscular lips that droop from her mouth. She holds the eyelock with Mike and says, "Let's go, Patricia."

And what the hell: Patricia's got everything she needs right here with her. Smokes. Purse. Money. If Fred, dear, were to take the Ovation back into the house and set it on its gig stand, where it belongs, why, we could go right away and leave you and *Magnuson* to your own devices.

THIS IS A comfortable evening, mid-sixties, windless, pleasant, and Mike and Fred head into it in a companionable, civilized way: They stop first at the tavern next door, The Elbow Room, and have a few tap Leinenkugel's, observing a gentlemanly distance between them on their bar stools, no elbows to the bar rail from these fellows, not here in the Elbow Room. When Mike's hanging with Fred alone, he behaves almost exactly the opposite way as he was just behaving around Patricia. Fred's a calm person, and he has a weird calming effect on Mike when it's just the two of them.

Fred says, "You certainly had your bombast and braggadocio out tonight."

"Ah," Mike says, "somebody's gotta put them women straight."

"I agree with you there."

Fred does genuinely agree, too—or at least he gives the impression that he genuinely does. Fred's got a way of doing that: agreeing with anything anybody says—a trait that makes Fred a master at endearing himself to people and making a good impression on people.

Mike says, "But I'm troubled, Fred."

Fred leans forward into the bar, directs his eyes toward Mike, tightens his lips in a profound, prepared-to-listen way. "Are you okay?"

"This thing with somebody shitting on my car, hey, it's eating at me."

"Well," Fred says. A weighty space of thinking. A barely perceptible roll of the eyes. "That's terrible."

Mike tries to get a laugh out of Fred. "You weren't the culprit, Fred, were you?"

But Mike doesn't get a laugh.

Fred takes a jagged drag from his smoke. "I don't think so, Mike."

Maybe they talk about a bunch of excellent stuff, maybe have fun, maybe find themselves having a better time than they've ever had in their lives, but years later the memory of it won't be clear in Mike's mind. Every Saturday night's the same and has been for a couple of years. This Saturday, that Saturday, it makes no difference. Caryn will go visit her mother or will stay at home and watch TV with the dog. Mike will go to Fred's house at five or six or so, and they'll hit three or four taverns on the way to the Joynt, and when they get to the Joynt there will be beers and shots of bourbon and sometimes a quick sneak into the alleyway behind the Joynt for a doobie or a bowl or whatever.

Somewhere in there, round about ten o'clock, Patricia will appear at the Joynt with Griffin. Patricia will be happily drunk by now, chain-smoking and bursting with alto laughter and brushing her hair back repeatedly with her hand, saying hello to the bartender almost in a shout and with a smile that twice exceeds the Government Daily Allowance for Joy. And now that Patricia has arrived—and she'll always say this—the party can begin in earnest. Which is the truth. She'll always have at least a hundred bucks on her, cash, and she'll let Fred spend as much of that money as he wants. He'll buy pitchers and more shots, always making certain Patricia's got her man's share of the booze.

And somewhere else in there Patricia will mingle up to Mike, look him in the eye with a vacant gleam, and she'll say, "I love you, Magnuson. You know that." And she'll hug Mike, jam her wet drunk nose into Mike's neck. Griffin will observe the hug and fold her arms and frown. Fred will observe the hug and be happy; he wants Patricia to be happy.

And Griffin will eventually strike up a conversation with somebody other than Patricia, usually a woman in jeans who's got a mind for feminism and a heart for the blues, and Griffin will occasionally heave a jowly glance in Patricia's direction, search for Patricia's approval, which will always come. Forever and ever.

And Fred and Patricia will take up a position near the jukebox, on wooden chairs that are built in to the wall, and Fred will listen to whatever's on Patricia's mind: something maybe about a foray tomorrow to Pier 1, or about how tomorrow's the day she's finally getting her shit together and sending some songs to Nashville, or about the pure heaven life's gonna be when Fred's done remodeling the house.

And Mike will investigate the evening's sleeping arrangements. These days, on any given Saturday night, Mike can scan the length of the bar and see at least six women he's at one time or another found himself in an unseemly position with. Which does not make Mike unusual here. The same's true of everybody at the Joynt on a Saturday night: Everybody's fucking everybody at the Joynt.

And if on these nights Mike pauses to reflect on his failure in life, how he used to be a dreamer, a guy with aspirations that not one of them has ever come true, he won't get maudlin. He's grown accustomed to being a failure. Maybe he's just not the type of guy meant to be a success. Which is cool. If you think about it. Besides, he's getting laid lots. What else can a guy ask out of life?

Sunday morning at nine or so, Mike takes his fishing rod out back of the house and spends a half hour pitching a yellow Kmart clothespin-spinner bait into Half Moon Lake. The bait's big, way too big for all the stunted bluegills that cluster among the weeds, but he's only fishing with one fish in mind, and sure enough he catches it. He lays the bait way out there, between a lily pad and a clump of weeds, and the moment he begins reeling in—Whammo, baby! Major splash! Mike's got himself a championship bass. He jerks the rod up, sets the hook good, and keeps the rod tip high, lets the bass run a bit, tire itself out so he can release it easily. But basically Mike just reels in the fish, reaches into the water, grabs the fish by the lip, and hoists it for examination. Mike should get excited here, but he doesn't. He's caught this bass probably fifteen times before. And this *is* a big bass, buddy. Twenty-one inches long. That's no exaggeration, hey: Mike took a tape measure to it once. And it's weighing something like seven, maybe eight pounds and is a dead weight in Mike's hand. The fish doesn't flip or wobble or nothing. Mike merely looks into its eyes, and it looks into Mike's. They know each other. The fish knows Mike will let it go, and Mike knows he will catch the fish again. They're a profound part of each other's lives. They give each other exercise, relieve each other's boredom. They might be in love.

ON TUESDAY, when it's time to leave for work on Tuesday, a thunder boomer rolls in, intense lightning and sheets of rain, and Mike can't be riding his bicycle to Jennico in this shit. Which is no biggie whatsoever. Because Tuesdays are paydays at Jennico. So Mike drives his Pinto through the rain and smokes and listens to tunes and feels his mind drifting into a pleasantly blank state that's always nice to have at the beginning of a shift. Tonight will be gravy.

He pulls into the Jennico lot at 2:30, and when he gets out of his car, his supervisor, a tall fellow named Rob McCarrie, is standing in the rain near Mike's back bumper and laughing himself blue.

Rob says, "Hey there, slick. You know you got a turd on your bumper?"

It has taken a pounding in the rain, has thinned from the large thing it originally was to a rectangle of brown no bigger around than a Butterfinger bar, but it's a turd nevertheless.

Mike wants to be furious, wants to run into the building, find a BFH—Big Fucking Hammer—and come back out and beat the crap out of his car, or out of the parking-lot asphalt, or out of anything. Twice in four days! But something about being at work and standing in the rain in front of his supervisor suppresses Mike's rage to a mean chuckle.

Mike says, "Looks like the Phantom Shitter has struck again."

LINE THREE is an extrusion blowmolder, a machine that makes detergent bottles, and it's more or less the same as seven other blowmolders in the shop, with the exception that Line Three is bigger than the others and is as a consequence more difficult to change over from one type of bottle setup to another. Tonight, Mike and Rob have to remove four hundred-pound molds from the Line Three, clean them, then install four different hundred-pound molds, hook them up to hoses, reprogram the electronic profiling for the machine, and then do what is known as "running the machine in," a process that, depending on the humidity and the air pressure and a million other factors, can take a full nine-hour shift, if everything goes right.

The work is difficult and requires strength and patience, and tonight's punch line to get through the grind is the Phantom Shitter. Rob really thinks that's hilarious. Keeps asking Mike to tell him the story again, starting with Kerm's on Saturday morning. Way too funny, is what Rob's saying. But the Phantom Shitter could be any joke on any night here at Jennico Inc. because the shifts are always the same: show up, do a changeover, get grimy, and try to make the best of things till midnight.

Blowmolding is situated in the back of the plant, and in between Blowmolding and Filling, where the jugs the blowmolders make are sent to be filled, there's the warehouse, stacked ceiling high with freshly blown bottles and pallets of detergent—filled, labeled, and ready to be shipped to stores in every corner of America, or so the management says in every Jennico newsletter. Also in the warehouse are these useful and entertaining factory tools: the forklift drivers. These are wiry men, with quick reflexes, who spin around the corners too fast and who think nothing of free-climbing a two-story stack of detergent skids to get a SKU number on the very top box. Mike figures they have a much better time at work than he does.

Always at 8:30 on payday, Scooter, one of the forklift drivers, cruises into Blowmolding on his forklift, finds Mike, and says, "the Big Jag." This means that after work they'll go to Hobbsie's Bar and drink nine hours' worth of drinks in the hour and a half before the bar closes.

Tonight when Scooter cruises into Blowmolding, after he

announces the imminent Big Jag, he says, "Somebody's been shitting on your car, hey?"

Mike laughs it off, but he stares for a long time into Scooter's eyes, searching him for guilt.

Mike doesn't really think Scooter's the type to defecate on somebody's car, but for chrissakes: whoever's doing this, it's got to be somebody, well, somebody with exceptional powers of waste withholding. Think about it: In order to take a big dump on Mike's car, you have to hold it in all day, no matter how bad the urge, and wait till you're *absolutely* certain Mike's asleep, which isn't till after about two in the morning, and you always have to know that no matter how late Mike went to sleep he'll for sure be up and kicking around by no later than nine in the morning. Whoever's doing this, hey, it's somebody who knows Mike as well as Mike knows himself. Maybe even better.

So the worknight passes, each half hour Scooter cruising in to confirm the Big Jag, each half hour Mike becoming progressively more irritated that he's got a psycho turd-dropper attacking him, stalking him, knowing his habits and his weaknesses, and by the time the shift's over and folks from work are gathered at Hobbsie's, Mike's frothing with paranoia. If he bellies up to the bar to take a shot with anybody from the crew, he'll say, "It wasn't you who shit on my car, was it?" If he looks at himself in the bathroom mirror and stares through the grime on his face to find his blue eyes, he'll say to himself, "Quit whining, Magnuson. Get over it."

WEDNESDAY. Mike wakes in the morning, goes directly to his Pinto, examines his bumper, and okay then. Good. Nobody's visited during the night's wee hours. Mike's relieved about that. So he wanders downstairs to his musty root cellar and his typewriter and his collection of used paperbacks, and he lights a cigarette and starts to type. He takes an hour or two and writes a story, not a very long one, about a fellow who works in a factory and who one evening plugs his toilet just moments before his big date arrives to eat supper at his place.

When Mike's done typing it out, he reads his little story over and decides that he doesn't have a knack for generating popular-type material; that's for sure. But hey: When Mike took Professor Rutgers's class, Rule Number Goddam One was *Write What You Know*. Mike figures he's doing what his teacher told him to do. He figures Professor Rutgers would be proud of him for making the effort.

Thursday night after work Mike rides his bicycle home, takes a quick shower, and goes to the Joynt to meet up with Fred. The crowd is thin—summertime in a college bar—and Fred's sitting in a corner table with Wanda Skalitsky. They have a pitcher of Leinenkugel's and an ashtray mounded with cigarette butts occupying the space between them, and they're looking very mellowed out. Wanda smiles at Mike, tells him to get a glass. Wanda is older than Mike by a few years. She's thirty or thirty-two, something like that. She's got scraggly black hair and wears glasses and has olive skin and has by God got false teeth, complete, uppers and lowers. She got her teeth knocked out when she was a teenager, training horses or cleaning horse stalls or something like that. False teeth, man. And they're seriously disgusting, too. They absorb the cigarettes she constantly smokes and make her mouth taste and smell like the ashtray she has in front of her right now. And Mike knows for damn certain her mouth is foul-tasting because he's been tasting it a couple-three times a month, sometimes a couple-three times a week, for the last two years.

On the wall behind Wanda and Fred there's a four-by-six-foot framed reproduction of an R. Crumb comic-book cover. *Plunge Into the Depths of Despair* is the name of the comic book, and on it there's a sad and withdrawn middle-aged couple in their living room, the man standing and staring out a window at a rainy day, the woman sitting in an easy chair, staring into a turned-off television.

The man says, "See if there's anything good on."

The woman says, "Why bother?"

Wanda says, "I'm glad you could join us, Mike. Tonight's a special occasion."

Fred nods and urges Wanda to explain.

"We're drinking to misery tonight," Wanda says.

Fred says, "To general misery."

Wanda fills Mike's glass from the pitcher, raises her glass, and Fred raises his, and they toast to being miserable forever.

But misery's a lot of fun. They drain a few pitchers, have a few shots, make fun of their lousy lives, have some laughs at the expense of the Phantom Shitter.

Fred says, "To the Phantom Shitter."

"Amen," Wanda says.

And Mike laughs his ass off.

WHEN BARTIME COMES, the three of them stand for a moment on the sidewalk outside the Joynt, and Mike offers to take Wanda home because, well, she lives four hundred yards down the road from him, in another city-owned duplex on Lake Drive, which is totally where Mike's going anyway. Fred looks at Wanda for a long time in a drunk and grim way, touches her lightly on the forearm. Says, "Have fun, Wanda. It's all been a lot of fun."

Fred walks off into the distance, a skinny taciturn figure in jeans and with his hands in his pockets. It seems to Mike that Fred's head, way out there under the streetlights, has a halo around it. Fred is a patient man, a guy who can let anything happen and not get worked up into a fury. Fred, Mike decides, is ten times the man he'll ever be.

He reaches his hand under Wanda's arm and begins guiding her to his car. "I sure like Fred," he says.

Wanda says, "He's wonderful, isn't he?"

A WHILE LATER, when they're standing outside Wanda's place, Mike decides they shouldn't go right in. He says, "Let's watch the lake for a while." And he leads her through her ratty backyard, past her small garden that she's usually too drunk or too depressed to tend, and they sit in the grass near the shoreline.

Mike says, "There's lots of history to this part of Half Moon Lake."

"I'm sure there is," Wanda says.

She leans into Mike's shoulder, and they cuddle like high school kids might on their first date.

In the middle of the lake the moon creates a streaky reflection over the weeds and the delicate wee-hour chop. A few ducks are out there, fussing about something, probably a muskrat swimming too close to them. Mike can see the lights illuminating the road that passes through Carson Park, and on the other end of the lake, blackness and small frogs singing. The end of the world.

THE NEXT MORNING at ten o'clock Mike rolls his bicycle out his front door. The skies—perfectly blue. The breeze—not a puff of it. He can't dream of a better day for cycling. He wheels his bike to the street, mounts it, and pedals away, not looking back, not thinking anything but how his pumping legs seem to be one with the world, how his bike glides out of Eau Claire and into the countryside, how strong he feels when he lifts from the saddle and charges the hills large and small. He *is* healthy, and he did make love last evening, the touching and tenderness lingering in his body and making him feel like maybe, just maybe, he's getting something wonderful from life, even if his larger dreams will never come true. He's happy.

When he gets home, he eats lunch—cold pasta and toasted wheat bread and two apples—and he takes Maroon the dog for a long walk through Carson Park, and it doesn't matter to him that when a squirrel appears ahead of him on the trail, when it scampers up the side of an oak and chatters, that Maroon is too stupid to know the squirrel is even there. Maroon can't help it that she's a stupid dog.

At 2:30 he mounts the bike again, strong and relaxed and ready for a six-mile spin toward another Jennico slog, and he turns back for one last glance at the house, at his Pinto in front of it. Sure enough: The Phantom has struck. This time there are *two* turds in an X-pile on the Pinto's back bumper.

Mike dismounts his bike, sets it on the ground, and strides with even, calm strides to his car, bends to the turds, sees that they've dried during the day. Must have been deposited here roundabout dawn.

He thinks about making fists and yelling at the top of his lungs, but he whispers instead. He says, "This is fan-fucking-tastic."

Maroon is sprawling near the maple tree, snoozing, twitching her paws and ears, dreaming about nothing in particular. The maple's leaves quiver in the faintest, tiredest way. Across Half Moon Lake, in the picnic area at Carson Park, a few children yip with glee. Eau Claire: the quaint life.

How's he gonna find who's doing this anyway? Hide all night in Maroon's doghouse or up in the maple tree, waiting for the Phantom to appear? Ridiculous. And he sure as hell can't call the goddam *police* and tell them somebody's been defecating on his car. The police ain't gonna be believing *that*. They're not *stupid*. And besides, what are the police gonna do about it? Take one of the Phantom's turds and do a chemical analysis of it and compare the results against sample turds submitted by suspects in the case? One of Fred's maybe? Or Wanda's? Or Griffin's? Or Caryn's? Or maybe from one of the dudes at work? Lordy. It's out of hand, is what it is.

Here's what Mike thinks: Fuck all of this. He's gonna leave the turds on the bumper, hey. That will freak the Phantom out completely. Like this: Here the Phantom comes, ready to drop his or her ass on Mike's Pinto, and yesterday's turds are still there. And nobody, not even Maroon, will take a shit on yesterday's turds.

ON HIS BIKE. Pedaling toward work. He's thinking how he'll spend his Friday evening being a productive citizen who appreciates making seven bucks an hour getting grimy and sweating and dreaming of Big Jags when work is done, and he's beginning to feel a swarm of rages gathering inside him. He's going through the he's-really-turned-out-to-be-a-piece-of-crud types of things a guy gets to feeling about himself when he's feeling sorry for himself. His pedal strokes become rough jabs at the ground. He summons all his leg-muscle power to crank the pedals hard and make the bike go faster, but he can't go faster. Angry strokes never make a bike go faster.

He rolls along Galloway Street, the road that passes Fred's house and the Uniroyal plant. He hears hollering coming from Fred's house, but he doesn't think much of it; there's always hollering coming from Fred's house.

He cranks down the three-mile flat north on Starr Avenue, toward the airport from which Buddy Holly once flew before going to Iowa and dying with Ritchie Valens and them. Toward Jennico. The horrible life beyond. He has a dim memory of the beach party he'd gone to years ago, the one where he floated a keg across the Eau Claire river during a lightning storm. He wishes for a time machine, a way to transport himself back to that moment in the driving rain, with the lightning crashing all around him. He wants to stay there in the rising river longer and die once and for all right then. For if lightning had fried his ass right then, he wouldn't have lived to be in the rut he's in now: work, booze, cheating on his old lady, turds on his car.

He comes to the railroad tracks that cross Starr Avenue near the VFW hall and the genuine honest-to-God World War II Sherman tank they got parked in front of it, by the flagpole, and Mike fixes his eye on the tank barrel, wishes it would fire at him, and while he's wishing, he bumps too hard over the railroad tracks, and the bump jars his water bottle loose from its cage. The bottle drops and wedges itself under the bike's back tire, causing the bike to slip as if it's on sheet ice. And the bike slips. And Mike topples to the street. His helmet bashes the asphalt.

He can see the curb next to him, the sand from which it's made sparkling in the afternoon sun. He can hear cars passing him, not slowing down to see if he's okay. He can feel himself breathing and sweating and can see a long scrape along his right leg, can feel that his elbow's been hammered good. But he can move. He wiggles his feet just to see if he can. And the sky: so blue. The asphalt: warm and pleasant. Stillness. Heaven.

Now a voice in the void: "Magnuson, I hope you're dead." This is Rob McCarrie, Mike's supervisor. "Because if you're not, you better get your ass off the ground and get on in to work."

Scooter's here, too. He says, "He ain't *dead*, Rob."

Mike says, "That's unfortunate."

Rob and Scooter help Mike to his feet, and Mike tests out his legs, discovers that he indeed can walk just fine, which means to Rob that Mike's good to go for tonight's shift. Mike examines his bike and notes that it hasn't received one noticeable scratch. Amazing. He sets the bike in the back of Scooter's pickup, and you betcha: it's heigh-ho, off to work we go, buddy. You shouldn't be riding that bike, Magnuson. What are you *thinking*?

THE MACHINES for once in a lifetime are all running properly, which means the night's cake and cookies. No changeovers. No busting ass and getting filthier than fuck. But Mike's not in a cake-and-cookies mood. Six hours after he crashed, and his body's seized up, achy, in need of serious lube. His elbow's bruised big-time yellow and still bleeding from the middle, and the scrape on his leg is hurting like an overused dick whenever he moves around and it rubs against his overalls.

The time: after nine, after lunch break. Mike's hanging in the mold room, cleaning the brass fittings on a sixty-four-ounce detergent-jug mold, removing the chiller-sludge buildup from them, killing time, trying his best not to think about anything, and being moderately successful at it, and Rob pages him over the loudspeaker.

He figures Caryn's calling because she sometimes does this time of night; something fires in her heart when she's getting ready for bed and realizes she's gone another week without seeing Mike once or talking to him once. Tough to be Caryn, isn't it?

So Mike doesn't hustle to the blowmolding office to pick up the phone. Besides, he can't really hustle anyway. His carcass is fucked up. Racked. He shuffles to the blowmolding office, kicks his feet up on the desk, and answers the phone.

This is not Caryn. This is Patricia Nelson calling.

"It's Fred," she's saying. Frenzied in her exponential-frenzy way. "You gotta come right away."

Mike glances at a calendar on the office wall. Miss Snap-On Tools. July. 1990. July is a brunette, frizzy hair, oiled legs and boobs, and she's wearing Daisy Duke jean shorts and staring at a Snap-On pneumatic impact wrench as if it's the love of her life. Today is July 17, and Miss July's been staring at that impact wrench for a long time.

Mike says, with a pained exhale, "What's Fred *doing*?"

Patricia says, *Oh my God* loud enough to sound like she's screaming it. "Fred wants to *die*! You gotta come and *save* him."

"I'll see what I can do," Mike says, and hangs up.

If Mike weren't at work, he'd never be saying *I'll see what I can do*. Away from work, he won't do shit for anybody; the thought never crosses his mind. But think about it: If Mike goes and does something about Fred, he can split from work early.

So Mike tells Rob that major troubles are up, and because tonight's a gravy night and Rob can handle things easy without him for the rest of the shift: Cool, man. Split. But just this one time, okay?

And Mike clocks out for the evening, dons his bike clothes, and commences a sore pedal through the darkness toward Fred's house. He follows the same route he took to work, passes over the railroad tracks, this time without jarring loose his water bottle. He's pedaling with calm, even strokes now. He feels no rage. He can't ever remember being angry, not once in his life. He's feeling free.

Aₙ ᴀᴍʙᴜʟᴀɴᴄᴇ and a couple of squad cars are parked at Fred's, their chaselights swirling and giving Fred's house and the tall maples around it a happy, Christmassy look. Ah, those bright whirling colors here on a dull night in July. Festive.

He's in a full lather from riding. The sweating and the cranking of bike pedals: it's eliminated the racks and agonies from his body. He's a new man. He leans his bike against a tree and makes his way through Fred's unfinished patio to the screen door that leads to Fred's kitchen, and just at that moment paramedics appear in the doorway, wheeling a gurney, and there's Fred on it, strapped in. He's not wearing his glasses, and his eyes are open wide and as clear as today's sky was. He's grinning, or maybe he's not grinning, but a policeman holds Mike back and won't let Mike get close enough to get a really good look at Fred.

The paramedics load Fred into the back of the ambulance, no problem. The guy can't weigh more than 140. He's a paperweight. A paramedic's dream.

Now Patricia appears on the patio, looking no more or no less haggard than usual, and before she climbs into the ambulance with Fred, she approaches Mike and offers him a set of car keys.

She jingles the keys absently. Says, "Too late to save the day."

"Sorry," Mike says. Gaspy-sounding. He's trying to come off worn out from the ride, but he's not worn at all.

Patricia says, "Doesn't matter. He didn't do it."

"Do what?"

Patricia shakes her head, hands Mike the car keys. Says, "These are for the Subaru."

Fred hollers from the back of the ambulance: "A screwdriver! Make sure Mike's got a screwdriver!"

A paramedic says to Patricia, "Ma'am, it's best we get going."

Mike knows what the screwdriver means; the Subaru's got a broken starter solenoid, and in order to start it, a guy has to open the hood and place a screwdriver blade between the starter and the solenoid, letting the spark pass along it: then the car will start.

Patricia climbs into the ambulance, and after a second pops her head out. Says, "Take the Subaru and follow me to the emergency room, will you, Mike? I'll be needing a ride home."

Mike says that's what he'll do, and the ambulance doors close, and a policeman, a thin fellow a few inches taller than Mike and a few years younger, a kid with a brand-new Criminology degree and a kickass new job, moves over to Mike and stands uncomfortably close to him.

The ambulance slowly rolls out of Fred's driveway and drives away in no hurry, its chase lights still whirling and making a beautiful jangly display on the leaves of the boulevard trees.

The cop taps Mike on the shoulder. Says, "You're a friend of those people, hey?"

"I guess you could say that," Mike says. He tinkles the car keys to prove it.

The cop says, "Buddy, those two are really something."

"That they are," Mike says. "Better than watching TV."

Mike lugs his backpack into Fred's house to change out of his bike togs and back into his work clothes. What the fuck: A guy can't be wearing bike togs to the emergency room, right? He takes a moment to reconnoiter. Some empty Olympia cans are in the living room, along with Patricia's guitar and a pile of song lyrics that she's written on legal pads. But otherwise the place is looking clean and dusted and innately civilized. If Fred indeed attempted suicide here, he didn't make a very spectacular attempt.

So fifteen minutes later, Mike's walking into the emergency room. Calm. Magnanimous. It's not Mike who fucked up. Not *this* time. And here's the situation: Fred's parents are sitting in the waiting room. Fred's dad, Dr. Lester, is rail-thin, like Fred, and has a coarse gray beard and wears little round T. S. Eliot glasses of the exact type Fred wears. He's a psychology professor at the university and is clearly the perpetrator of Fred. He rises in a rickety way to shake Mike's hand,

and Mike takes the hand and links eyes with him—weary eyes, black bags hanging under them, but the whites are as white as white can be. Dr. Lester hasn't been crying.

Mike says, because he knows he has to say *something,* "What did Fred do?"

"We don't know," Dr. Lester says. "We're happy at this point that he didn't take pills." Dr. Lester knows the drill with these things; psychology professors are the type who do. He says, "They'll give him seventy-two hours on Ward Five, I'm sure. Then he'll be reevaluated and released, is my guess."

Now Patricia appears in the waiting room, smiling a huge, put-on-for-her-in-laws smile. She stands by Mike but doesn't look at him, merely at Fred's dad.

She says, "We can come in and see him now."

Fred's mother gets to her feet, grasps her husband's arm, and they follow Patricia out of the waiting room. Patricia turns to Mike, rolls her eyes to suggest that this is *really* tedious, dealing with in-laws. She tells Mike that he should come along, too. Fred will *really* appreciate seeing him.

THEY GOT FRED in a curtained-off cubicle, sprawled on a narrow examination bed and staring at the ceiling. He's wearing a hospital gown, his chest hairs exploding from the neck line. He's looking normal enough. He levels his eyes at his wife, his mother, his father, his drinking buddy. Says, "How *is* everybody this evening?"

Mike doesn't think. He instantly says, "Great. I got off work early."

"That's terrific," Fred says, his voice exactly like it always sounds.

Then Fred turns his eyes to his dad. "Looks like I'll get out Monday morning."

"That's the standard procedure," Dr. Lester says.

"Then I guess I'll be an outpatient for a week or two."

"Correct." Dr. Lester lapses into a deep ponder, scratches his head in a gesture of professorial thought. "Which psychiatrist has been assigned to you?"

"Gunderson, I think."

"Oh. He's very good. Very good."

They're discussing this shit the way they might discuss hiring somebody to do yard work or to fix the car. Routine stuff.

Two male orderlies arrive with a wheelchair; they're going to wheel Fred to the elevator and get him situated on the hospital's fifth floor. The Psych Ward. Ward 5. Fred stares long at Mike, one of those deep Fredlike glances that Mike's never before understood, but Mike can understand perfectly what Fred's eyes are saying tonight: *Look at my loveless life.*

Fred's feet are protruding from the sheet he's under. He's wearing nice rag-wool socks, warm wool, expensive socks, quality workmanship, comfortable, and for some reason Mike leans forward and gently grasps one of Fred's big toes, wiggles it like this little piggy went to market and ended up with a horseshit life.

Then the orderlies load Fred into the chair and wheel him away.

Mike drives Patricia home and doesn't bicker with her. Hey: It's *her* car. And she's panicky and crazy, of course, shifting from one mood to another, shouting "Oh, my God" one moment then laughing or whispering the next. But Mike refuses to toy with her, to goad her, to make sport of her instability. Nope. He ain't doing that to her anymore. He says, "Look, I'll be home all tomorrow. Call me the instant you need something."

Patricia's overjoyed. "See?" she says. Touches his leg. "We're friends after all. We're like *family.*"

Even when Griffin arrives to be with Patricia in this darkest hour, Mike is a pleasant person. He takes Griffin aside and tells her, "She needs you right now more than she ever has. Be there for her."

Be there for her. Mike's too overcome with pleasantness to recognize the irony in saying that.

So Patricia gives him the Subaru for the weekend; he does own his own ride, his Pinto, and Patricia knows this, and my God she just *can't* drive at a time like this, but really she just *can't* be shuttled around town in a tainted vehicle. Which Mike totally understands. He doesn't want a tainted vehicle, either.

SATURDAY he sleeps through the day, doesn't notice Caryn taking the dog with her to her mother's, doesn't do anything but saw logs and rise every few hours to pee, and he doesn't bother going outside to see if the Phantom has struck. He's sleeping off eight years of being an asshole. Which is remarkably easy.

AT SIX IN THE EVENING, Patricia calls, says everything's okay with Fred. He's in fine spirits, is eating and sleeping and has attended group therapy this afternoon, which Fred's dad is saying is a wonderful sign. Still, Fred's dad has worries. Fred's dad's thinking there's good cause to extend Fred's commitment to Ward 5 beyond the state-mandated seventy-two hours.

Mike says, "Are they gonna keep him for a month or something?"

"Maybe," Patricia says. "But he'd like to see you tomorrow. At one o'clock. We'll go together. That okay?"

Mike tells her everything's going to be fine, that he's there for her no matter what. One o'clock's great. Then he hangs up and sleeps again.

TOWARD DAWN he's slept all the sleep out of himself. He's dreamed and tossed and turned and sweated through the sheets and shivered while they dried and dreamed and tossed and turned and sweated and shivered all over again, and he's feeling fresher than he's felt in years. He gets out of bed, tugs on a T-shirt and a pair of gym shorts, puts on a pair of shoes, and goes outside.

The night is black and star-freckled, maybe a half hour till the first spits of light spread through the trees from the east. Near the lake, crickets and frogs yammer softly, become quieter with each passing moment. In the far distance, not a single vehicle moves. Sunday morning predawn, the last instant before Christ returns for His weekly visit, and Eau Claire is dead.

Mike inspects his Pinto's back bumper; the X-piled turds are still there, which means either (1) leaving them there actually *did* deter the Phantom, or (2) the Phantom has yet to appear. Up and down the alleyway, nothing moves, and Mike listens hard into the darkness, searching in the void for the truth in a Sylvia Plath line Professor Rutgers once read in class: "The sweet deep throat of the nightflower." He knows this kind of pitch-dead dark is sweet indeed, full of possibility, for this is the hour of the Phantom.

No sound down the alley. Not the slightest flutter in the nearby trees. The lake: glass, not one duck or muskrat swimming out there. He hides himself behind a bush near the alley, near the corner of the fence, stands there as motionlessly as he can and tunes his ears to the night, to the approaching crunch of the Phantom.

And the Phantom approaches. Shuffling steps. Light. Indiscriminate. Human steps. This person isn't in any hurry: a few steps, a sound like scuffing at the asphalt, maybe kicking at a pebble, a few more steps. Now the steps even out, assume an easy stride toward Mike and his bush, and sure enough, not ten feet from Mike, the steps halt.

A Zippo flashes, and there, lighting a cigarette, stands Wanda Skalitsky. She cups the flame with her long-fingered hands, the flame highlighting the elegance of her cheekbones—a scraggly woman out here smoking in the night's last deep throes of darkness.

Mike moves from behind the bush, clears his throat to announce himself.

Wanda shrieks, throws out her arms, in the process dropping the Zippo, which dings distinctly on the asphalt. "Jesus, Mike. You scared me." She bends to the ground to find the lighter, but she can't find it. Too dark out to see.

Mike goes to her and bends to help her, and sure enough he finds it right away, and when he hands it back to Wanda, she lets her fingertip slide gently along his thumb.

She says, "I'm glad you found that. That's not mine."

"Whose is it?"

"Fred's."

There. Fred.

They don't say anything for a time. They lose themselves in an awkward, eye-rubbing moment thinking about him.

Finally, Mike says, "You heard about it, then?"

Wanda says that she has.

Another lost moment. Sure. Fred deserves all the lost moments he can get.

Mike says, "Whatcha doing walking around this time of night?"

"Couldn't sleep." She pops open the Zippo and thumbs absently at the flint, producing an occasional tiny spark. "Thought I'd take a walk."

"I couldn't sleep either." For reasons Mike can't understand he reaches for Wanda's hand and holds it, pulls it so she's face-to-face with him: her body, smooth and olive, her brown tangly hair that's soft to the touch, hair that Mike's touched so many times before. No way. Wanda simply *can't* be the Phantom.

Mike says, "I don't have any sleep left in me."

"I understand." She senses something urgent and sad in his grip on her hand, she must, because she lets go and takes a few steps away from him, backpedals to the center of the alley. "Everything's gotten too crazy."

A ways away, a robin begins singing in a maple tree. Light begins smudging into the eastern sky.

"I'm going home now," Wanda says. "See you some other time."

"Yeah," Mike says. "Some other time."

And she walks away. Mike doesn't watch her go, keeps his eyes instead on the spreading blue light in the east, how it seems to intensify the darkness, to give it shapes and depth and sound, more robins singing, a duck somewhere out on the lake erupting in anger. Wanda has just dumped Mike. Simple as that. Over with. Two years, they've been living on the same street, rendezvousing a few times a week, gentle to each other when they were alone, caressing, saying gentle words. Mike's been in love with Wanda all this time, and there you have it, buck: It's over.

WHEN DAYLIGHT is full and bright blue Mike goes inside, sprawls on the couch, and watches cartoons. A couple of Bugs Bunnies. A couple of Daffy Ducks. A Foghorn Leghorn. The cartoons make him smile, always have. He relaxes. He feels okay. And hey, he doesn't really *love* Wanda. He's bullshitting himself if he thinks he does. He just *fucks* her once in a while. Ain't no point getting mopey over her.

A MOVEMENT outside the window. A commotion. Splashing. Mike hears a kid hollering, and then sees him. The kid's got a cheap fishing rig—a Zebco push-button spinning outfit, which is one level above your Snoopy pole—and the kid's in the process of horsing Mike's prize bass to the shore. The bass surges and jumps and swashes and makes great gouts of weedy foam. The bass must know it's not Mike who's hooked her this time.

Mike bolts outside as quick as he can, runs around the house, and appears beside the kid, who has in the interim managed to drag the bass on shore. She flops and twists and is in the process getting covered in a disease of slimy grass blades. Mike bends to the bass, gently grasps her lips, and hoists her. The fishhook's in one corner of her upper lip, a piece of worm there. Jesus. She's gone through all this, and she still hasn't got to eat the goddam worm. Up and down the lip are various holes and nicks and ragged gashes from all the times Mike's caught her before.

The kid is scrawny and grinning so hard he can't say anything.

Mike says, "She's a nice fish."

The kid keeps grinning, looks like he's just about to weep for joy.

Mike says, "Now let's put her back in the lake."

The kid contemplates the lake, the fish's freedom; then he looks down the shoreline, where a man in a feedcap and a flannel shirt is running this way. The kid yells, "*Do* something, Dad! This guy's taking away my *trophy*!"

Mike doesn't give a fuck about trophies. He bends to the water and dips the bass in. He keeps hold of her lip, moves her back in forth in the shallows, trying to restimulate the gills, but she's not responding. She's been topside too long. She twitches now and then, but that's it.

The dad in the feedcap grabs Mike by the shoulder. Says, "What the hell do you think you're doing, buddy?"

Mike doesn't like to be grabbed, and he jerks himself erect, the bass still in his grip, and heaves her into the man's face. "This," Mike says, "is *my* fish."

"Give me a break," the dad says. "You didn't catch this fish."

The dad isn't quite Mike's size, but he's thick about the shoulders and has something recessed and murky about his eye sockets that gives Mike pause. Might not be smart to provoke this guy much more than he already has.

Mike says, "I live here." He points to his duplex, which the dad regards, takes in the ratty shingles, the rusted-through gutters, the dirty windows, the shabby shrubs.

The dad says, "You *own* this?"

Mike doesn't say anything. The bass flexes. Her dorsal fin expands, once, and contracts. *Old friend, you're dying.*

The dad says, "What kind of asshole are you?"

In the bass's eyes, something—Mike swears it's instantaneously—smears and becomes opaque, her death's milk-film appearing in the black buttons of her eyes and spreading across them, as if she knows the time's come to quit going on. *Let the kid have me*, is what she's decided.

"I'll tell you what I am," Mike says. "I'm the usual kind of asshole." And he hands the bass over to the dad and walks away, heads back around his house to go back to the junk heap inside.

He hears the dad say to his son, "I'm proud of you, Tommy. You're a fine fisherman."

Pᴀsᴛ ɴᴏᴏɴ. Maybe a quarter past. It's almost time to go pick up Patricia and take her to visit Fred on Ward 5. But he doesn't want to go anywhere. He's not ready. He wants to think about things for a while, a few days, a week. To treat that kid that way! Jesus! The kid didn't know any better. He couldn't possibly have known the intricate relationship and mutual understanding Mike had going on with the bass. He was just out there on a sunny day wetting his worm for a while, hoping to catch a bluegill or two, and, whammo, he caught the biggest bass he would ever catch in his life. And there was Mike: ruining everything.

He showers, scrubs and scrubs at his hands, but the fish-slime smell won't go away. It lingers there on his fingers, mixes with the creased-in Jennico blowmolding grease and hydraulic fluid, sinks into the cuts and crusty calluses on Mike's hands. He puts on clean clothes, washes his hands again, this time with Comet Cleanser, but still his hands smell like bass.

Pᴀᴛʀɪᴄɪᴀ ɪs sᴇʀᴇɴᴇ, placid, nothing jumpy about her whatsoever. She hugs Mike when he arrives, squeezes him with all her strength, buries her nose deeply and wetly into his neck. She doesn't smell like bass. She smells of sandalwood and lilacs. She's the best-smelling woman Mike's ever known.

She says, "Let's be calm and try not to upset him."

Calm. Sure. Mike is calm.

Wᴀʀᴅ 5 is partitioned from the fifth floor elevator foyer by a plate-glass wall, in the middle of which is a glass doorway and several-foot glass hallway, at the end of which stands a security guard. He's mid-

dle-aged, grizzled but not paunchy and not wearing a gun on his uniform belt. He sees Patricia first, smiles at her. Heartfelt. Patricia's
pupil-less eyes must display to him the kind of profound concern a
wife with a husband on Ward 5 should have. But when the guard sees
Mike—ratty hair, beard, bloodshot eyes, torn shirt, grimy gym-
teacher shorts and old factory-filthy shoes—he tenses up.

Patricia approaches the guard's counter, puts her hands on it, and
identifies herself as Fred Lester's wife, and she identifies Mike as Fred's
best friend, which information seems to bother the guard. He frowns
at Mike, but says they can go ahead and sign the visitor's book and
wait for Fred over there in the sunroom for a few minutes.

The sunroom isn't particularly sunny. Two picture windows with
mesh woven into the glass allow in a feeble version of the afternoon
blaze. Cigarette smoke hangs before the window and everywhere in
here, over the institutional sofas and straight-backed chairs and end
tables that hold up institutional lamps. Several patients sit on the
sofas, smoking and chatting grimly with friends or family. One patient
is a young chubby trailer-court woman, no more than twenty. She's
wearing a baggy flannel shirt and blue jeans, has bags under her eyes
and smokes in panicky, cram-in-the-nicotine drags, and she's talking
with an older woman of the same build and haircut and wearing the
same type of flannel shirt and jeans. The patient's mother. The only
way Mike can tell for sure the younger one is the patient is because
she's wearing a pink hospital wristband.

The patient says, "To hell with Jimmy. He'll never change."

"I know it," the mother says. "But what can you do?"

A bubble of thought and cigarette smoke hangs between them,
remains there in a chasm of quiet, a smoke-eater's fan spinning,
nurses chatting with each other in codes, in murmurs, patients coughing somewhere in the recesses of the ward's corridors, and here's Fred
all of a sudden: He's wearing his regular jeans, his regular reserved
smile, and sunken eyes.

He takes a seat next to Patricia but doesn't take her hand. He fixes
his eyes on Mike. Says, "How's the Subaru running?"

"Fine," Mike says. He can't look at Fred. The mother and daughter are leaning back in their sofa cushions, new smokes lit, gazing through the window mesh at the day. "Or once she gets started she's fine, Fred."

"The Subaru," Fred says, "has always been a difficult vehicle."

"I imagine," Mike says.

A quiet spell passes, Mike staring at Fred's hospital wristband, Fred noticing, adjusting it over his wrist bones, Mike averting his eyes.

Finally Patricia brushes her hands together and stands. "So. It's nice we're all together. Mike's like *family* to you, Fred. Isn't he?"

Fred stands, too, but doesn't respond to Patricia, doesn't look at her, doesn't make any attempt whatsoever to register her presence. He moves to the window, presses his hands to the glass, and gazes out. "Mike, you know what *defenestrate* means?"

"What's that?"

"It means to jump out a window."

Mike rises automatically, steps toward Fred. "That's enough of that kinda talk, Fred."

"Don't worry, Mike. I couldn't defenestrate anyway. I'd have to *transfenestrate*, which means to jump *through* a window, not jump *out* of one."

Mike shouldn't laugh, but he does. And he says, "So if a guy in the movies gets thrown through a window he's *transfenestrating*?"

"Exactly."

The mesh in the glass dulls the glint on the cars parked in the parking lot five stories below, but they sparkle nevertheless. They're so tidy, so neat in their rows, so small. Mike sees his life, a thing he knows only in flashes—a phantom, a friend on Ward 5, a broken-off affair with a woman who wears dentures, a big bass dying—and he can't say anything at all.

But Fred can. "*Transfenestrating*," he says. "That's always been the sticking point for me."

MIKE SUCCESSFULLY jimmy-starts the Subaru with the screw-driver, gets the spark to pass through it from the starter to the sole-noid, and he closes the hood, climbs into the driver's seat, sets the screwdriver on the dashboard. Patricia is crying—not theatrical tears, just flat-faced, stare-straight-forward tears. Mike reaches a hand to her shoulder and touches it, massages it, and she leans into him, holds him and weeps into his shoulders. She doesn't shudder or shake; her eyes merely leak. Mike clenches with her like this for a long time, five minutes maybe, till, just like that, she pulls away, runs her hands through her hair, and exhales herself back together again.

"Enough of this moping around already," she says. "Let's go to the bar."

THEY GO TO THE JOYNT. Of course. This is nearly three o'clock, Sunday afternoon, a beautiful summer day when people should be outside playing Frisbee or swimming or gardening or doing anything else but hanging in the tavern. But the Joynt is packed. Folks line the bar and sit at the corner tables, by the picture windows, drinking pitchers and eating peanuts, tossing the shells on the wood floor. The afternoon light is strong and shining into the barroom, bleaching the darkness, giving it a washed-out look, like everybody here is drinking in a black-and-white movie.

Mike and Patricia make their entrance properly. Smile at everyone. Say hello to those who say hello. They find themselves two stools in the center of the bar, between the bathrooms, and order a pitcher of Leinenkugel's. And they drink happily. And if everybody in the bar knows that Fred's on Ward 5 for the weekend, which they probably do, nobody lets on. The Joynt's not a place for all that; this place is for kicking back and getting smashed and being obnoxious and laughing and having a great time.

So for several hours Patricia and Mike kick back and get smashed and have a few laughs. Sometimes Fred, the subject, comes up, but usually only in passing. Patricia's explaining all the vagaries of her career in music, what she hopes will happen. She figures on going to Nashville with Griffin and trying to get some regular gigs, and if she and Griffin can't make it as recording artists, they sure as hell can write songs for people.

"They're good songs," Patricia says.

Mike agrees. Sure. They're good. What the hell.

And Mike's got dreams, too. He gets into explaining his hopes for a better way of living. He says, "We all need to love each other a little more."

Patricia is so taken with this notion that she throws her arms around Mike's neck and kisses him on the lips, a friend's kiss that lingers a moment into the lover's zone, into the time when Mike breathes himself goofy with Patricia's lovely sandalwood smell and feels in her soft nose brushing against his the final release of everything bad he's ever done. He's going to be a better friend to his friends now. He's going goddammit to start *caring*.

When they let go of each other, they do the shrug-and-grin thing folks do when they've kissed each other and, well, liked it a lot, and bam: A voice bellows directly behind their bar stools.

"Now I know what you do when I'm not around," the voice says.

It's Griffin. She's got on a black T-shirt that stretches over her big shoulders nearly to the point of ripping. She lifts a heavy hand to her glasses and adjusts them on her nose, as if to see better the atrocity of Patricia Nelson and Mike Magnuson sitting together and getting along in the bar. *Kissing in the bar, for crying out loud!* Griffin's cheeks flush from the eyes down to the jowls, and her lower lip distends in a disgusted sneer. She glares at Patricia. Says, "It's always about *you*."

Patricia's biggest problem: She doesn't possess the ability to think things out. Listen to what she says: "You're looking thinner today, Griffin."

Stupid.

Griffin's cheeks turn into beefsteak tomatoes. "Don't pull that with me, Patricia. I'm the fat piece of shit you can trample on when you can't find anybody else to trample on."

Patricia says, "I am *trying* to be nice."

Griffin wags a fingertip toward Mike. Says, "You wanna be nice? You can start by losing Mr. Asshole here."

"Oh," Patricia says, and meets eyes briefly with Mike, tries to smile officially. "Mike went with me to see Fred in the *hospital*."

Mike's guess: She's trying to elicit sympathy from Griffin.

But Griffin doesn't have any. She says, "Like I'm saying, it's *always* about you."

Patricia turns to the bar and musters a cheery voice to order a glass for Griffin, and while the glass is on its way, she says to Griffin, "See, it's not always about *me*. I'm getting you a beer."

"Great," Griffin says. "Get the fat bitch a beer. That'll shut her up."

Patricia says, "Just trying to be sociable."

"Try harder." Griffin folds her arms and waits for Patricia to try.

And Patricia does try. The bartender gives her an empty glass, and she hands it to Mike, who in turn fills it from the pitcher and hands the glass to Griffin.

Mike says, "I think we're all having a hard time."

"Everybody but *you*," Griffin says and cuts a sudden laser-beam glance into Mike's eyes. Her face bulges with loathing, and in the moment when she's just taken the glass from Mike, when he hasn't yet withdrawn his hand, she seizes Mike's hand, his right hand, the hand that held the gigantic bass by the lip this morning, and she draws it to her nose and sniffs it.

Mike yanks his hand away, but this is too late. Griffin's detected the scent of an unimaginable crime. Mike's hand smells of Patricia, her sandalwood-oil perfume, and of dead bass, the combination of which, well, what else can Griffin think?

She doesn't speak. She merely lifts her beer glass high, leans toward Patricia, and dumps the beer on top of Patricia's head.

Patricia extends her arms and holds absolutely still, stares down at the beer dripping from her hair to her lap.

Griffin says, "Now you're paying attention to *me*."

Up till now, nobody in the bar's been paying attention to *them*, but now Patricia begins to wail. She bawls full-out, full-throttle, three-year-old-throwing-a-tantrum style. A hush spreads through the bar, and people stare, and Patricia bawls and bawls.

Drunk. Mike's as bagged as potatoes in Kerm's. But nobody would know it. He instantly does the correct thing: He takes action. He gathers his cigarettes, the Subaru keys, and Patricia, and leads her, still bawling, out the back entrance of the Joynt, and they stand for a moment in the alley, trying to collect themselves.

Patricia shakes, blubbers. *Oh, my God. Oh, my God. Oh, my God.*

Dusk is setting in, a yellowing in the western sky, and Mike can see sparrows flocking together for a night in the treetops. The sparrows chip and chatter.

Mike puts a hand on Patricia's shoulder, slick with beer. "Listen, we'll go to my place for a while and cool out. Griffin won't think to look for us there."

Patricia's crying reduces to a sniffle, and she tries to smile. She's feeling better. "You have beer at your house?" she manages to say.

"Got a few," Mike says. "But we can stop and get some more on the way home, if that's what you want."

Now she stops crying entirely, takes his hand. Says, "I'd like that, Mike. Thanks. I mean, for everything."

Before Mike can say *Anytime* or *No Problem*, the Joynt's back door slams open, and Griffin's there, redder than ever, looking bigger and nastier than ever.

She speaks to Patricia. "Let's get something straight: You are *not* leaving this bar with Mike goddam Magnuson."

He's a man of action. He leans to Patricia's ear and whispers, "Just do what I say, all right?"

Patricia nods that she will, and Griffin takes offense.

"What did you tell her, Magnuson? Ignore the fat bitch? Is that what?"

Mike says, "Griffin, you gotta calm down. This is ridiculous."

Griffin says, "You are *not* taking Patricia with you. That's all there is to it."

Mike says, "We're leaving, Griffin, and there's nothing you're gonna do about it."

Mike's been playing this correctly so far, but now he's made a serious mistake. He's threatened Griffin. The worst thing he possibly could have done. And here comes the fallout: Griffin shoves Mike in the shoulder, hard, much PSI tonnage thrust behind the shove, nearly knocking Mike over, and she lunges for Mike's hand to grab the keys.

She says, "Don't fucking tell *me* there's nothing I can do."

Patricia screams, puts her hands to her head.

But Griffin isn't going to get the keys. Mike's got his thumb slipped through the chain ring. "You ain't getting these keys," Mike says. "So leave it be."

He takes Patricia by the arm and begins leading her down the alley toward the Subaru. She's bawling, shuddering, not able to speak. She's saying, "Waaaaaaaa!"

But Mike tugs her along and keeps his weight lowered, making ready in the old freestyle wrestler's way to keep his balance, to stay on his feet in case Griffin rushes at him again.

And Griffin follows, maintains a steady course a short distance from Mike's shoulder, her 275 pounds of anger and hate at point-blank striking range, but she doesn't pounce and doesn't utter a sound, doesn't even seem to be breathing. Mike picks up the pace, pulls on Patricia to speed up, and she does, and Griffin adjusts her steps to maintain her range.

Above the alley, over the trees: dusk. The nightfall reverberates with the partying sounds of Water Street coming briefly alive on a summer Sunday night—car doors slamming, young men hooting and whistling, young women giggling—the bars filling up with folks who've spent their Sunday picnicking or water-skiing and being beautiful carefree people for whom beautiful summer Sundays are made.

Here's the Subaru, silvery gray in the fading light on the corner of

Third and Water. Mike bends to the driver's door, sees across the street a mixed-sex pack of college students, tanned and grimy from a day at the beach, loafing toward the bar, and he unlocks the door and opens it. He pops the hood latch, retrieves the screwdriver off the dashboard, and stands to face Patricia and Griffin.

Griffin's moored on the boulevard, nothing in her eyes, her mouth slack, hands balled near the vast pockets of her jeans. Patricia's at Mike's shoulder.

Mike whispers into Patricia's ear: "Take the wheel. When I jump the starter solenoid, pump the gas, okay?"

"I know what to do," Patricia says. Her voice: a maudlin flute mixing with the music of the Water Street dusk.

When she slides past Mike to get in, Mike whispers, "And lock the door."

Patricia does as she's told, and now Mike raises the hood, and when he's got it propped open and bends over the engine to touch the screwdriver to the solenoid, Griffin makes her move. She lowers her shoulder and slams into him at a run, knocking Mike back from the car. But he plants his leg and doesn't fall. Griffin reaches across his chest and tries to grab the screwdriver, and Mike stops thinking. He lurches forward with a tremendous push of his legs, puts his shoulder into Griffin's tits and drives her back from the car, drives her so hard that she loses her balance, and she smashes hard on to the boulevard grass and rolls on to the sidewalk.

She struggles to get back on her feet, giving Mike time to bend over the engine, place the screwdriver on the solenoid, and you betcha: The engine sparks to life.

Here comes Griffin again, a bull charge, which Mike ducks under and again shoulders her weight backward, knocking her back down on the sidewalk. But she's right away rolling over and getting ready for another run at him.

Okay, so he drops the hood closed and goes to the passenger door. There's Patricia's arms flailing inside the car, reaching to the lock to let him in, and there's Griffin on her feet again, hitting a run around the car, and this time when she bashes into him, Mike dives into her with everything he's got, grabs her legs and dumps her NFL style. She squirms on the way down, twists her body so that when Mike's got her mashed into the ground, his head's only a couple inches from her face. The horror: Her lips look like they're the size of hammer-handles from this close. For a second he ponders just going ahead and punching her right between the eyes, the force of which, because he works full-time hanging hundred-pound molds, would take her head clean off. But he doesn't punch her. He pushes himself off her and bolts back around the car to try to get in.

When he opens the door, he lets out the pierce of Patricia screaming, and before he maneuvers himself into the small Subaru seat, he notices some people who have gathered across the street to watch the fight. He goes totally limp, is embarrassed suddenly, and in this instant he gives Griffin her opening. She grabs him by the back of the collar and the back of his gym shorts and with fantastic strength she pulls Mike away from the car door, and he falls, and his knee slams into the curb, jolting him with such pain that he pancakes forward onto the street. Before Mike can recover, Griffin crams her hands around the waistband of Mike's shorts and yanks them down to his ankles and over his shoes. There. She's pantsed him.

He's never believed silence could truly exist in the world—always he's heard something, some noise, some music in the world's goings-on—but he knows silence is real now. He can see Griffin, expressionless, soundless, leaning into the Subaru and coming back out holding the car keys and tossing the car keys across the street, near the people who've gathered to watch. He can see those people alternately smiling and looking shocked and disgusted, but no, there's no sound. Everything shut down. There's the dusk-blur in the sky, the daylight fading but still there.

Look how the lummox rises! He's in his underwear, and on the other side of the Subaru: Griffin. Grinning a fat grin. Waving Mike's gym shorts in the air like Neville Chamberlain waved the peace agreement he'd made with Hitler in 1938. *This is peace in our time*!

The people across the street are laughing their asses off. Griffin is laughing her ass off. Even Patricia is.

So Mike beats feet out of here. He runs across the street and into the alley and heads down the alley toward home. The light: Sure, it's good. He can see just fine, which means anybody out here can see him just fine. Out here in his skivvies, beating feet. But it's funny, hey. Without shorts, he can really run. This is the first time in his life he's been able to run fast. So that's what he's thinking about—how it's so cool he can finally run fast—not about Griffin or Patricia or the Joynt or Fred or the Phantom or Jennico.

A block from his house, the alley ends, and there's Lake Drive, the last stretch toward home, and he doesn't pause to see if anybody's around: He keeps on running, picks up the pace to a sprint. Long strides. Best strides ever. And right when he reaches the fence by Maroon's doghouse, he turns back to check out the distance he's just sprinted, and there's three children, maybe six, maybe eight years old, playing in tall grass on the far side of Lake Drive. They're pointing at him and laughing and saying something he doesn't recognize. He looks down at his underwear and sees that in all this running his personality has worked its way free of its trap door, and there it hangs: bobbing in rhythm with his heavy breaths.

Mike speaks to his personality: "You old sea dog, sometimes I wish I'd never met you."

LATER, he's inside his house, soaped and showered. He's got on fresh underwear and T-shirt and shorts and socks, and he's feeling fine, and Caryn's not back from her mother's yet, but she probably will be in a while. He cracks open a Leinenkugel's and sits at the kitchen table with the lights off and listens for sirens, but none ring out.

The phone rings, though. Patricia's calling from the Joynt.

"I'm okay," she says.

Mike can hear through the phone line the boisterous bar, the jukebox, the good time being had by all. He says, "I'm okay, too."

"Griffin's calmed down now. We're going to be fine."

"Great," Mike says. "Wonderful."

Patricia says, "But I gotta tell you, Mike, Griffin's telling everybody you beat her up. I don't think you should come down here for a while."

Mike says, "Don't worry about it, Patricia. I'm done with the bar."

He's not done with the bar, of course—he's got a thousand drunken nights ahead of him before he's got drinking out of his system—he's simply done with the bar for this particular evening.

The next day he's back into his routine again: bicycle ride in the morning, bicycle ride to work just before three. He works, eats, sleeps, drinks, collects his paycheck and spends it. He gets along.

And Fred gets released from the hospital. He goes home to Patricia, refuses the medication prescribed for him, which is cause for great concern to Patricia and to Fred's parents, but they needn't be concerned. Fred resolves never to drink again, and he's successful at that. He remains sober and alive for years and years.

Mike never does find out who the Phantom Shitter is. The Phantom never strikes again, and after a time Mike forgets about it. He goes on to other things, and the Phantom does, too.

And Mike never finds out exactly *how* Fred tried to kill himself, either, but he does discover why he tried.

A long time before Fred ends up on Ward 5, almost a year before, on a dull Tuesday night, Fred and Mike meet at the Joynt at about ten o'clock for drinks and whatnot. This is summertime. The barroom's nearly dead, maybe ten folks lining the bar and minding their own business. Every fifteen minutes or so, the jukebox plays a random tune, just to remind everybody that it's there and ready, for a few quarters, to sing. Fred and Mike take to their stools at the far end of the bar, near the back, near the pool tables and the narrow hallway that leads to the back door, which is open tonight, revealing the slack blue light of the moonlit alley. They drink pitchers, smoke, and talk. Convince themselves they're *somebodies*.

So Mike starts to talk about how he's been carrying on with Wanda Skalitsky: stopping by to see her late at night, holding her exquisite soft hand, getting her naked. And maybe because Mike used to have such rotten luck with women when he was a young pup out of high school, maybe because now he's scoring big-time and regular, he feels the need to brag about sleeping with Wanda in the same way that a hunter might describe bagging a trophy whitetail deer.

He tells Fred about the things she does when he makes love with her—the way she holds her head, how she coos and giggles and takes her false teeth out and sucks his cock—and Fred's listening in that way he's always had of listening: smiling, offering encouragement and sympathy.

What Mike doesn't know now—and won't know for many years—is that all this time he's been sleeping with Wanda, Fred's been sleeping with her, too. Fred's been visiting her sometime during the day, or early evening, when Mike's at work, and Mike's been visiting her later, after midnight or after bartime. He *should* know this right now. He should be able to see Fred and Wanda when they're at the Joynt or at parties or wherever: how they seem like such good friends with such intimate knowledge of each other, touching each other on the arm when they speak to each other, giving each other knowing nods when they part. Sure, it should be obvious to him, but he can't imagine Wanda Skalitsky needing more man than Mike Magnuson, which if you think about it is a good thing. Mike used to be a complete pussy about women; now he's got confidence.

So here are the fellows doing Tuesday night at the Joynt: two men, one married, one as good as married, both cheating on their mates with the same woman. Mike's the guy who boasts about it. Fred's the guy who lies back in the weeds, keeping his secrets, soaking in the irony of it all.

After an hour or two, headlights appear in the bar's back doorway. They blaze through the narrow hallway, giving it a searing white glow, like the open gangway of a spaceship in the movies.

Fred and Mike look to the light but without much interest. Headlights behind the bar are nothing unusual.

But maybe this *is* the movies. An alien figure *does* appear in the hallway, a hazy silhouette moving toward them. This is a woman, with scraggly hair and wearing a flannel shirt, hobbling and dragging a large object along the floor. This is Wanda Skalitsky emerging from the light and hobbling toward the pool table, and the object in her hand is a three-foot table lamp that's got no shade and no bulb. She's using this lamp for a cane, hobbling with her good right leg and dragging the left. Her left leg is broke clean, halfway between the ankle and the knee, her foot dangling above the floor like it's swaying in an afternoon breeze.

"Hurt my leg," she says. "Need to get to the hospital."

Mike says, "How did *that* happen?"

"Fell," Wanda says. "I'm clumsy."

Fred stays quiet, sips his beer, and doesn't stare at Wanda's broke leg, the darkening of the skin at the break.

Wanda says, "Can one of you guys take me to the hospital?"

The pitcher, it's three-quarters full. The glasses: both full. Somebody's finally put a few quarters into the juke: James Brown is singing "Sex Machine." Everything is beautiful here. It will always be too beautiful here.

Mike says, "Jesus, Wanda. If you could drive yourself to the bar, you don't need *us* to drive you to hospital."

Fred doesn't object, doesn't look up from his beer. "Right," he says. "Mike's right."

Wanda says something then—not angry or sad: just words—but Mike will never remember what it is. She shuffles herself around and begins rehobbling the narrow corridor filled with white light back to her car.

After her headlights pull away, the bar redarkens, and Mike quotes Ezra Pound: "What thou knows't well, thou loves't well."

And Fred knows the next line. "The rest is dross," he says.

And they drink till bartime.

Mike has never known what he's living for, no less what constitutes worth dying for, but Fred Lester is a person who professes ideals and tries to embody them. Former president of the Eau Claire Feminist Alliance. Founding member. He's sensitive to women, supportive of his wife's right to take the lead in their marriage. Fred's life is about being good to women. It's about trying to think like women think. But right now, on this dreary Tuesday night, with Wanda making her own broken-up way to the hospital, Fred must know deep down that he's a lummox after all. This is news for Fred, and he can't bear it. Mike, on the other hand, he's known this all along.

BUT WANDA makes it all right. She gets her leg put in a cast, gets crutches, and after a time the bone heals. If she resents Mike and Fred for what they've done to her, she never lets on that she does; she keeps sleeping with each of them for another year.

AND FRED makes it all right, too. He festers, escalates his sadness and his drunkenness. One day he pulls a crazy, gets sent to Ward 5, admits that he's got to make some major changes in his life. He quits drinking. He stays married to Patricia, at least for a few more years, but even after they divorce, he remains her best friend in the world. He even helps her pick out her wedding dress, when she remarries, a long time later. Fred may have sunk to an embarrassing point in his life, but he gets over it. He goes beyond it. Fred is capable of becoming a better person. Good for him.

 AND AS FOR Mike Magnuson, goddammit, he gets better, too. He makes it through life just fine. He always has a job, and he's always got plenty to eat and always has a roof over his head. He never gets rich, but so what? Give him some beer money and some friends who like to yuck it up with him, hell, he'll be happier than the proverbial pig in shit. Catch him on a Sunday afternoon in the fall, when he's watching the Packers play on TV and wearing his Packers jersey and his Cheesehead, and you'll know he turned out okay. He'll be hooting and hollering and laughing and telling stories about all the raunchy stuff he used to do, and you'll probably think he's a goodhearted guy, which is true: That's who he is. He's a goodhearted guy.

Sometimes he tries to make sense of his life, and when he does, he'll usually try to reduce his life to a useful maxim: *You can take the lummox out of the tavern, but you can't take the tavern out of the lummox.* Or *You can't take what the lummox did at the tavern out of the lummox.* Or *You can take the man out of the lummox, but you can't take the lummox out of the man.* It's something like that, something that's true but he can't quite figure out how to say. Hell, he's having a beer right now, a few beers actually. If you got a problem with that, take it up with the management.

Look, Mike's a middle-aged man now. He's married, has kids, a mortgage, car payments, credit cards, and he works at a place where people call him Professor Magnuson. He makes his living teaching young folks to make something of themselves, which he can only do because *he's* made something of himself. He's all grown up. And it was a long, long time ago when Fred tried to kill himself. Mike and Fred were in their mid-twenties then, the time of wildness and turbulence and unpredictability, and by extension every person reaches a point in their twenties when they discover once and for all who they really are, what their limits and strengths are, and thereafter, if they're going to amount to anything, they'll buckle their butts down and do what's necessary to succeed as adults. When that moment came for Fred, he gave a suicide a go, failed at that, and then succeeded at being a sober person. When that moment came for Mike, he discovered that he's your typical guy guy, your guy-with-a-spare-tire guy, et cetera, and if people can't tell that there might be a little more to Mike Magnuson than the way he *looks*, they're probably assholes.

So ONCE upon a time Fred Lester gets into some trouble, and once upon a time Mike Magnuson is sage enough to identify the cumulative horrors that got Fred into trouble because Fred's troubles have been essentially the same as Mike's. The way they've been carrying on: gone too far, gotten too crazy. Enough's enough, hey. So consequently, while Fred's getting better, at least for the first nine months of his getting-better period, Mike's trying to get better, too. Fred stays sober. Mike tries to get drunk less than he did before. Fred refocuses his energy on being an understanding and supportive husband. Mike tries to quit cheating on Caryn.

That's right: He tries. Sure, his flesh eye remains a roving thing, probably in the way that all men's always will. And a few times in there he consents to hold hands or to smooch in the tavern with this woman or that, and one snowy Wednesday night in January he moseys over to Wanda Skalitsky's house and wrestles around with her just the way they used to, in the good old days, but hey: It's just that one time. Mostly, Mike's figuring that Caryn, well, that he's got to lose Caryn, that he just doesn't love her, doesn't even *like* her. But at the same time he's figuring that the best way to get a suitable replacement for her is to refrain from being a habitual cheater. Sounds horrible, doesn't it? Suitable replacement. The perfect woman. But that's what our guy's thinking. And he's thinking that whenever this perfect woman does come along, he's going to do everything right for once. He's going to be honorable. He's going to behave like a gentleman. He's going to be honest and forthright and courteous, and if he can do this shit, and the perfect woman is cool about this shit, he can begin with her a wonderful lifelong relationship with, as the Hallmark-minded people of the world might say, the right foot forward.

Here's a magnificent truth Mike used to hear regularly in the factory break room: "Wish in one hand, shit in the other. See which one fills up first." Nobody—no philosopher, no poet, no physicist, no economist, no leader of nations—has ever said anything more profound.

Mike wishes for the perfect woman to come along, the one for whom he's going to be a perfect gentleman, and she comes along. Now, he knows what you're thinking: You're thinking he's going to say that once upon a time Magnuson falls in love with the perfect woman and that she ends up ruining him for all time. You're wrong. He's not about to say something like that. She does come along, but as a direct consequence of his association with her, his life does not get ruined. What happens is that this perfect woman has a bunch of ideas she's picked up at the university, and when she applies them to Mike, he learns the truth, corny as it may seem, that sets him free. He learns that just because folks go to college, that doesn't mean they're geniuses. He learns that a lot of educated people are full of shit. Oh, and he learns that if the perfect woman comes along, there ain't no way in hell she's really perfect.

So okay, okay: Years ago, twenty-five jobs ago, a dozen girlfriends ago, back when Mike's living with a woman named Caryn who owns a dog named Maroon and when he's making his living pulling a wrench in a plastics factory full-time, back *then*, he takes to hanging around with a woman who's the star of the English Department's graduating class. She's read her prerequisite truckload of books and then some—novels, books on thought and culture and politics, the whole spectrum—and now she's finished with her undergraduate rigors and is preparing to go off to graduate school to study the theoretical underpinnings of literature.

You know her. Or you know somebody like her.

She's not what you'd call an *original thinker*. For instance, if she's seen an R-rated movie featuring violence and brief nudity, she'll point out that women always comprise the nudity quotient, bless their hearts, and that men always perpetrate the violence quotient. She's correct: The skin is female skin, and the person shooting the gun or kicking the dog or kidnapping the sweet innocent child is, more often than not, a man. Horrible. But it's not as if she's come up with this idea on her own. Somebody's told her this shit is how she's came to thinking it. But she sure has got a bunch of thinking going on anyway. She's got a catalog of socially responsible material i n her brain. She says she completely understands and can quantify the vagaries of ethnicity and social class and gender and how it all mixes into something she can see functioning on the streets of Eau Claire, Wisconsin. This gives her power. She says that type of thing. She says she can feel power in knowledge. Her education gives her this, and power gives her a future.

Mike's got an education, too. *And* a degree. But he doesn't believe his schooling is a source of power. No way. All that matters to Mike is that when he's hanging with this English-department woman, and she's talking, and she's *always* talking, the talk she talks is a solar system away from the time clock, from the production-figure babble, from the cuts on the knuckles when a wrench slips off a nut, from the sore feet, from all the man-for-low-wages misery that makes up his forty hours a week. If he's with this woman, he's happy.

ONE THING, sure enough, leads to another. Mike grows close with this woman, becomes friends with her, talks with her sometimes late into the evening about Faulkner and Dostoyevsky and shit like that.

And it comes to pass that they are about to end up in that biblical together so much literature ends up being about. They are in love, for real, in the classic-literature, soul mate sense of love, the kind of spiritual love the Brontës wrote about, and they know, just like in the Brontë books, that *something* is going to have to be done about it.

And the Brontës will tell you that transforming love from a theoretical thing to a physical thing, that kind of stuff takes time. And

Mike's pleased that it takes time. He hasn't attempted to hold this woman's hand, or to smooch with her, or any of that lowbrow crap. If there's going to be contact, she will have to initiate it. So aside from the fact that Mike's been living with another woman for six years and is plotting in a large way to leave her forever, Mike is truly behaving like a honorable gentleman.

Finally, one crystalline night in June, when they know what they have to do, they go to the Joynt and drink, then Mike takes this woman for a walk across town and up the steep pitch to Space Mountain, the cemetery that overlooks the valley, the place where he used to go years back to smoke dope with his roommate Joe Murphy. This night is pleasant, sixty-five degrees and dry, and overhead the stars are brilliant and true.

They sit on a log up there and talk and take in the scenery. The view seems, just like it always has on nights like these, as if it's from the cockpit of a spaceship hurtling through the void—the streetlights and the car lights and the lights from the radio towers and the lights spanning the heavens, and all those points of moving, blinking, remote life in the valley's bottom—and they chat about the nice, safe things that educated people chat on and on about: Aesthetics, epistemology, hermeneutics, subjects with fancy names and slippery meanings the defining of which will eternally entertain folks who have taken some fancy classes at college.

Somewhere in there she reaches for his hand, takes it, and says, in the manner of asserting a postulate, "I love you."

He doesn't respond right away, just grips her hand, runs his thumb along hers, a pause that she takes to mean she needs to elaborate further on her conception of love.

She says, "But I have some reservations."

He doesn't flinch at this. He can understand why a woman would have reservations about him. He's been a lout for many years, and this is no secret to most people he knows.

She releases his hand then and says that she has prepared in advance for this moment. She's sought professional advice on this. And who else would a fine student like her seek out for advice but her favorite professor? She's gone to see a man called Dr. Dinardo, a man who is the English Department chair.

Dr. Dinardo, such is his specialization in literature, takes a skeptical view of the nature of men and their dubious manly ways. He knows that men are forever up to no good, not only in matters of the heart but in all matters political and spiritual and cultural. He knows men *always* have something suspect and ulterior about them. Human history has proved this to be true. Dr. Dinardo is not a woman—he's got a wife and a kid and everything—but he's proud to call himself a *feminist*. His profession is to think like women do. His most popular course is titled *Jane Eyre* and Her Literary Daughters.

The woman says, "So you want to know what Dr. Dinardo said about you?"

Mike does. He really wants to know.

"He said you are a very traditional male."

"What did he mean by that?" Mike says.

"He meant what he said. He's a concise man, I should think."

Something dramatic should happen now: a shooting star zipping across the horizon, the moon dimming, something. But the night merely keeps on with what it's doing, being a twinkly thing that will forever be, from this vantage point up high, a twinkly thing. The night doesn't give a damn what Dr. Dinardo says, and it never will.

Mike can imagine Dr. Dinardo at the moment of passing judgment on him: the thoughtful pause, the downcast tug at the Marxist beard, the eyes rolling with extratextual distaste at a bust of Charlotte Brontë on his office bookshelf. "Mike Magnuson is a very traditional male."

Check this out, Dr. Dinardo: The traditional male is a superintendent of school's son, a boy raised in Menomonee Falls, a suburb of Milwaukee, Wisconsin. He's raised with opera on the radio, and with Wagner and with Mozart and with Aaron Copland. He can play Bach fugues on the piano when he's eight years old. When he's twenty, the traditional male lives in the traditional abandoned school building with the traditional drum set and the traditional underage alcoholic girls, and he ends up working in a group home and getting one of the residents stoned and in the process inadvertently causing his traditional death. When the traditional male is twenty-one, he reads Proust and lives in a house with the traditional lesbians and goes to college and gets a degree and works in a plastics factory and engages in the traditional-male pastime of reading poetry and novels and discussing subjects with fancy names and slippery meanings and on and on.

And this is the truth Mike learns: The woman who's just told him she loves him, she can't help it that she parrots the words and ideas of her professors; she's just being a good student, which doesn't at all mean she's a bright person, merely a person who believes what her professors say. But Dr. Dinardo, a man with power over others, a man who spreads ideas that young people parrot, he's a person with the profoundest sort of ignorance, judge-a-book-by-its-cover ignorance, don't-know-his-ass-from-a-hole-in-the-ground ignorance. Dr. Dinardo sees what he thinks is a traditional male, and he believes that here is a bad person, a person for whom society no longer has any use, but how the fuck could Dr. Dinardo possibly know, just at a glance, what's inside another person's heart? Fuck *him*.

The next night, Mike goes to Hobbsie's Bar after work, drinks too many beers, and embarks upon a brief and sloppy series of hog-wrestles with a gal named Bertha, a custodian on the Jennico day shift and a mother of two, who's got enormous boobs she's fond of flashing at folks late at night, when she's full of beer and feeling skittish in Hobbsie's parking lot. Bertha smells like the pine-oil tanks she cleans all day, and she swears and drinks and belches like a lumberman. The only thing she knows about, say, Blake or Joyce is that they're married, they're friends with her cousins, and that she thinks they run a fishing resort somewhere near the Canadian border. Mike and Bertha will get their bodies maneuvered into some obscene position or other, and Bertha will be saying "Fuck my shit hard, baby," or something equally eloquent, and Mike will be thinking this: Hey, a guy may *look* like a lummox and *act* like a lummox, but deep down inside him he can be anything he wants. A guy can enjoy the Berthas of the world *and* enjoy reading Marcel Proust. And if the Dr. Dinardos of the world can't see how these two characteristics can exist in one person, they really do have their heads up their asses.

But that's all later on, all some other starry summer night.

On Space Mountain, with the educated woman who's just said she loves him, Mike can see how the Eau Claire streets below are slow veins, one car driving here, one car driving there. He can see the lights in the Eau Claire houses, all those traditional homes. He can see the fixed points freckling the firmament, something that will never change. He can see his freedom coming on.

He reaches for the woman's hand and holds it.

He says, "I love you, too."

And he's certain she has no idea whether he does or doesn't.

AUTHOR'S NOTE

The author wishes to note that the events described in this book happened a long time ago. The people he used to hang out with are probably far different now than they were then, so to prevent embarrassing these people, he admits to altering the truth in the following ways:

1. He has changed the names of the people who appear in this book, and in some instances he has taken the speech and behavior of any number of people he knew and combined these characteristics into a composite person.

2. He has attributed specific remarks to people who undoubtedly did not say in real life exactly what they say in this book. He intends their remarks to be approximations, in subject matter and in tone, of what they actually said.

3. He has time-compressed several sequences in this book and has periodically changed locations of events he describes. He has removed certain people from certain events, too.

The author nevertheless maintains that this book constitutes an accurate record of his experiences. He insists that all this shit really happened.